The Political Economy of State-making in

post-Apartheid South Africa

The Political Economy of State-making in
post-Apartheid South Africa

Sihle Moon

AFRICA WORLD PRESS

TRENTON | LONDON | CAPE TOWN | NAIROBI | ADDIS ABABA | ASMARA | IBADAN | NEW DELHI

AFRICA WORLD PRESS
541 West Ingham Avenue | Suite B
Trenton, New Jersey 08638

Book design: Dawid Kahts
Cover design: Ashraful Haque

Library of Congress Cataloging-in-Publication Data:
Names: Moon, Sihle, 1967- author.
Title: The political economy of state-making in post-apartheid South Africa / Sihle Moon.
Description: Trenton, New Jersey : Africa World Press, 2017. | Includes bibliographical references and index.
Identifiers: LCCN 2016059383| ISBN 9781569025079 (hb : alk. paper) | ISBN 9781569025086 (pb : alk. paper)
Subjects: LCSH: South Africa--Politics and government--1994- | South Africa--Economic conditions--1991- | Economic development--Political aspects--South Africa.
Classification: LCC DT1971 .M66 2017 | DDC 968.07--dc23
LC record available at https://lccn.loc.gov/2016059383

Dedication

For
Ethel de Kaiser
and
Adrian Leftwich

This book is dedicated to my friends and mentors, both killed by cancer. Although they could not stand each other, I owe them both a huge debt of gratitude for their constant support and confidence in me. May their souls rest in peace.

Contents

vii

Abbreviations

AAC	Anglo American Corporation
AB	*Afrikaner Broederbond*
AHI	*Afrikaanse Handels Instituut*
ANC	African National Congress
BAD	Bantu Affairs Department
BCM	Black Consciousness Movement
BSA	Business South Africa
CODESA	Convention for a Democratic South Africa
DEP	Department of Economic Policy (ANC)
GATT	General Agreement on Tariffs and Trade
GDFI	Gross Domestic Fixed Investment
GDI	Gross Domestic Investment
GDP	Gross Domestic Product
GNP	Gross National Product
GEAR	Growth, Employment and Redistribution Strategy
GNU	Government of National Unity
HSRC	Human Sciences Research Council
ICU	Industrial and Commercial Workers Union
IDC	Industrial Development Cooperation
IFP	Inkatha Freedom Party
IMF	International Monetary Fund
ISCOR	Iron and Steel Corporation
ICU	Industrial and Commercial Worker's Union

MDM	Mass Democratic Movement
MERG	Macro-Economic Research Group
NAD	Native Affairs Department
NEF	National Economic Forum
NEM	Normative Economic Model
NIEP	National Institute for Economic Policy
NECC	National Education Coordinating Committee
NUMSA	National Union of Metal workers of South Africa
NUM	National Union of Mine workers
OECD	Organisation for Economic Cooperation and Development
OPEC	Organisation of Petroleum Exporting Countries
PAC	Pan Africanist Congress (of Azania)
RDP	Reconstruction and Development Programme
SAAU	South African Agricultural Union
SACOB	South African Chamber of Business
SACP	South African Communist Party
SABRA	South African Bureau of Racial Affairs
SADF	South African Defence Force
SAF	South African Foundation
SANCO	South African National Civic Organisation
SSA	Statistics South Africa
SSC	State Security Council
TEC	Transitional Executive Council
TRC	Truth and Reconciliation Commission
TRIPS	Trade Related Intellectual Property Rights
TRIMS	Trade Related Investment Measures
UDF	United Democratic Front
UNDP	United Nations Development programme
WTO	World Trade Organisation

Preface

The 1994 democratic breakthrough in South Africa generated a great deal of excitement and expectation internally and globally. After all, it was surmised, here was a country whose history, politics, social structure and connection to the global economy, presented fascinating possibilities for effecting equity based growth and development. Furthermore, the electoral victory of the African National Congress (ANC) that had openly declared its preference for a Keynesian, state-led approach to social and economic development, only added to the sense of expectation. The various progammatic documents associated with the ANC (Freedom Charter, MERG and the RDP), all underlined the primacy of the state in driving an inclusive developmentalist project that would lead to shared prosperity and an end to inequality, poverty and rampant unemployment. This, of course, despite the predominance of a neo-liberal anti-state orthodoxy, the general feeling and expectation- internally and externally, was that the post-apartheid elites would 'give it a real go'. For this and other reasons, a project devoted to the analysis of the rise and fall of the RDP (and by extension, state-led growth and development) is absolutely essential.

The central argument of this book is that the only way to address the massive socio-economic challenges inherited in 1994 was going to be through a developmental state led by a determined developmental elite. Its principal task was going to be two-fold. First, navigate a hostile global ideological and intellectual environment that preferred, favoured, facilitated and actively supported a neo-liberal growth and development agenda (especially in the global south). Second, the new leadership had the unenviable task of meeting huge internal pressure and expectations for employment-creation, poverty eradication and a determined plan to tackle shocking levels of inequality in South Africa.

Twenty years down the line, it is now opportune to conduct a thorough-going and forensic analysis of South Africa's prospects for developmental state-making in the early to mid-1990s. The book is thus about the failure of a developmentalist state project in post-apartheid South Africa in the period under consideration, and the political explanation for such failure. Moreover, it shows that the Reconstruction and Development Programme (RDP) was a crucial moment in South Africa's drive towards a state-led growth and development strategy and an equitable and sustainable democratic future for all. However, the successful evolution of the RDP into a developmental state project was thwarted by inimical internal and external political factors and circumstances. These include but are not limited to (1) the absence of a cohesive developmental elite to drive the political and economic changes called for, (2) the continued resilience and ideological hegemony of the neo-liberal agenda in the new South Africa, (3) an elite negotiated pact that severely constrained developmental prospects, (4) the absence in the ANC of a coherent ideological agenda as a countervailing force to neo-liberalism and several other factors besides. As ever, the contingency nature of political processes, mean that there were both constraints and opportunities. How were these negotiated and towards what strategic and political ends? These are some of the critical questions desperately crying out for answers, and it is with answers to these questions that the various chapters in this book are concerned.

Earlier (and arguably much successful) experiments with developmental state-making in East Asia, had shown that developmental states are not there for the taking. Instead, as Castells (1992) has shown, successful developmental state-making is a function of understanding and ability to negotiate fundamentally complex political factors and circumstances. This is what has shaped the urgency, thrust and pace of developmental strategies through state and appropriate institutional arrangements. I show that to really understand the spectacular collapse of the RDP and with it, the diminished prospects for radical state-led development in post –apartheid South Africa, one needs to go back a hundred and fifty odd years. In that history is to be found fascinating analytical material about the South African state, its character, culture, structure and above all, the accumulation strategy that created, drove, and continue to sustain it. There are, thus, important continuities and discontinuities to be explored, analysed and explained.

Many attempts have been made by various political scientists, historians and economic historians and economists to account for what is generally viewed as a sudden and spectacular about face of the ANC leadership, as far as economic policy are concerned. Most of these accounts are in the main conspiratorial, putting too much explanatory weight on the subjective at the expense of the objective factor and vice versa. These, I argue, are generally of limited explanatory utility and what is more, they are, in the main, thin on analytical rigour. This is not surprising given the history of the country and the emotions it generates. Nonetheless, to illuminate the full range of factors and circumstances accounting for the policy somersault in South Africa's developmental trajectory, requires the deployment of a comprehensive analytical method. To do this, I make use of the Strategic Relational Approach, at the centre of which is the notion of 'strategic and intentional actors'. What is the significance of this in probing the political economy of state-making in South Africa? It is simply this: structure critically informs political behavior (policy choices, ideological positions etc.), but it does not determine it. Also, agents are not helpless victims of structure (their contexts), instead, they act intentionally and strategically. So, the answer lies in understanding the process as a dynamic and mutually reinforcing relationship between structure and agency. To summarise: actors in concrete socio-economic and political processes more often than not act strategically. Their actions are rarely arbitrary, but are based on a careful calculation of the broader context within which they operate. Such calculation takes into account the possibilities and constraints inherent in the said context. Therefore, political and state actors are more likely to choose a course of action that is informed by the strategic assessment of the relevant context (Hay,2002:129).

Such an analysis of the period will, in turn, throw up several other really useful analytical variables, including but not limited to the following: the role and place of power in the analytical equation; the contingency nature of political processes, and, of course, structure and agency and how all of these variables interact and conspire to give rise to certain political and ideological outcomes and not others.

The Idea behind the book

The process of writing this book started around 1999, as a PhD project. The primary research material, including interviews with key personalities was all done in the early 2000s (both in South Africa and the UK). Politics being what it is, I accept that the views of some informants may have changed in the intervening seventeen odd years. Nevertheless, these are reflected here such as they were at the time of the interviews. There is, furthermore, no doubt that since then, new political variables have become salient in the South African socio-economic and political landscape, variables that were less prominent in the late 1990s and early 2000s. Those variables include (but are not limited to) the following: corruption; spotlight on leadership; dynamics within the ANC-led alliance; state and business relations; the impact of the global recession on the South African economy; the spotlight on state owned enterprises; the South African labour market and failure of the education and skills system and many others besides. Although the initial temptation was to update the earlier material in ways that captured these new and emerging developments in the political landscape, it occurs to me that a project focused on the politics that defined and set in motion the current socio-economic framework is a good context-setting point of departure and worthy of independent analysis. As I see it, there are two critical analytical intellectual gaps this material fills. First, I'm fascinated by the analytical angle taken to examine the ideological foundations, character, culture and operations of the Apartheid state. Its characterization as a form of developmental state (with all the caveats), is an important intellectual contribution at a time when comparisons between what the apartheid state did for Afrikaners (all social classes) is increasingly being compared with what the post-apartheid state is failing to achieve for the black majority. Second, the politics that gave rise to a brief flirtation with the RDP (and the possibility of a radical state-led growth and development trajectory), do require proper definitional clarity. Far too often, the analysis of this period and the complex internal and external processes that shaped the resultant outcome, is insufficient and unsatisfactory. True, therefore, there is a whole range of new (and not so new) political dynamics in the South African landscape crying out for analysis and examination – it seems to me that these are matters secondary to the current endeavor of tracing and explicating the roots of and reasons for the current socio-economic framework. At any rate, the current maladies cannot be properly understood outside decisions and policy choices made in the early and mid-1990s. For that reason, (in the hope that a second project will be undertaken to deal with the new developments), this book shines the spotlight sharply on the political economy of state-making in South Africa (past and present).

Acknowledgements

This book is a product of many years of research, teaching, political debates and active involvement, in the struggle to end apartheid (in various capacities). Such involvement includes leadership roles in the national student movement that set South African politics alight in the 1980s. My few years at the ANC Head Office [Shell House] in charge of policy development was certainly an exciting and hugely fulfilling period. In some respects, it was deeply disappointing and eye-opening. The central role I played in shaping policy and leadership for the 1997 Mafeking Congress of the ANC, gave me access to the inner-most thoughts of leading left elements of the ANC/SACP/COSATU alliance. Living in a foreign country is, at the best of times, extremely difficult, especially for activists. In this regard, I would like to thank my family for making things ever so slightly easier, without their unconditional support, it would have been impossible to do the research on which much of this book is based. During my time in England, colleagues and friends from East Asia, Latin America, Russia, the Caribbean Islands and Greece contributed immensely through debates and shared experiences. I am grateful to the Department of Politics and the Post-War and Reconstruction Department at the University of York, for creating such a robust and intellectually stimulating platform. Interestingly, the collapse of the Greek economy was predicted in those debates more than fifteen years before it actually happened. Such was the quality of the research and the foresight of the individuals involved. There is quite a long list of people to thank and, as ever, a few might not make it in this list for reasons to do with space, I am profoundly grateful to all of them. The Centre for the Advancement of Scholarship and the University of Pretoria, Ethel de Kaiser, Adrian Leftwich, Alex Callinicos, John Sharp, Sibusiso VIl-Nkomo, Keith Hart, Patrick Bond, Langa Zita, Phillip Dexter, Delekile Klaas, Naph Manana, Thenjiwe Mthintso. Although all of these individuals contributed in various ways to this book, I take full responsibility for the final product.

Sihle Moon

CHAPTER

1

The Problem

Introduction

The role of the state as society shaping, organizing and coordinating institution has come under increasing academic and intellectual attack in recent times. Indeed, there is a growing body of literature extolling the demise of the state as a central organ for managing domestic and global socio-economic and political arrangements. There are several quite plausible reasons for this declining confidence in the role and place of the modern state in directing internal and external economic and political affairs. Some of these include the perceived powerlessness of states in light of globalization and transnational capital, in other words, the world is characterized more and more, by the dominance of borderless finance capital and stateless corporations (Weiss;1998). The state, the argument goes, has lost its centrality in the face of an increasingly complex world (including international terrorism, increased financialisation and the role of technology). Following Smith (2009), I suggest that much of this debate is based on American and European case studies. Even there, the obituaries of the role and place of the modern state are pre-mature and predicated on a failure to see the changing nature, adaptability and variability of the state (Weiss, 1998; Smith, 2009). Instead of their purported collapse, states respond, interact (with domestic and global phenomena) differently across space, time and policy area (Smith, 2009:90). And, as ever, there are still strong anti-statist voices based on the neo-liberal Washington consensus. This is despite its spectacular fail-

1

ure in the past thirty years or so, to respond to the most basic human development requirements of significant sections of the population both in the global south and north. Secondly, there is limited empirical evidence to demonstrate that these 'endist' approaches have any real traction in the developing world. After all, the state in the developing world whether strong, weak, democratic, authoritarian, developmental or non-developmental, predatory, clientelistic – remain a critically important institution for understanding the past, present and future developmental prospects of countries in the global south. Accordingly, the political economy of state-making in South Africa provides illuminating definitional clarity and is a useful lens through which to understand the economic and political choices of the South African leadership elites before, during and after the demise of legal apartheid.

The principal preoccupation of this book is two-fold. First, I discus, analyse, explore and underline the politics associated with developmental state-making, in a variety of historical and geographic contexts. This is done to demonstrate the centrality and primacy of politics in developmental state-making processes. Second, and guided by the above analysis, I interrogate post-apartheid South Africa's state-making dynamics, using East Asian developmental states as touch-stone. A running theme throughout is the fundamental recognition of the significance of ideology in developmental state-making. The complexity of the subject matter necessitates the deployment and definition of other key variables for a better organisation and structuring of the empirical and secondary material that has driven the research in this work. This chapter is essentially a context-setting and definitional chapter, concerned to deal with the following key variables: the South African state, the centrality of ideology and political processes, developmental state and prospects in the current global conjuncture, the role of structure and agency in understanding state-making in South Africa. The last section is a chapter break-down of the book. First, the South African state.

The South African state- historically

The modern South African state is essentially traceable to the formation of Union in 1910. It is a product of complex, historically specific, geo-political and internal socio-economic phenomena and epiphenomena. These include but are not limited to: the discoveries of minerals; the Boer war; Lord Milner's 'reconstruction period' (and its implications for race relations and politics); the need for cheap labour to fully exploit the potential of the mines; the need to create political and social stability; and the facilitation of peace between the English and Afrikaners. Crucially, white unity and mineral extraction were to rest on the high degree of economic exploitation and political oppression of blacks (Legassick, 1974a; Dubow, 1995; Swanson,1995). Furthermore, these complex factors required an enormous super-structure of labour relations, pass laws and influx control measures which in turn called for an intensely *estatiste* (state-centred) system from the very outset (Gann and Duignan, 1981:5). Chapter two shows that despite its anti-statist rhetoric, the National Party:

> depended for its own political ascendency on the construction and maintenance of a massive and sprawling state structure and a significant state economic role. The Afrikaner hegemony of over four decades was predicated on a strategic, if at times blunt, use of public sector power and patronage (Munslow and FitzGerald, 1997; 43).

All these factors significantly inform the character, content and developmental possibilities inherent in the post-apartheid state. For, as will be shown in the chapters that follow a developmentalist state culture, history and heritage facilitates rather than hinder prospects for developmental state-making. Indeed, the constitutive elements of the state at its inception do not necessarily disappear with the passage of time. Instead, their influence can still be felt many years later. Thus, "states carry their parentage and birthmarks with them throughout their lives, as do domestic political forces in each state" (O'Meara,1996:43).

This analysis has important implications for the analysis and understanding of the South African state, its politics and developmental prospects. First, it implies a dynamic and historical conception of the state, one that views the state as a historically specific form of power, and a product of its own concrete geo-political and socio-economic circumstances (ibid). For this reason, chapter two is devoted to an historical analysis of the politics of the segregationist and apartheid South African state, capturing continuities and discontinuities in its development. Such a forensic and clinical analysis of the history, politics, relations (internal and external), what persist and what new elements are discernable in such relations, has immense explanatory force. It is also vital in bringing to the fore the full range of political issues that inform state-making in South Africa, historically. A second implication for the South African state, and states in general, is a definition and approach to analyzing the state that does not (as do many political commentators) confuse the state and government. Contrary to being individuals and groups of individuals (political parties), the state is defined as a social relation which reflects and reproduces all the socio-economic and political conflicts inherent in wider society (Jessop, 1982). More directly, the state is to be seen as an ensemble of institutions and organisations whose socially accepted function is to define and enforce collectively binding decisions (Jessop, 1990; 341). Thus, a full understanding of the workings and operations of contemporary state systems requires the examination of the interactions and relations between and within such institutions and organisations. In a word, what is required is an examination of the *politics* of the state under consideration.

A third and very important implication of O'Meara's characterization is the variability, adaptability and dynamic nature of states. This means that the state is an ongoing and continuously changing structure of power, responding to domestic and external pressures. Some states navigate this twin role (domestic and global) well, others not. It is precisely the differential response or powerlessness to respond to such pressures that sets developmental states apart from other state types. Developmental states are so-called partly because of their ability to skilfully manoeuvre their way around such pressures, in pursuit of their primary goal of economic growth and social development. Linda Weiss (2000), in response to the oft-lamented demise of the state, has shown that the 'endist' assertions confuse the considerable changes to the modern state with its demise. She puts it thus: "with some exceptions and in spite of some significant changes over the past decade or so, the tenacity and adaptability of national institutional arrangements are more impressive than their purported erosion" (2000: 22).

More than anything, this speaks to the durability of state structures, culture and traditions, and by extension, the difficulty of transforming old state institutions, structures and traditions.

It is, thus, also the case that those political elites that inherit state systems with a developmentalist state culture, notably South Korea, Taiwan and post-apartheid South Africa, experience fewer difficulties in pursuing development themselves (Maundeni, 200: 93). Whether or not developmental state construction succeed, is determined (among other things) by the ability of the new state elites to engage creatively and intelligently with complex political and geo-political pressures and expectations (internal and external) that accompany regime-change and transitions. I will show that there are several variables that have generally determined the success of developmental state-making process. They include the availability of a developmental elite, driving a developmental agenda (project) and how they tackle the ever-present structural constrains at hand. South Korea, Taiwan and apartheid South Africa (for some time at least), provide comparative material against which prospects for developmental state-making in post-apartheid South Africa can be assessed. Above all, the assessment of such prospects is guided by a firm recognition of the centrality of politics in state-making processes.

Prospects for developmental state construction

Although the term 'developmental states' first made its debut in the social science lexicon with Chalmers Johnsons' (1982) ground-breaking research into the Japanese state (MITI), the idea of activist and interventionist states is not new. Its provenance can be traced back in much earlier works, including Karl Marx, in his characterization of the 'relative autonomy' of the state, Fridrich List and Alexandra Gerschenkron, on late development.

Fridrich List (1885) was inspired by the German experience at a time when England was the dominant global economic power. For List, late developing countries cannot expect to follow, step by step, the path of economic growth pursued by nations before them. Instead, they would need to pursue growth and accumulation strategies designed to enable them to catch-up with the rest of the industrialised world. His mind deeply exercised by Germany's seeming blind mimicking of the English development path, List expresses his frustration thus: "there is therefore a real danger that the strongest nations will use the motto of free trade as an excuse to adopt a policy which will certainly enable them to dominate the trade and industry of weaker countries and condemn them to a condition of slavery" (1966:24).

For this reason, List advocated a path of development designed to avoid such obstacles for Germany and other late developers in Europe, in order that they could catch up with England. This path was characterized by a departure from *liasse affair* economic policies and the introduction of active state involvement and monitoring of trade and commercial activities of the country.

Later on, Alexander Gerschenkron (1962) and also of German extraction, took time to consider the development prospects of the newly liberated or politically independent countries in Africa. Like List, Gerschenkron was skeptical and deeply suspicious of the development paths the former colonisers were encouraging and actively supporting in the post-colonial countries, he warned:

> …in a number of important historical instances, industrialization processes, when launched at length in a backward country, showed considerable differences, as compared with more advanced countries, not only with regard to the speed of the development (rate of industrial growth), but also with regards to productive and organisational structures of industry which emerged from those processes (1962: 7).

For Gerschenkron, therefore, special measures had to be taken by the new post-colonial states. Specifically, they needed to adopt a developmental strategy in Listian mode. This means that the only way for the newly independent African states to avoid the pitfalls of developmental failure, was through the construction of institutional state structures poised for active and pervasive involvement in driving the catch-up processes with the advanced countries.

More recently, Charles Tilly came to a similar conclusion while examining the process of state formation in 17th and 18th century western Europe. In that study, Tilly cautions those social scientists and economists trying to understand the developing world by introducing misconceived models of western experience as the criteria for political development (1975: 4). According to Tilly, these models are misconceived for a number of reasons but principally because: "European experience could have been a lucky shot, an aberration, a dead end, or simply one among many paths open to 'modern government'. Therefore, major political transformations which occurred in the past may not repeat themselves in exactly the same way" (ibid). This analysis also speaks to the need for the developing countries to base their developmental strategies firmly on their own concrete experiences, needs, and contemporary local and international challenges. For these are dynamic and highly shaped by place and time. Central to such strategies, therefore, is the construction of state types suited to the challenges of developing country transformation, reconstruction and development. There are, thus, important implications arising from the work of List, Gerschrenkron and Tilly. At the core of their conclusion is the idea that there is no beaten path to economic growth, social development and equity, instead, these take place in historically specific circumstances, informed by and confronting unique sets of challenges and opportunities. Furthermore, far from the state being counterproductive in the development edifice, it remains a central force for change and development.

An important part of the new state elite's task is that of deliberately and consciously setting out to be at the centre of the socio-economic and reconstruction agenda. To do this, however, capacity, meritocracy and capability are critical elements. In this context, the market is systematically monitored and guided in such a way that it works in the putative interest of, and not against the broader socio-economic goals of the country. Gordon White had this in mind when he put forward the view that, in the developing world, the state has become the primary mechanism for overcoming certain major constraints inherent in the domestic and international context of the new nations (White, 1984: 997). Post-apartheid South Africa, emerging as it does, from one of the most abominable racially exclusive socio-economic systems, was uniquely placed to launch an extraordinary state-led countervailing development strategy. Of course, the continuities and discontinuities would have to be clearly defined, understood and underlined. For, after all, the apartheid state was going to bequeath important developmental state features for the new elites. Also, this would have to be a comprehensive plan for economic development, firmly rooted in the country's concrete experiences and the experiences of other developing countries, both success stories (East Asia) and the not so success stories (much of the rest of the developing world). It is shown in chapters five and six that in the final analysis, the success or failure of developmental state construction hinged on the internal and external pressures and expectations confronting the RDP and its implementation. Such pressures and how they were managed or not managed (in the interests of development for all), speaks to the materiality and centrality of politics in the process of initiating and driving processes of economic growth and development. Put differently, politics constitute a crucially important explanatory and analytical variable in the state-making processes investigated in this book.

Therefore, an important conclusion arising from the above discussion is that there is absolutely nothing automatic or inevitable about the formation of developmental states. Such states are not there for the taking. Indeed, were this the case, the Global south would be a completely different place right now. Instead, the success of developmental state-making rests on the political challenges confronting state and political elites, and their ability to navigate complex internal and external pressures (Chang and Kazul-Wright,1998).

Global Context and Developmental State-making

Much of the anti-statist and state denialism is predicated on and can be roughly divided into two broad schools of thought. First, there is the neo-liberal inspired approach. This approach essentially posits the view that states are spoilers and the less we have of them the better- they are most certainly bad for the economy and often bad for politics (individual freedoms, choice etc). Accordingly, the remedy for these maladies lies in significant reductions in the role of the state by way of de-regulation, privatization and checking public spending on social services etc. The second school of thought is best viewed as a sub-type, a strand of the globalization approach. The central argument here is that the sheer scale and volume of cross-border flows, technological advancement, financial and trade openness, have left the state vulnerable to the vicissitudes of global markets. This state of affairs, the argument goes, has left nation-states impotent both as power actors in the global and domestic arenas but also, as sites of economic accumulation. This being the case, therefore, why bother with political and economic projects whose success rely on institutions whose significance and relevance, as global and domestic players is, at any rate, declining?

These questions are dealt with in detail in later chapters. For now, the point is to provide a succinct foretaste of the central counter-argument. Of course, the point of this exercise is to underline not only the endurance and adaptability of states in the current global economic conjuncture, but crucially, their centrality in the definition of alternative growth and development paradigms (especially for the global south). Nevertheless, the forthcoming chapters will consistently seek to argue and demonstrate that the global accumulation strategy associated with neo-liberalism is fundamentally flawed and unsustainable, moving forward. It cannot and has been unable to replicate itself (certainly in the past twenty odd years, both in the developed north and the global south). In this regard, the financial crises of Mexico in 1991; East Asia in 1997; Russia in 1998; Brazil, Argentina and Turkey in 1999-2001, followed by the global stock market crash of 2001 – all tell a story of a broken system. One in urgent and desperate need of re-organisation and fundamental overhaul. In this respect, the Great recession of 2008 is not (as the neo-liberal economists and other apologists would have us believe), a momentary 'blip'. Instead, the system is desperately crying-out for change and the state (especially in the global south), will have to be at the centre of such efforts at re-organising the global regime of accumulation. What is more, it is foolhardy for economists and policy actors to expect growth and developmental plans, predicated on this flawed logic to succeed in, say, post-apartheid South Africa. I show, instead, that the construction of institutional arrangements (associated with the developmental state), is possibly the only way for post-apartheid South Africa to reverse continuing and growing high levels of poverty, entrenched inequality and rampant unemployment. I also show that in large measure, the statistical evidence demonstrate that these trends have not been reversed by post-apartheid policies – instead, there has been a palpable increase. This has to do less with exogenous factors (although these do play a role) and more with bad policy choices and bad politics.

The second school of thought advances the idea that the financialisation of global trade and investments has led to the vulnerability of the state to these developments. Thus, leaving state actors and state-led policy processes (notably industrial strategies), inadequate in the face of runaway (borderless) finance, trade and investment movements (Fingleton, 1995:155). I argue, in this regard, that the impact of these developments on the role and place of the state is grossly exaggerated. And, at any rate, any impact global phenomena can and do have on the state cannot be and is not even. Instead, several studies have shown considerable unevenness in the response of states across place and time. Significantly, however, I also show that instead of ending, state's responses have demonstrated adaptability and variability. In other words, the claim of a collapsing (declining) role for states is too general and is not supported by available empirical evidence. There is evidence, instead, of counter-tendencies towards the enhancement and re-positioning of states and state power in the current global setup. At any rate, in politics (endogenous or exogenous), there is always room to maneuver. Another problem with this approach (as distinct from say, the neo-liberal approach, which actively advocates for lean and mean states, de-regulation etc), is that it inadvertently subscribes to the TINA (there is no alternative) approach. I argue instead that there is an alternative and states (organized and structured along developmental statist lines) are an intrinsic part of such alternatives.

The domestic environment and developmental state-making

Internal political conditions refer to all the factors that are critical to the construction of developmental states, including but not limited to: leadership, institutions, the role and impact of interactions between the state and civil society. In this respect, the RDP was crucial for mobilizing South Africa's different social classes around an integrated programme for economic development and equity, and this was a vitally important condition in the creation of socio-political stability. Comparatively speaking, chapter two shows that apartheid state-making was also predicated on the mobilization of a broad spectrum of Afrikaner social classes, around the development of the *Volk*. In addition, the RDP went a long way in cementing and consolidating unity and cohesion, not only within the ANC-led alliance, but also within the more diverse Government of National Unity (GNU). This cohesion within the South African leadership would be vital in ensuring that the RDP implementation process was unencumbered by conflict, vested interests and squabbling at the political top. But, a coalition around RDP implementation would have to be enduring and single-mindedly adhered to by all involved. So, the question arises: Was this the case in the South African context? And more importantly, what was the real content and dynamics of the coalition around the RDP?

At the same time, there were also negative internal political factors, which conspired with international pressures to frustrate the successful implementation of the RDP. These included the nature of the institutional arrangements set up to coordinate RDP implementation (Turok, 1999: 63). Another crucial weakness concerned the lack of adequately trained personnel within the bureaucracy to deliver a project of the scale and size of the RDP. Institution-building has been a critically important aspect of developmental state-making in East Asia (Leftwich, 1996; Evans, 1998). It is, thus, important to establish the extent to which, if at all, RDP institutional arrangements corresponded to the model advanced by developmental statists. Also, the relative strength of civil society organs in South Africa during the 1990s raises important questions regarding the desirability of strong non-state actors in the construction of the type of developmental state that emerged in East Asia. The object here is thus to compare and contrast the politics of the RDP against the politics of East Asian developmental state construction. Moreover, the shift from the RDP to GEAR is given the same critical assessment.

The Approach

The exploration of East Asian developmental states will be organized around seven key themes, the same themes that will be used to assess replicability and prospects in post-apartheid South Africa. The first theme relates to the global context and whether this promotes or hinders developmental state-making. The second has to do with the role and place of a developmental leadership to navigate both the external and internal environment in pursuit of developmental objectives. Thirdly, the focus is on state-society relations and how these can facilitate or undermine effective developmental state construction. The fourth theme has to do with institutional arrangements and specifically the institutions that have come to be associated with successful developmental state formation in East Asia. The fifth theme explores the bureaucracy, while the sixth focuses on redistribution and equity. The last one and the one that runs throughout this document has to do with the role of ideology in determining, shaping and conditioning the character and typology of states. While in no way discounting the role of the subjective factor (room to maneuver), it is important to underline that the character and substance of any developmental state-making process will, in the final analysis, be determined and coloured by the ideological framework that guides it.

The centrality of politics in developmental state-making

Much of the literature seeking to explicate the South African transition has been analytically limited and lacking in explanatory force largely because politics and political processes are not placed where they belong – at the centre of such analyses. Instead, there is a tendency to focus on a single explanatory variable at the expense of a comprehensive and forensic analysis of the incredibly complex socio-economic and political phenomena (and epiphenomena) that define that transition. Typically, developmental state skeptics will focus on the non-replicability of the geo-political and strategic realities that facilitated and gave rise to the East Asian developmental states. Alternatively, the new global economic dynamics and their hostility to state-led and driven processes are advanced as intractable obstacles to developmental state construction in the current period. Yet, others underline the unique nature of the institutional arrangements, these are supposedly unique to the culture of East Asian peoples. Yet, to gain fuller insights into the workings and interactions of all these (and other) variables, one needs to conduct a thoroughgoing forensic analysis of political actors, their interactions with each other, against each other, and with the structural and institutional arrangements within which they operate. For this very reason, politics and political processes are the central basis of analysis deployed to engage with the fundamental business of this project – the RDP and its developmental prospects. And in turn, the RDP (and political processes around it) is the touch-stone against which is tested and analysed the dynamic interaction between power, structure and agency, to explicate both its demise and the reasons thereof. The literature is awash with reasons why the construction of a developmental state in South Africa is either undesirable or an unsustainable proposition. Although this literature is engaged with in far more detail later, We might as well succinctly consider some of the key arguments.

In an otherwise useful and insightful review of the developmental state debate over the past three decades, Fine and Stoneman make the assertion that in Southern Africa "the economic conditions which confront the region are far from conducive to progressive interventions by the state in pursuit of developmental goals, given low growth, budgetary constraints and how these have been handled domestically and internationally (1996:7). Several problems are inherent in this way of approaching the problem. In the first instance, Fine and Stoneman fail to enlighten their readership as to their conception and definition of a developmental state. Consequently, it is not clear what analytical instruments and specific yardstick is being used to arrive at what Mkandawire (1998) has referred to as an "impossibility thesis". Secondly, is not the whole developmental edifice all about the triumph of state elites over such adversities as sluggish growth, budgetary constraints and how these are actively counter-acted domestically and globally. Indeed, the very idea behind the construction of developmental states has, historically,

11

been inspired by the pressing need to 'catch-up' – in the process surmounting precisely the constraints that Fine and Stoneman are alluding to. Chalmers Johnson clearly understood this when he made the point that "developmental elites are generated and come to the fore because of the desire to break out of the stagnation of dependency and underdevelopment" (1987: 140). Thirdly, and crucially, insufficient attention is paid to the analysis of specifically political factors to examine the replicability of East Asian developmental state experiences in the Southern African region. For such a political examination would demonstrate that in politics, the constraints noted by the authors invariably come with constraints and opportunities. In other words, there is always room for maneuver. And the decision to use such room or not, is in the final analysis a function of politics.

In an approach reminiscent of the reductionism they claim to avoid, Fine and Rustomjee (1996) elected to subordinate politics to economic processes. Such analysis may well be analytically credible in other contexts, but in South Africa, where politics has played such a central role in shaping and defining the socio-economic landscape, failing to give due prominence to politics can hardly suffice. For Fine and Rustomjee, politics:

> can only be adequately understood on the basis of a more complex analysis of the structure and functioning of the economy itself. Only then can political change be related to the prospects for economic change and the issue addressed of whether there has or can be an economic transition, or break with the past, corresponding to the political transition that has already occurred (1996:4).

It seems to me that South Africa's prospects for development can best be assessed by deploying a far more complex set of analytical instruments, that take on board both the institutional and structural constraints and the dynamic interplay of these with agential (political) factors. Such an approach would find that there is a dynamic and mutually reinforcing relationship between these variables. Thus, not only is an approach that subordinates politics to other variables of limited analytical utility, but it also confines to the background the most dominant and critical variable in understanding developmental state construction – politics. Indeed, developmental state-making is essentially about the nature of leadership, the state, state institutional arrangements and their interaction with various social actors – domestically and abroad, and the state's capacity to deploy its power in aid of economic development. In essence, therefore, developmental state construction is a fundamentally political process.

Other approaches have sought to treat the 'African continent' or Sub-Saharan Africa' or indeed, the 'African state' as an historically, political, economically and socially undifferentiated monolithic entity. The historical specificity of developmental states is brilliantly captured by Pempel (1999), where he shows that within East Asia, South Korea, Japan and Taiwan, although each was developmentalist in character and content, each state also confronted very different and unique internal and external challenges. In the case of Japan, the time period was very different. In certain respects, even the outcomes of development for each state, notably the extant of authoritarianism, nationalisation and protectionism, were different (199:149-153). In this context, Mkandawire's (1998) otherwise sober analysis of the developmental state's replicability sets itself the impossible task of contesting an 'impossibility thesis', which holds that 'Africa' is incapable of constructing developmental states (1998). The reality is that Africa is not an economically and politically undifferentiated entity, and what is more, there is neither concretely nor analytically an 'African State' against which Mkandawire's assertions can be tested. At any rate, prospects for developmental state construction and replication can only be derived from the analysis of concrete socio-historical and political conditions of country-specific realities. States are, after all, historically specific forms of power and rule, uniquely shaped by internal and global pressures. And this, in historically determined space and time (O'Meara, 1996: 41). Other Analysts who subscribe to this view of an 'African state' include Aron, who argues that:

> The state in Africa has come full circle to the small government of pre-colonial days; but with additional hysteresis effect from past shocks of a seriously depleted current institutional capability (1996:117).

The critical contribution of my approach to the developmental state debate and the discipline of politics more broadly, is that this assessment is not conducted on the basis of some indeterminate set of 'African conditions', but on the grounds of the concrete socio-economic, political and historical realities of pre-apartheid, apartheid and post-apartheid South Africa. At any rate, all these contributions to the debate seem to underplay a critically important variable in the politics discipline and practice- contingency.

The Primacy of Politics and Contingency

The debate around developmental prospects and replicability of developmental states is quite often undermined by a poor recognition of contingency. In other words, there are views, as we have shown in the foregoing pages, where structural and institutional constraints are presented as so intractable that the outcomes are certain – no developmental states in the current order of things. Alternatively, the limitations of agency are presented as iron-cast and non-negotiable. The common error in both instances is the assumption that in concrete socio-economic and political life, there are phenomena that are pre-determined, whose outcomes are certain and by extension, there is no room for manoeuvre. I underline contingency to explain not only the phenomenal growth in East Asia in the 1960s and 1970s, led and driven by the developmental elites in those countries, but I also show the role of contingency in the drive by Afrikaner elites to build a state type that was going to be responsive to the putative needs of the Afrikaner *Volk*. And, contrary to the dominant view that the demise of the RDP can be explained away by invoking the hegemony of neo-liberalism, I show that there was nothing certain or inevitable about the outcome of events in that process. Instead, the key players were conscious and strategic agents, who were fully aware of their options, the complex and contingent realities of 1990s South Africa. So, not only is there always room to manoeuvre, but leaders are strategic actors (with sufficient information), who choose their policy paths intentionally. They consciously make certain policy choices and reject others.

In order to set the scene for an outline of the key arguments and hypotheses of this project, it is important to delineate clearly the conceptual approach adopted here. To this end, some disclaimers are in order.

Some disclaimers

In the first instance, this book does not seek to argue that the experiences of East Asia can be mechanically transplanted to South African conditions. On the contrary, there is recognition that a South African version of the developmental state would necessarily be significantly different to the East Asian models. There are reasons for this. A South African model would be a product of its own peculiar socio-economic, political, historical and geo-strategic circumstances (as was the case with East Asian varieties and indeed, the partial, if distorted, Apartheid state).

Second, the human rights violations, specifically the suppression of the working classes, so characteristic of East Asian developmental state, is an unsustainable and probably unworkable option in the South African context. This is due to the fact that, unlike in East Asia, South Africa boasts an extremely powerful working class, highly politicized and one that played a major role in the eventual defeat of political apartheid. In South Korea and Taiwan, on the other hand, the strong state predates the evolution of the working class and bourgeoisie as significant social actors. Therefore, a South

African version of a developmental state would have to subscribe to Linda Weiss's model, where the political system is supportive rather than repressive (200:23). This necessarily implies a state whose legitimacy is earned through its developmental programmes, and not one that is violently imposed.

Third, it is not necessarily the argument here that thoroughgoing and systematic state intervention is a sufficient condition for the realization of South Africa's developmental and reconstruction needs. It is, however, the view that such state intervention is a necessary condition for the success of such projects. Moreover, this kind of intervention is not only viewed as an economic exercise, but also a profoundly political process aimed at far-reaching reconstruction, socio-economic and political development, which is seen as crucial in the context of South Africa.

Fourth, the analysis deployed here is not blind to the role played by the geo-strategic and political realities of the 1950s and 1960s in facilitating and shaping the state forms that emerged in the East Asian countries being discussed here (notably, Japan, South Korea and Taiwan). The cold war situation certainly gave these countries unprecedented access to western support, both in terms of military and financial aid. Jung-en Woo, for instance, notes that between1946 and 1976, the Americans injected $12.6 billion into South Korea, while Taiwan received $5.6 billion in the same period (1991:45). If the $3 billion coming from Japan and other international financial institutions is taken into consideration, then the total amount received by South Korea can be fixed at $ 15 billion (ibid). The 1990s presented a completely different and unique set of circumstances, with constraints and opportunities and by extension, room to manoeuvre.

Ideological Orientation

Gordon White and Christine White et al (1983) provided very interesting and stimulating examples of socialist oriented versions of developmental states in China, Vietnam, North Korea and other states. Moreover, there are valuable lessons to be drawn from these experiments with developmental state-making. However, the phenomenal success of the capitalist versions has been undeniable by comparison. Gordon White notes in this regard "in the eyes of their socialist competitors" and many contemporary left-wing economists in the region, economic progress in Japan, South Korea and Taiwan, has been superior to that of the socialist developmental states (1983:9). Thus, although ideational factors matter and are critical in determining success or failure in developmental state-making, so too, do plans, strategies, leadership, performance (in a word, a dynamic interaction between power, structure and agency). At any rate, it makes sense to evaluate the developmental capacity and potential of the South African state on the basis of what actually obtains in that country, which is a capitalist socio-economic order. Ideas and the ideological frameworks around which various developmental projects are structured are an important and critical explanatory factor. It is precisely for this reason that ideology (regime of accumulation) is identified as an important theme in our understanding of the developmental state thesis.

Why Ideas matter in developmental state-making

Many state actors, policy makers and economists continue to hold on with religious fervour and dedication to the supposed virtues of the neo-liberal ideological framework. This, despite its hopeless failure in large parts of the globe, to attend to the most pressing human development requirements, not to mention its proclivity to drag entire economies into damaging recessions. Moreover, almost thirty years following the fanfare surrounding the Washington consensus' stabilize, liberalise, privatize and reduce the role of the state aphorisms, economic performance, growth and development in many of the beneficiaries of these policies, remain dismal. However, reading the news on print media, television anywhere in the world today, one would be forgiven for thinking these policies were the very epitome of growth, development, equity and universal plenty. On the other hand, however, many of those opposed to the damaging role of neo-liberal policies on the global economy continue to hold on to doctrinaire notions and approaches to economic growth and development that have not, quite frankly, lived up to the egalitarian, growth and developmental promises of the ideological frameworks. And more disappointingly, the left has failed to put forward a comprehensive and sustainable critique of the failures and fundamental flaws of neo-liberalism. And, as a consequence, despite its damaging effect on almost every facet of life today (economy, trade, environment, poverty, inequality, education, health services and much more besides), the neo-liberal ideology remains the most dominant global intellectual, economic, social and environmental framework. Global problems and solutions are crafted and framed along the same lines.

What many critiques of the developmental state idea have generally failed to pay attention to, is its critical contribution to ideology. Not only does it provide a fundamental refutation of many of the axioms of the neo-liberal approach, but it also exposes the flaws in actually existing socialist state models. Above all, developmental state approaches open the way for a desperately needed heterogeneity in state-making, economic growth and human development perspectives. There is yet another reason why ideology matters in state-making processes. First, historically, all developmental elites have come to power armed with radically new and different sets of ideas. For there was appreciation that the current ideological framework was designed to sustain the current social and power relations. Despite their eschewal of communism and possible Chinese occupation, both South Korea and Taiwan (but especially, Taiwan), structured their party (Koumintang) and state very much along Marxist lines. Essentially, these developmental state experiments are a lesson in how to deploy the state-market dialectic, in the putative interest of society as a whole, growth and development.

Second, and this is crucial for the South African case, ideology matters because developmental state-making inherently imply fundamental change and transformation. This means that the current accumulation strategy will and must be disrupted and overhauled, for it is at the service of specific class and social beneficiaries. Thus, a critical measure of the success or failure of developmental state performance is the extent to which the underlying ideological framework has been overturned and the extent to which the dynamic between winners and losers has been affected. This will typically involve class formation and class annihilation, this process is discernible both in the destruction of landowning classes in South Korea and Taiwan, but also the formation and consolidation of finance capital, agricultural capital and the ideological nurturing of the Afrikaner working class in apartheid South Africa. Therefore, ideology matters in effective developmental state-making processes. Not all is doom and gloom. Though few in number and though not strictly adhering to the Japanese or South Korean developmental state models, it is nevertheless encouraging to see a growing number of states that consciously (sometimes not so consciously), insist on working outside the dominant global ideological framework. Some of these countries are located in East Asia, the middle East, some are rich in oil some have no primary products to speak of, some are still volatile as they emerge from war situations while some are relatively stable, all are dealing with complex internal and external socio-economic and political difficulties (including the effects of the global recession, corruption, financialisation etc). However, what is really common among this group of countries is that they have all generated average annual rates of growth (GDP per capita) of 7 % and more, consistently over a period spanning twenty-five years (1989 – 2015). Iraq has been at war for most of this period and is expected to average 7.2 % five year compound annual growth, with an unemployment rate of 16.1 %. Lao People's Democratic Republic (a former communist state) is expected to grow at around 7.5 % in 2015, while in Qatar (despite the decline in international oil prices), growth remains robust at 7.3% in 2015. Cambodia is looking at 7.3 % in 2015. There are other similar stories, as figure 1.1 below clearly illustrate.

Gross Domestic product – average annual % growth

Country	1999 - 2000	2000 - 2009	2009 – 2013
Cambodia	7.0	9.2	7.0
China	10.6	10.9	8.7
Indonesia	6.0	7.6	6.9
Iraq	10.3	3.8	8.1
Lao PDR	6.4	7.0	8.2
Qatar	11.1	13.5	10.2
Singapore	7.2	6.0	6.3
South Africa	2.1	4.0	2.7
Vietnam	7.9	6.8	5.8

Source: World Development Indicators (2015)

Apart from their politics, which are geared to growth and development (and their obvious impressive growth rates), there is one other really fundamental common attribute between these countries. The growth and development prospectus (ideology), has for one reason or other eschewed the dominant neo-liberal template. Could it be coincidental that the few countries that steer clear of prudence and stabilization policies are the only ones that seem to be making waves, even in the middle of one of the most devastating global recessions for eighty-five years? It seems to me that economics, economic theory, policy making and international development practice has much to learn and would be thoroughly enriched by enquiry into the growth and development determinants of these countries. I suggest that an ideological approach characterized by a heterodox policy mix (much like Japan, Korea and Taiwan did in an earlier period) is behind this *difference*. I have added South Africa in the list to underline the contrast. So, ideas and how such ideas are packaged, the policy packages and politics that emerge from such ideas do shape the character and content of states (and state-making processes).

Summary

To summarise, the central argument in this work is that the Reconstruction and Developmental Programme (RDP) constituted a critical instance for state-led and equity-based developmentalism in South Africa. Moreover, the shift from the RDP to the Growth, Employment and Redistribution (GEAR) strategy represented the passing of this opportunity and the abandonment of a state-led developmentalist path. This shift in strategic policy was a reflection of the absence of developmental state features, which was a consequence of internal and external pressures on the construction of a developmental state type in 1990's South Africa. At the same time, however, the policy direction ultimately adopted by the ANC is essentially and fundamentally a function of contingency and strategic intention. Both driven by ideology and politics. This is, by no means, an *Afrophobic* take on South Africa's developmental prospects. Far from it, the idea is, instead, to show the limitations of the current prospectus and to advocate for a re-imagination of the South African transition, guided by a different politics and a different ideological framework.

The Structure

The developmental states of East Asia have been remarkable and rare examples in the modern world of how rapid growth and relative equality may be combined in developmental strategies, which take the active role of the state to be one of their most important features. The central argument of the book is that active and intelligent state intervention (along East Asian lines) was going to be essential if the legacies of apartheid were to be transcended in the years after it became a democracy in the 1990s. I shall argue that the RDP of 1994 represented just such a hope and vision, combining a plan for growth and development with redistribution, which would be driven by the state in its role as catalyst, manager and senior partner in the economy. The RDP also reflected real continuity with key elements of the fundamental political and socio-economic philosophy, and the goals of the ANC, as contained in the Freedom charter of 1955. Moreover, an interventionist state of the kind envisaged by the RDP did not constitute a sharp break with the traditional form of the South African state. For the rise of Afrikaner political power from the 1920s, and its control of the South African state apparatus from 1948, represented an interesting, if narrowly racist and exclusive, example of developmental statism. However, the demise of the RDP and its institutional apparatus (however imperfect), and its replacement by the GEAR strategy in 1996, meant that this opportunity has been missed, leading to the abandonment of the state-led developmental strategy, with bleak implications for South Africa's immediate future. If we are to understand how this process unfolded, we need to understand developmental strategies and their outcomes in political terms. For just as the rise and modification of East Asian developmental states needs to be understood in a political context, so too, does the brief life of the RDP and its replacement by GEAR, with regard to both the internal and external political relationships of post-apartheid South Africa. This is the central analytical concern of this book.

Chapter One has outlined the problem to be analysed and explained. The chapter has sought to provide definitional clarity and background to the key concepts and variables dealt with in the rest of the chapters of this book.

Chapter Two explores the developmental and interventionist function of the apartheid state. Apartheid state political processes are analysed to demonstrate the developmentalist (albeit racist and exclusionist) form of the apartheid state. The chapter ends by suggesting that a developmentalist and internventionist state culture is not new to South Africa, and that in some respects, the foundations for the construction of a more inclusive state-led developmental processes were already in place.

Chapter Three sets out to identify the social, economic and political legacies of apartheid in order to show the extent of the developmental and redistributive deficit confronted by the new democratic post-apartheid state elites. The land issue, labour market and the economy are used as case studies to draw attention to the continuities and discontinuities between the apartheid and post-apartheid human development socio-economic status. The chapter concludes by demonstrating that, in the main, the continuities overwhelm the discontinuities and that as such, a fundamental overhaul and re-framing of South Africa's socio-economic problems is called for. And crucially, only some form of developmental state (led by a developmental leadership) can effectively deal with and overcome these legacies through a growth and re-distribution strategy, and that the RDP (in large measure) represented just such a strategy.

Chapter Four is essentially an introduction of the Reconstruction and development Programme. It seeks to isolate the key structural factors that defined the character and ultimate shape of the RDP. The chapter concludes by asking whether, given the immense structural constraints, the politics of the RDP left any room for manoeuvre in the form of a radical state-led economic policy frame-work.

Chapter Five focuses on the key agents whose activities defined the politics of the RDP. This is essentially a political analysis in which I focus on the roles and limitations of RDP politics, as a platform from which to launch a developmental state project. The chapter notes that the politics of the RDP were characterized by a pervasive presence and articulation of special interests, and that these interests articulated by the social actors were notorious for their conflictual character. Furthermore, until 1996 (when GEAR was unveiled), the new state elites sought to adopt a neutral stance and even underplay fundamental ideological difference within its ranks, this only served to further polarize the policy arena and sow mutual distrust. Not until the introduction of the GEAR did decisive and assertive leadership emerge with respect to economic policy. Only the direction of this new-found firm leadership represented a significant departure from the RDP. I conclude by noting that important aspects of the political features associated with the emergence and success of the East Asian developmental states were not present in the RDP process. Certainly not in sufficient strength to lay the foundations for the construction of a developmental state in South Africa.

Chapter Six accounts for the demise of the RDP in political terms. To this end, the external and internal factors, the structural and agential factors at play in the collapse of the RDP are examined to explain this collapse. The chapter concludes by noting the centrality and primacy of politics and political processes in the success and failure of developmental states in general. The chapter also concludes with specific reference to South Africa, that in the complex inter-play of structural, agential and power dynamics, the battle for the heart and soul of a developmentalist RDP was lost. Moreover, the answer for the demise of the RDP is to be found precisely in these interactions.

Chapter Seven presents the overall conclusions, by drawing out key themes of analysis. These include themes that were not prominent in the 1990's but which have in the intervening twenty years made themselves prominent features of the post-apartheid political landscape. I argue, first, that a combination of structural and agential factors and political circumstances conspired together to severely limit developmental state prospects in 1990's South Africa, whatever may have been the vision and hope of (at least some of) the new political leadership. Moreover, external pressures exerted a powerful influence against the RDP and its state-led developmentalism. However, there is always room to manoeuvre. Policy choices and broader economic policy direction taken was intentional by a leadership elite conscious of the suit of policy options available to post-apartheid South Africa. Second, as regards the debate over the primacy of structural or agential factors, my analysis suggests that the two mutually reinforce each other in shaping socio-political and economic processes and outcomes. Third, therefore, the study confirms the primacy of politics in the building of developmental states, and helps to explain why such states cannot simply be constructed to order. Finally, I conclude more speculatively (and in light of the worsening situation twenty years into democracy) that the demise of the RDP represented a tragic occurrence for South Africa's growth and development prospects. Without some kind of developmental state, committed to both equity and growth, and able to bring both about, one can anticipate only very slow and sluggish growth. In the context of a democracy with a robust civil society, one must therefore also anticipate deepening tensions (especially labour unrest, service delivery protests and student and youth disaffection), and hence increasing political instability.

The next chapter delve into the state, political and economic history of South Africa, in order to explore and analyse pre-1994 state-making processes. The central argument is that apartheid economic and state history provide important insights into the political economy of state and developmental state-making in South Africa.

CHAPTER

The Apartheid State:
its Role and Character

Introduction

This chapter focuses attention on apartheid economic development and state-making processes. It is a comparative analysis which draws attention to moments of developmental state-making in pre-1994 South African state and economic history. The chapter is also a deliberate invocation of the developmentalist state approach in explicating the awesome levels of state involvement in the economic and social development of Afrikaners in particular and the South African economy more broadly. Indeed, the phenomenal growth of the role of the Industrial Development Corporation (IDC) after 1948 was consistent with the apartheid state's policy of creating and assisting industries of economic and strategic importance in its programme. Moreover, the real gross domestic product (GDP) between 1948 and 1971 increased more than three-fold, while the average annual increase in gross national product (GNP) was more than double the rate of population growth, and average real per capita incomes had risen at the rate of over 2.5 per cent per year, in the same period (SARB Quarterly, various).

Exploration of the apartheid state as a moment in developmental state-making in South African state history has three important implications for the overall project. First and foremost, it places the history and politics of state-making in South Africa in historical perspective. Second, it shows important parallels between the politics of the apartheid state and politics of developmental state-making in East Asia. Third and crucially, it underlines the significance and materiality of ideology, politics and political processes in developmental state failure or success. The concern is therefore to shine the spotlight on a rarely explored aspect and explanatory factor in our understanding of growth and development processes that characterized South Africa at least until the mid-1970s. This is that the apartheid state's pervasive interventionist strategies on behalf of key sections of the Afrikaner community constitute an important explanatory variable, for a fuller understanding of the character, role and evolution of that state.

The chapter deals with five focal areas thus: Class formation and mobilization; the Cape-Transvaal ideological tendencies; Repression and mass action; International dimension and state intervention in the literature. First, however, a brief history and provenance of the apartheid state.

Racial Segregation Historically

The real impetus for the creation of the Union of South Africa, and hence the modern South African state is traceable to the discovery of minerals in the 1870s. Before these discoveries, South Africa was only of strategic and geo-political significance. However, after the discoveries, the country came to be seen by its British colonisers as a huge potential capital market. Moreover, before the formation of Union in 1910, present day South Africa was divided into various states and state-like entities, notably, the two British colonies: the Cape and Natal and the two Boer republics: Transvaal and Orange Free State. Additionally, there also existed a number of "autonomous African polities of varying sizes and political and military capability (Marks and Trapido, 1987:3).

The discoveries of diamonds in the Orange Free State in 1867, and gold in the Transvaal (both Boer republics), heralded the replacement of local agricultural capital with direct imperial capital (Legassick,1974: 260). The success of deep-level mining activities in particular demanded large scale capital inputs that were just not accessible locally. Successful exploitation was thus destined to rely on predominantly foreign inputs. For instance, foreign investment in mining activities between 1887 and 1913 amounted to 125 million Pound Sterling, with less than fifteen per cent of the shares held in South Africa itself (ibid).

Therefore, the conquest of the Transvaal and the Orange Free State by the British must, in the first instance, be seen as a response to the needs of deep level gold mining: the need for a drastic reduction in labour costs, and crucially, for a state with wider geographic powers and greater efficiency than the Transvaal land owners (Legassick, 1974: 261). Consequently, after a rather costly three-year long South African war (Anglo/Boer war, 1899-1902), both needs were met with the formation of the Union of South Africa in 1910 (Hepple, 1966; Fisher, 1969). This, in turn, set the scene for the formation and consolidation of the modern South African state, the central focus of this section.

The work of David Welsh (1971) on the Shepstonian policies in Natal, Maynard Swanson (1977) on the bubonic plague and segregation in the Cape, and Martin Legassick (1995) on Lord Milner's role in the reconstruction period, are all thoroughly illuminating and fascinating pieces of research and truly path-breaking in their contribution to the segregation-apartheid debate. These interventions are important if only because they helped convincingly to repudiate a major theme in liberal historiography on this subject. According to this view: "...the tragedy of race relations in South Africa reflects the capitulation of English speakers' flexible views to the harshly doctrinaire approach of Afrikaner nationalism" (Beinart and Dubow, 1995:6). Such analyses of South African history are, of course, fundamentally flawed and thoroughly misleading, as the architecture of racial capitalist policies are traceable to periods way before the advent of the apartheid state in 1948.

Segregation depicted more that the mere spatial separation of the races because of prejudices and attitudes of the white colonial administrators. Instead, it underlined the ideological rationalization, economic functions and legislative-administrative policy that conspired to give rise to segregation in the period under consideration. Lord Milner, the British Administrator of South Africa in the 'reconstruction period' (between 1902 and 1910), was determined to enunciate institutions and policies that would guide the new Union of South Africa. Central to this project was the satisfaction of the labour needs of the gold mining industry, the advocacy of racially exclusive residential areas and amenities, and the political representation of whites and blacks by separate means (ibid: 47). The views of Lord Milner expressed in his address to the Johannesburg Municipal Congress in 1903 are instructive:

> The white man must rule because he is elevated by many steps above the black man...Which it will take the latter centuries to climb and which it is quite possible that the vast bulk of the black population may never be able to climb at all...One of the strongest arguments why the white man must rule is because that is the only possible means of gradually raising the black man, not to our level of civilization- which it is doubtful whether he will ever attain- but up to a much higher level than that which he at present occupies (cited in Marks and Trapido, 1987: 7).

The reconstruction period under Lord Milner therefore saw the introduction of many of the strategies and policies that would constitute the hallmark of the apartheid state's own policies in later years. These included the allocation of African reserves, the control of urban influx through pass laws and the manipulation of tribal chiefs as agents of the colonial state. For these reasons, therefore, the advent of apartheid essentially represented a tightening of segregationist labour controls rather than a departure from it (Legassick, 1974b). On the other hand, the same reconstruction period can be used to explain the country's legacy of a hierarchical and racially segmented labour market structure. On the other hand, there was the need for highly skilled and experienced workers, and these were inevitably whites from England and elsewhere in Europe (Marks and Trapido, 1987).

The early 1900s constitute the formative period of segregationist policies, the catalyst, however, was the eruption in that period of the bubonic plague in the Cape. Research has shown that, on the pretext of controlling the spread of the plague, the colonial authorities removed thousands of Africans from the city centre to Uitflugt (now known as Ndabeni). Of significance is that: "By September 1901, the plague had receded in Cape Town, with 806 cases and 389 deaths of which sixty-nine were whites, 244 coloureds and seventy-six Africans" (Swanson,1995:31). It is therefore not clear why it was only Africans (who seemed to pose a much limited danger) who were moved to a resettlement camp, unless one probes deeper. Once the epidemic was arrested, the Cape authorities did not return those who were moved to Uitflugt. Instead, it was deemed prudent to transform the said resettlement camp into a labour bureau, that would respond to the labour needs of the Cape's white employers (ibid). To facilitate controlled, but easier access for employers, African labour was facilitated through a dompass system to employers who required and thus applied for such labour.

Afrikaner farmers looked to apartheid as a system that facilitated state intervention to ensure an equitable distribution of African labour between urban and rural areas. This was hardly different to the way that Lord Milner's administration actively intervened to cater for the labour needs of white employers in 1900s or the United Government instituted racially repressive policies in order to satisfy the labour needs of the mines. Segregationist policies are thus in many respects, a precursor to apartheid and their genesis should be located firmly in British Administrative policies in the 1900s. Swanson has also shown that the manner in which Africans were treated during the bubonic plague in the Cape was not an isolated incident. In fact, it was official policy for the 'sanitation syndrome' to be used as pretext to control the movements of Africans. A Dr. Banard Fuller- a Cape Town Medical Officer is quoted in Swanson's work: "these uncontrolled kaffir hordes were at the root of the aggravation of Cape Town slumdom brought to light when the plague broke out…it was absolutely impossible to keep the slums of the city in satisfactory condition". At the same time, British Administrator of the Transvaal, Sir Godfrey Lagden, responded to Indians residing in central Johannesburg thus: "the lower castes are as a rule filthy in habit and a menace to the public health" (cited in Swanson, 1995: 28-30).

Two factors are worth noting from the above analysis. First, segregationist policies were related to both economic imperatives and the racial prejudices held by different British authorities in South Africa. Second, the continuities between segregationist policies and apartheid policies are undeniable. In fact, any doubt about the provenance of apartheid policies and the continuities with earlier British Administrators' race policies, is dispelled by a careful analysis of key legislation passed during Milner's reconstruction period.

The legislative terrain

To give legal force to Lord Milner and his South African Native Commission's ideas, a plethora of segregationist laws were passed by the new Union of South African parliament. Of these, three stood out as confirming the 'cheap labour thesis' as advanced by a number of historians and economic historians (Wolpe, 1972; Legassick, 1974a). And, as ever, these laws responded to the deeply engrained racial prejudices held by the different British Administrators (and the general population) for some time, but were only systematized into a coherent strategy during Milner's time (Legassick, 1974a; Dubow, 1995; Swanson 1995). Above all, the Union's segregationist policies sough to cement the shaky unity between the English and the Afrikaner white communities. This unity was to be predicated on meeting the labour needs of both the mining sector and the agricultural sector on the one hand, and on protecting the white man, especially the unskilled Afrikaner lower classes, from black competition on the other (Innes, 1984; Terreblanche and Nattrass, 1990).

The mines and Works Act No 2 of 1911

This piece of legislation essentially discriminated against black mine workers and specifically targeted their advancement into more skilled jobs. More specifically, the law stipulated thirty-two categories of work in the mines that were strictly reserved for white workers. These categories included the driving of elevators, blasting of explosives, mine management, mine overseeing, mine surveying, mechanical engineering and engine driving (Wilson, 1972:11). This law essentially sealed the inferior status of black workers for it set the tone for the statutory colour bar thereby defining South Africa's labour market for the next hundred years. Indeed, the recent Marikana upheavals have brought these conditions once again into sharp focus. The employers were, in the main, supportive of this law, as long as it did not interfere with their access to cheap black labour in the unskilled categories, where the need was most acute. Black wages in the mines remained roughly constant between 1911 and 1972, thereby contributing significantly to the lowering of production costs in this sector (Wilson, 1975:23). White workers were attracted to the mining sector because higher pay and more highly skilled jobs were reserved for them. Moreover, the state was determined to ensure that the provisions of the Act were strictly adhered to. The Act stipulated that "any person who contravenes any provision of this Act or any regulation, or who fails to comply with the terms of any notice or instruction given by an officer of the Mines Department under this Act or any regulation…will be liable on conviction to a fine not exceeding hundred pounds or … imprisonment for a period not exceeding a year" (1911: 390-392). More than hundred years later, the South African labour market has yet to completely rid itself of the oppressive and iniquitous effects of this legislation.

The Black Labour Regulations Act No. 5 of 1911

This regulation is related to the above, but had the added dimension of imposing control over black labour. It made it an offence for a black worker to break his contract with one employer, say in a gold mine, and move to a manufacturing company that offered better wages. The legislation also prohibited employers from enticing a black worker contracted elsewhere with the promise of higher wages (Innes, 1984: 68). In order to properly police and control black workers, this piece of legislation provided for the registration of all work seekers with the relevant employer recruitment agencies. Furthermore, the employer recruiters themselves had to be registered with the Native Affairs Department and had to ensure that a worker was only registered by the employer who recruited him. This helped the authorities to keep track of the numbers of blacks residing in 'white areas' and to get a good sense of where labour needs were. However, the issuing of passes to such registered workers was not only about identification, it was also about the Native Labour Regulation Act's desire to systematize pass controls in the labour districts by regulating recruitment, employment and housing. The mines favoured this legislation principally because of its divisive effect between black and white workers. For, it helped to "inhibit the emergence of common purpose and helped preserve the economies of the migrant labour system. White racialism also provided a convenient rationale for the regimentation of the black workforce" (Crush, Jeeves and Yudelman, 1991: 80). The penalties for breaking the contracts were severe, including imprisonment and hard labour (Act 15:1911). Moreover, as the preamble to the law suggests, it also sought to extend and consolidate the various pre-Union laws with respect to "regulation and recruitment, employment, accommodation, feeding and health conditions of native labour" (ibid). This last point denotes the origins of these laws in the 'reconstruction' and earlier periods, and crucial to the segregationist agenda was the desire to separate the different races geographically as well. In this connection, the Native Land Act was promulgated.

The Native Land Act of 1913

This legislation essentially prohibited Africans (except for certain categories in the Cape) from owning land outside areas designated as 'native reserves'. These areas constituted 7.3 per cent of the country's land, and were supposed to be home to some 87 per cent of the country's population (Lipton, 1985; Nattrass and Terblanche, 1990). Moreover, the central force behind this legislation was the need for cheap labour and to respond to the racial prejudices of the white population for the races to be separated. Principally, however, the idea was to squeeze Africans into these reserves in order to force them off productive land which would in turn compel them to seek work in white controlled farms, mines and commerce. In this connection, the Land Act gives the Director-General the task of identifying:

> As soon as maybe after this Act, what areas should be set apart as areas within which natives shall not be permitted to acquire or hire land or interests in land. Which areas should be set apart as areas within which persons other than natives shall not be permitted to acquire or hire land or interests in land (1913:438-440).

Therefore, apart from separating the races, the 1913 Land Act also fulfilled a different role, namely that of supplying the white industries with large quantities of cheap black labour (Wolpe, 1972; Legassick, 1974). What is more, all three pieces of legislation taken together underline the same basic proposition advanced by Swanson, Legassick and Wilson: that much of the apartheid legislation, even if not directly introduced by the apartheid state, at least has precedents set by previous British Administrators. Furthermore, these laws, in large measure, confirm Legassick's proposition that the key to understanding apartheid and segregationist legislation on issues of franchise, land and labour, should in the final analysis be sought in the cheap labour needs of capital (coupled with, but secondary to the racial prejudices of the instigators of such policies). So, the same socio-economic logic has driven the suit of policies enacted by both the British Administrators and the apartheid state.

In the next section I set out to show not only that the drive, logic and motivation behind the apartheid state's repressive labour policies were the same as those that drove segregation, but I also discuss the specific politics of apartheid state-making that made the general framework attractive. It is the same politics and political factors that gave the regime of accumulation a specifically Afrikaner nationalist flavour. Therefore, the crucial innovation was the anchoring of an Afrikaner nationalist development agenda within the broad structural and institutional framework of a racial capitalist accumulation strategy. I seek to discuss the National Party's post-1948 innovation by looking at how its support among the different Afrikaner social classes was mobilised and constituted. This survey will also serve to explain the almost unswerving support that apartheid and apartheid policies continued to receive from most members of the Afrikaner community. I also show that, over and above the systematic mobilization of this community around an Afrikaner development agenda, the apartheid state project was also linked to the brutal oppression and strict regulation of the rapidly proletarianising African population. In this connection, the rise in the numbers of African employees in the post-war period is instructive, for it was in large measure directly responsible for the unity of purpose forged among different Afrikaner social classes. These classes were for different reasons threatened by the rapid urbanization, militancy and numerical superiority of Africans in South Africa's urban centres.

The following statistical information illustrates that these fears were not baseless. Trade Union membership rose from 264 000 in 1939 to 419 000 in 1945, whilst the number of registered unions grew from 139 to 203 in the same period (Simons and Simons, 1983: 554). More importantly, the Non-European Trade Union Council represented 119 unions at the end of 1945, with a total membership of 158 000 organised workers. Also, the manufacturing sector, the fastest growing economic sector in the post-war era, saw the number of African workers rising by a phenomenal 57 per cent in the same period (ibid). Hence, by deconstructing the Afrikaner community along class lines, it becomes apparent in what way each class and class fraction stood to benefit from supporting the apartheid capitalist agenda.

Agricultural Capital

The second World War production demands turned out to be a watershed period for South African manufacturing. For the first time, this sector contributed more to Gross Domestic Product (GDP) than did mining or agriculture. Manufacturing output grew 81.6 per cent from 1939 – 1944, and the use of local materials rose from 51, 7 per cent of input in 1938 to 60 per cent in 1945 (BTI, 1945: 153). It was precisely because of these developments that the number of black workers, both skilled and unskilled, grew so phenomenally in the manufacturing sector and, in the process, undermined the cheap labour needs of Afrikaner dominated agricultural capital. Thus, there was phenomenal growth in the manufacturing sector, especially during the second world war period. At the same time, this growth was accompanied by a massive urbanization of blacks from rural areas and those who left the farms and mines for better wages.

This development frustrated white farmers with respect to their labour needs and deepened insecurity among white predominantly Afrikaner workers. As Muller and Jones (1992) observed in their study of the performance and status of the agricultural sector in relation to other sectors of the South African economy in the mid-1940s: "Agriculture was occupying a declining role in the economy until 1948, when the National Party's victory in the general election of that year installed a farmer-sympathetic government" (1992: 129).

In preparation for the 1948 general elections, the Nationalists latched onto this sector. It was after all a huge potential constituency, since Afrikaners enjoyed numerical superiority in all provinces with the notable exception of Natal (Davies, O'Meara and Dlamini, 1985: 18). The grievances (that needed to be packaged into an elections manifesto) essentially revolved around shortages of cheap labour and the powerlessness of agricultural capital in controlling and keeping such labour. And, importantly, agricultural capital had no resources or capacity to compete with the higher wages offered by employers in the manufacturing sector in the urban centres, where most of the potential black work force was flocking. A second problem for this sector lay in the pricing of their products. Prices for agricultural products were rapidly dropping as gold and manufacturing increasingly took centre stage in South Africa's economy. Agricultural capitalists were thus anxious for a government that would be sensitive and responsive to both problems:

product pricing and need for cheap labour (Posel, 199; O'Meara,1996).

This anxiety was illuminatingly demonstrated by the 1944 meeting between the Minister of Native Affairs, Mr. Van der Byl, and a special delegation of the South African Agricultural Union. In that meeting, the farmers requested a "long term policy to encourage and develop the division of the native population into two main groups: agriculture and industrial" (cited in Morris, 1977). Two years later, the South African Agricultural Union was only able to report that "little progress has been made in the long term proposal of the Union to encourage and develop native labour into two main groups in order to ensure a fair distribution of labour between agriculture and industry" (ibid: 21).

Afrikaner farmers made various demands off the United Party government throughout the mid-1940s: "farm organisations required increased state control of the African labour market, the displacement of squatters and the use of emergency regulations to compel squatters to take up work on white farms, removal of 'loafers' and 'idle' Africans from the urban areas and their forced relocation to white farming areas." (Greenberg,1987:35). The various pre-1948 governments in turn, showed little sympathy for the 'repressive' and racial solutions advanced by the farming community" (ibid). All the while the government was making similar interventions for mining and manufacturing capital. Accordingly, the key issues in the National Party's campaign for both the 1948 and 1953 general elections centred around apartheid, labour needs and anti-communism.

To address the labour needs of the agricultural sector, a rigid form of influx control was envisaged to ensure an unlimited supply of cheap black labour. This would be achieved through a strict implementation of the pass law system (that was already in the statute books), thereby controlling the movement of blacks and systematically directing them to farms (O'Meara, 1996: 29). To ensure that existing legislation hit the right spots, The Natives Laws Amendment Act of 1952 and the Natives (Abolition of Passes and Coordination of Documents) Act of 1952 were promulgated. Taken together, these two amendments required Africans to have worked in the 'white areas' for ten years or more before acquiring the right to remain in those areas. Also, they provided for the establishment of labour bureaux to control and move the unemployed 'loafers' and 'idle' to areas of need (usually remote white farms far away from the urban centres). In short, the movements and employment status of Africans in the urban areas were to be tightly monitored, thereby making it easier for farmers to get hold of excess labour. Although the laws seemed relatively straight forward in the statute books, in practice it was a completely different story. Africans experienced these laws in the most repressive and humiliating ways, being caught by the police with the wrong or incomplete papers often meant spending time in cells whilst the system slowly decided your fate. So, the advent of Nationalist Party rule brought forth a period of major state innovation and growing state presence in the South African labour market. That government also set out to fashion a state apparatus and legislative framework designed to respond more effectively to the labour needs of agricultural capital.

With respect to the pricing problem, the Nationalist government would revive the agricultural control board (also already in the statutes), which were set up under the Marketing Act of 1936, to protect agricultural prices from fluctuations. Once in power, of course, the National Party government made good on both promises. The Maize Board and other agricultural control boards, whose role had changed due to the exigencies of war to that of food rationing (lower prices), were reorganized to protect prices. In this regard, the producers price index for maize rose by more than 50 per cent between 1948 and 1954, while that of meat increased by 82 per cent between 1948 and 1956 (Department of Agriculture, 1958). Consequentially, agricultural production rose by more than 50 per cent between 1948 and 1960 (Brand and Tomilson, 1966: 45). Such had been the relationship between Afrikaner agricultural capital and the Nationalist Party. The new regime had a firm and very reliable social base in this class, not only for electoral purposes, but also for the broader socio-economic and political agenda of Afrikaner nationalist development. However, in order to be effective, other Afrikaner social classes had to be brought on board.

The Afrikaner Petty Bourgeoisie

One fraction of the Afrikaner petty bourgeoisie was composed largely of teachers, academics, newspaper editors, civil servants, religious leaders and small businessmen. Many people who fell onto this group were also members of the Afrikaner Broederbond (Afrikaner Brotherhood), a secret organisation formed in 1918 to cater for the interests of the Afrikaner Volk (Bunting, 1986: 54). The Broederbond was essentially an economic movement formed to improve the economic fortunes of Afrikaners, and the key obstacles were characterized as English monopoly capitalism and African political domination. These two issues were aptly depicted in the Afrikaans media as 'Hoggenheimer' (a racist and anti-Semitic symbol that caricatured English monopoly capitalism), and *oorstroming* (inundation), referring to the danger of black domination (O'Meara, 1996: 34). These two ideas constituted the central thrust of the National Party's work among this section of the Afrikaner community.

In this respect, therefore, the relative improvement of the economic status of black people, facilitated by the growth of the manufacturing sector during the war years, was seen by the Afrikaner intelligentsia as a potential threat to their political and economic survival. More so in view of the fact that white wages were stagnant in the same period. In sharp contrast to the relatively stagnant earnings of white labour, the index of average real earnings of Africans employed in private manufacturing rose from a base of 1, 000 in 1938 to reach 1, 533 in 1945/6 (1983: 239). The increased black unionization and increasing militant demands for political rights were seen, by the Afrikaner elites, as a direct challenge to the position of Afrikaners in the country.

This group wanted, above all else, to see an Afrikaner nationalist government in power that could stem both economic and political threats posed by Africans on the one hand, while challenging the economic status of the English speakers relative to the Afrikaner on the other. The Nationalist Party was seen as a perfect vehicle through which to pursue these aspirations. Deborah Posel (1999), in a detailed study of the public and civil service under apartheid, noted how the possibility of more blacks being employed in order to stem the massive staff shortages in the civil service, startled the Afrikaner employees. Therefore, despite their many grievances "the prospects of having to compete for their jobs against a huge black pool must have been a rude reminder to white civil servants that their meal ticket remained with the National Party." (Posel, 1999: 115). Despite the provisions of the law, prohibiting active political party membership, thousands of Afrikaner public servants remained loyal and active participants of the National Party (ibid).

The Bantu Education Act of 1953, which provided for an inferior system of education for Africans and Promotion of Bantu Self-Government Act of 1959, also provided for the exclusion of Africans from political participation in 'white' South Africa, were legislation designed to respond to the fears of the Afrikaner petty bourgeoisie.

The second fraction of the Afrikaner petty bourgeoisie consisted of small Afrikaner finance, commercial and manufacturing capital, mainly dominated by the Broederbond and other aspirant commercial and financial capitalists. These included the founders and leadership of the South African National Life Assurance Company (SANLAM), which was formed in 1918, and the South African Trust and Assurance Corporation (SANTAM), formed in 1919. The key concern here was to build Afrikaner commercial and industrial enterprises capable of competing and surpassing their English counterparts. For these ambitious plans to succeed, the group needed capital, and lots of it. The key source of this capital was the Afrikaners themselves. To this end, strategies were designed to appeal to all the different Afrikaner social classes. They wanted to see a rate of profit in the agricultural sector, the surplus of which would be redirected and re-invested in other Afrikaner commercial ventures (Welsh, 1974: 259). Furthermore, they wanted to see the employment conditions of Afrikaner laboring classes improved in terms of both salaries and the general availability of employment opportunities. The workers would in turn be encouraged to use the Afrikaner banking and insurance organisations to save their money. This capital, too, would be invested in the Afrikaner nationalist developmental project. This group was also concerned by the potential threat posed by black political and economic demands. The realization of these demands would lead to competition with Afrikaner workers' employment and earning prospects. At a political level, the realization of black demands for political rights would undermine the possibility of an Afrikaner nationalist government – a possible instrument for the articulation of the economic aspirations of Afrikaans speakers. An Afrikaner nationalist government in power would give the access and control they needed over the economic apparatus of the state.

Once in power, many aspects of this agenda were swiftly implemented and achieved. Terblanche (1989), for instance, makes the point that : "the government's policy of promoting Afrikaner interest was very successful. In 1946 the per capita income of Afrikaners was less than half that of English-speakers. By 1970, after many years of government pampering and patronage, it has increased to 70 per cent" (1989: 13). Such therefore, was the position of the Afrikaner petty bourgeoisie in the broad frame of Afrikaner nationalist and capitalist development. To complete the broad multi-class alliance that brought the apartheid government into office, the role of the Afrikaner working class was imperative.

The Afrikaner Working Class

The main issue for the unskilled and semi-skilled Afrikaner working classes was the growing competition they faced from black workers, which, as we saw in the foregoing sections of this chapter, had been intensified by the second world war labour needs of the manufacturing sector. Moreover, the growing strength and militancy of black trade unions threatened the relative job security hitherto enjoyed by white workers, against black competition (Innes, 1984: 143; Lipton, 1985: 196). Unsurprisingly, therefore, most white workers resented the set back to what they regarded as their natural right to precedence over blacks. In an endeavour to protect their privileges, many of them voted for the National Party in the 1948 general elections. A number of factors contributed to this sense of insecurity and alienation among white workers.

First, many white workers were lost to the different sectors of the economy because of pre-war military recruitment. Employers (because of cost considerations) were rapidly abandoning the old racial allocations to certain positions. Cheaper black labour was being engaged in positions traditionally recognized as the sole preserve of whites. By 1945, the proportion of blacks in such positions had increased by an incredible 57 per cent (Innes, 1984: 143). Secondly, the exigencies of war meant that wage rates did not have to keep up with the rise in prices where this would affect the prosecution of the war. These exigencies included the compulsion of workers in "the engineering industry to work fifty-four hours per week, the status of skilled artisans in a number of industries was 'diluted', making them easily replaceable. Over and above this, managers in some industries could insist on overtime without overtime pay" (Davies, 1979: 299). Consequently, real wages in many sectors were affected negatively. As a matter of fact, in his work on this subject, O'Meara discovered that "For much of this period, the real wages of white workers actually fell.... the brunt was borne by the lower strata of wage workers, particularly those in the mining industry" (1983: 239).

An additional factor was that many rights of workers were removed in support of the war effort, strikes in particular were not tolerated. Would be strikers were subjected to violent repression. For instance, in1940 white women workers were baton-charged and tear gassed back into their tobacco factory and compelled to work. The same treatment was meted against sweet workers in 1942 (ibid). Furthermore, as a war time measure, government appointed a Controller of Industrial Manpower with wide ranging powers. These powers were used to extend minimum working hours in certain industries with no overtime pay. All these factors created an extremely discontented Afrikaner working class, many of whom did not even support the war (or were partial to the Germans). This, among other things a function of a strong anti-British sentiment engendered by the Anglo-Boer war. And so, the organisers of the National Party utilized these grievances and resentment to mobilise this section of the Afrikaner community.

All major economic sectors of the South African economy experienced serious fluctuations in terms of wage increases in the period between 1939 -1945. Although the combination of these factors led to increasing despondency among Afrikaner workers, none riled them and was as contentious as that depicted by the rapid erosion of their privileged position relative to the black workers. This fact made apartheid policies, which promised the perpetuation of the colour bar in industry and white supremacy in all spheres of society, very attractive to the Afrikaner worker

The electoral victory of the Nationalist Party in 1948 proved an important turning point for Afrikaner workers, especially with respect to wages. White wages rose more rapidly than black wages in the period after the 1948 elections. Nattrass (1990) advanced the view that the growth rate of white wages relative to black wages was such that "the white share of the wage bill increased from 61 per cent to 63.4 per cent, despite the decline in the white share of employment from 32. 3 per cent to 27 per cent between 1948 and 1960 (1990:113). Moreover, the apartheid state tightened the 1937 Amendment to the Industrial Conciliation Act. This law provided for the determination of wage levels by industrial councils. The wage rates of blacks were affected because this law also systematically discriminated against them, by allowing the determination of high minimum wages for certain categories of employment. This, of course, also negatively affected those employers who employed blacks in such positions.

Furthermore: " for white labour, apartheid remained beneficial. It provided an effective closed shop with protection from competition and undercutting by blacks. It also provided the white working class and lower middle classes with preferential access to resources such as welfare benefits, housing and education with social status and...considerable political power to protect their privileges" (Lipton, 1986: 8). Such state nurturing went a long way in securing the support of the overwhelming majority of this group. This was also consistent with the argument that the apartheid state pursued a socio-economic agenda around which Afrikaners were being mobilised. Therefore, black workers were kept at an inferior position in terms of their conditions of work, their prospects for promotion to more skilled jobs, and in terms of wage increases. Black trade unions were not recognized by the apartheid state until black workers forced such recognition through rolling industrial action, starting in Durban in the early 1970s. In this regard, JB. Schoeman (Minister of Labour), un-apologetically proclaimed "I want the native trade unions to disappear...I have made that perfectly clear.." (HA, 1953: col.1899-19/08/53). Instead, therefore, black trade unions were thoroughly suppressed through a suite of repressive measures available to the state not excluding the infamous Suppression of Communism Act of 1950 (Simons, 1983: 595). Such was the role and significance of the Afrikaner working class both in the National Party's victory and in its future development plan.

However, for the apartheid state's political and economic agenda to succeed, it was crucial to contain the threat brought forth by the growing black opposition and mobilization. To deal with this problem the state instituted a number of laws, notably the Suppression of Communism Act of 1950, the Settlement of Disputes Act of 1953 and of course, crucial to the state's agenda, the Separate Development Act of 1957. Combined, these laws added to the existing arsenal of measures implemented to thwart all black political activity in 'white' South Africa, and to consign any political aspirations to the rural slums as provided for by the Separate Development Act of 1957. With the black threat out of the way, the scene was set for a thoroughgoing Afrikaner nationalist socio-economic development programme.

The Apartheid State – Its Socio- historical Foundations

There is sufficient consensus among South African economic and political historians that the socio-historical and ideological foundations of the apartheid state are traceable among other things, to the rise of Afrikaner nationalism, and the economic aspirations this engendered (Welsh, 1974; Moodie, 1975; O'Meara, 1977 and 1996; Giliomee, 1979 and 1989; Davies, 1979; Uys, 1989). The intensity of Afrikaner nationalist passions is in turn traced firstly, to the Boer experiences during the Great trek and their often acrimonious contact with various African tribes while escaping British control in the Cape (Marks and Trapido, 1987). Another crucial aspect relates to the Afrikaners' experiences during the Anglo-Boer war (1899-1902), which led to the death of many Afrikaners and the humiliation of the Volk (Hepple, 1966; Welsh; 1974). Since all "nationalisms need enemies, the Afrikaners' enemies were British imperialism and indigenous blacks" (Uys, 1989: 206). The socio-economic pressures associated with the war, were a particularly strong catalyst for the rise and development of a particular type of anti-British Afrikaner nationalism. Moreover, it represented a particularly painful and humiliating chapter in Afrikaner history, not only because it ended in defeat for Afrikaners, and the annexation of their territories, but also because the horrific treatment suffered by those directly affected, scarred the whole Volk for a long time.

The following breakdown of Afrikaner casualties of the war illuminate the point: of the 26 000 Afrikaners who died in the concentration camps, more than 20 000 were children under the age of sixteen, 4 177 were women, while only 1 676 were men (Fisher,1969: 197). Actual Afrikaner casualties sustained in the battlefield amounted to 7000 men. Over and above this, at the end of the war, those who survived were confronted by devastation and destruction of their homesteads and animals. The exigencies of the war situation coupled with drought and cattle disease also led to the massive displacement of Afrikaners from the platteland, compelling them to move to

38

the urban centres of South Africa, in search of alternative means of living. On arriving in such centres, they found their arch-enemies, the English in full control of all aspects of life, commerce, industry and the public sector (Welsh, 1974: 251). In the work places too, there seemed to be a preponderance of an English speaking industrial working class, with a well-established tradition as industrial artisans. They were moreover, well organized in their trade unions which had set traditions and ways of doing things.

This situation, too, contributed to putting the Afrikaner worker and potential worker in the precarious position of having to fit into an unfamiliar culture and politics, thereby accentuating the feeling of alienation (ibid). The political and economic hegemony of English speakers meant that their culture, language and English business and commercial traditions predominated, much to the resentment of the Afrikaners. Therefore, the nature of the apartheid state must, in part be located, understood and explained in terms of conflicts, resentment and drive by Afrikaner elites to catapult themselves out of this miserable state of affairs. There was a burning desire to surpass the English in all social spheres and this factor is an important explanatory variable for understanding the provenance and character of the apartheid state. As O'Meara underlined:

> Following the Anglo-Boer war, British colonial hegemony fashioned economic, social and cultural relations in such a way as effectively to exclude those defined as Afrikaans-speaking whites from ownership of capital in all sectors bar agriculture, and leave most Afrikaner speakers with the deep sense of resentment (1996:44).

The apartheid state's imposition of protectionist barriers, and the provision of concessionary finance to many Afrikaans owned industries, is an important demonstration of the practical articulation of the state's preoccupation with developing Afrikaner capital at the expense of an 'even-handed' mediation role by the state between capitals. Legassick (1975) also showed how Gencor, the first ever Afrikaner owned mining company received its first industrial contract from the state owned Iron and Steel Corporation (ISCOR). Seidman (1994) too, observed that on assuming office, the National Party government moved many of the state organisation's financial accounts to Afrikaner owned banks, as such state deposits in Afrikaner owned Volkskas bank increased fivefold between 1948 and 1955 (1994: 80). Indeed, Grietjie Verhoef noted the same tendency in her study of the growth of South African financial enterprises from 1950. Explaining the Volkskas' rapid expansion in this period, she state:

part of the explanation for Volkskas' asset growth lies in the expansion of parastatals, such as Eskom, Iscor and Sasol, that had given part of their business to Volkskas (Verhoef, 1992: 130).

The other 'enemy' of Afrikaner nationalism in the post Anglo-Boer war period was the black population (a group they considered to be racially and culturally inferior). What accentuated the feelings of resentment and humiliation was having to compete with blacks for jobs in the unskilled categories, principally in the mines. Moreover, the cheap rate of black labour relative to white labour (a cheapness particularly facilitated by the Masters and Servants Act of 1856), meant that employers increasingly preferred the more cost effective black labour over Afrikaner unskilled labour. Because of their numerical superiority engendered by deteriorating conditions in the reserves and active recruitment by the Chamber of Mines, blacks posed a serious problem to Afrikaner employment chances in the unskilled categories (Innes, 1984:63). The establishment by the Chamber of Mines of its own Native Labour Department in 1893, specifically to recruit blacks from the reserves, underlined the difficulties confronting unskilled Afrikaner work seekers, and the employers' preference for black labour (ibid). Of significance, from an Afrikaner point of view, were the obstacles blacks posed to Afrikaner employment and social advancement in the cities.

Secondly, and related to the above point, was the prospect of a numerically dominant black populace. This presented a major threat to Afrikaner freedom, economic and political development, since it would mean that the Afrikaner would forever be caught between English economic dominance and black numerical and by extension political dominance, something that surely consign Afrikaners to the economic and political fringes of South African society. This, too, is an important defining feature and explanatory variable of the character and role of the apartheid state. This was acted upon in the apartheid state's consolidation of segregationist policies, and establishment of 'separate development' through self-government and 'independent' Bantustans (Legassick, 1974). Such policies, above all else, were about checking black oorstroming (inundation) in 'white areas' thereby securing the political future of Afrikaners in South Africa. This was reflected in the apartheid state's deep commitment (even when it did not make sense economically) to block black access to land and citizenship in the urban centres.

Meeting Afrikaner Economic Aspirations

The Afrikaner elites were anxious to meet the economic aspirations of their chief constituents. This, however, had to be achieved within a broadly capitalist framework but one that would be overhauled in such a way that it refocused and reproduced a different socio-economic agenda. Nevertheless, the racial capitalist framework was largely deemed appropriate for the achievement of the elite's broad objectives. Thus, to the extent that the capitalist content of any state is determined by the extent to which it creates, maintains or restores the conditions required for capital accumulation, the apartheid state was a capitalist state (Jessop, 1982).

However, in the South African context, one needs more than just to establish the state's maintenance and restoration of capitalist relations. There is always the added need to explore the particular factors that gave the state its peculiarly complex racial capitalist dimension. In this regard, there is the added requirement to explicate the particular form taken on by the apartheid state – one rooted in an Afrikaner nationalist ideological discourse. One way of going about such an exercise is to look at the class basis of the Nationalist Party in the early years of its existence. Such an investigation reveals two ideological tendencies in the evolution and interpretation of Afrikaner nationalism over the years. It reveals, moreover, that the tensions engendered by these different interpretations were resolved by an approach (to capitalism) that sought to take on board the interests of all sections of the Afrikaner community. One of these tendencies espoused an openly capitalist brand of nationalism based on creating a stake for Afrikaner corporate interests within the wider and more inclusive (of Afrikaners, of course) accumulation framework. The proponents were mainly Cape based and relatively affluent. On the other hand, the northern provinces put forward a more exclusivist brand of nationalism, one quite suspicious of capitalism, something they associated with British imperialism and greed. These two, I suggest, were welded together, and given concrete organizational, ideological and policy expression in the 1939 Afrikaner People's Economic Congress. The National Party, formed in 1914 in the Cape, therefore has its origins and ideological outlook in these two tendencies. In what follows, I discuss each tendency, in turn.

The Cape

In the Cape the driving force behind the Afrikaner nationalist project and thus the National Party had always been the wealthier farmers, on the one hand, and the small group of financial capitalists associated with SANLAM. Contrary to the Transvaal brand of Afrikaner nationalism, the Cape nationalist's interpretation revolved around economic prosperity for Afrikaners and catching up with English capital. In other words, they were not opposed to the English for their capitalists' ways, what was objectionable was what they viewed as English monopoly capitalism and marginalization of Afrikaners from the economic system. Indeed, one of the economic movements' key leaders, explicitly set out this perspective in a speech to a conference: "the aim of a struggle against capitalism does not mean that you are opposed to capital as such The [Afrikaner nationalist] movement is against the system which concentrates capital in a few hands" (cited in O'Meara, 1983: 151). There were, however, other factors that defined the Cape group notably, the brutal suppression of the 'rebellie' and the execution of its key ring leaders notably, Japie Fourie in 1914 (Uys, 1988: 207). The rebellion was essentially about Afrikaner opposition to what was widely (within the Afrikaner community at least) viewed as an unjust English war. Opposition was further intensified by the support enjoyed by Hitler's policies among important sections of the Afrikaner community and its elites. The 'poor white question' was also a major factor for the nationalists based in the Cape, for in the last instance, and judging by the available statistical information, the poor white question was essentially and fundamentally a poor Afrikaner question. The Carnegie Commission Report on the poor white problem in South Africa estimated that by 1929, out of a total of about a million Afrikaners, more than three hundred thousand were very poor. This meant that they lived on a pauper level, while an equal number were poor but lived slightly above the pauper level (ibid). Their state of poverty was in turn attributable to a variety of factors and circumstances, including the rinderpest epidemics of the 1890s and the ravages of the Anglo-Boer war. These calamities invariably forced the Afrikaners to the urban centres where their dire state of poverty was prominently displayed. This set the Cape nationalists in motion.

The principal concern of the Cape elite was to tackle the Afrikaner's lack of self-reliance, and lack of vocational and industrial skills. These disabilities were described by De Kiewiet aptly thus: "at the base of white society had gathered, like a sediment, a race of men so abject in their poverty, so wanting in resourcefulness, that they stood dangerously close to the natives" (cited in Giliomee, 1979:146). In order to counteract precisely this state of affairs, the Cape leadership launched a number of pioneering projects, the aim of which was to both advance their own bourgeois aspirations, while at the same time, seeking to uplift the Afrikaner under classes. The Mutual Life Association of the Cape of Good Hope, had started as a relatively insignificant stokvel around 1845. As part of an Afrikaner economic renaissance period, the Mutual Life was being consolidated and positioned as a serious Afrikaner business concern. It is common cause that the Mutual Life Association of the Cape of Good Hope has, over the decades, metamorphosed into the Old Mutual Group, a globally recognized assurance and financial entity. The other economic projects included a publishing house, the Nasionale Pers, which was founded as a propaganda platform from which to clearly articulate and promote the interests of Afrikaners in their mother tongue. To this end, the first Afrikaans newspaper, Die Burger, was established and similarly, two insurance companies, SANLAM and SANTAM, were established in 1918 and 1919 respectively, as launching pads for even more ambitious investment initiatives. Naspers, SANLAM and SANTAM are today very successful and recognizable global brands. Further investment commitments were also made in the wine and funeral industries, through the formation of the Kooperatiwe Wjnbours Vereeneging (KWV) for the wines, and Afrikaanse Begrafnis Onderneming Beperk (AVBOB) for the funeral services (Giliomee, 1979). These too, have grown to become hugely significant South African brands, with global foot prints. Among these pioneering men from the Cape, can be singled out W.A. Hofmeyer one of the key leaders and intellectuals who saw the need earlier on to: "develop a national consciousness into a business consciousness… and pursue this vision with iron determination" (cited in O'Meara, 1983: 96).

Through the party's political structures and Die Burger, an extensive propaganda campaign was initiated to pursue Afrikaners to support these new Afrikaner –owned establishments. This was designed to foster desperately needed self-reliance and also give the Afrikaner both self-respect and dignity, in relation to both English speakers and blacks in the country. From a developmentalist state perspective, the primacy of both politics and political processes and the creative manner in which the National Party's 'developmental leadership' manipulated these is remarkable. The essence of this strategy is captured in a 1921 SANLAM chairperson's report, and it reads:

> SANLAM is an authentic institution of the Afrikaner Volk in the widest sense of the word. As an Afrikaner, you will naturally give preference to an Afrikaner institution. I would just remind policy holders that we are busy furnishing employment to young Afrikaners, and training them in the insurance field. We hereby intend to provide a great service to South Africa. If we want to become economically self-reliant then we must support our own institutions (cited in O'Meara, 1983: 98).

In important ways, the capitalist origins and intentions of the apartheid state's orientation were firmly established in this early period already.

The Transvaal

In the Transvaal, the main constituency of the National Party was drawn from white labour, Afrikaans speaking petty bourgeois elements and former farmers (who were displaced by the agricultural sector's commercialization, drought, crop failure and by the Anglo-Boer war). The other major grouping in the Transvaal's membership came from the Afrikaans speaking farmers. In this part of the country, the Afrikaner Broederbond (Brotherhood) was the leading think-tank of the National Party and Afrikanerdom more broadly. So, the Broederbond:

> was always an urban petty bourgeois, northern dominated grouping, they provided the leadership and ideological cadres for a party which they saw as the guarantor of their interests (O'Meara, 1976:161).

Through the national Party therefore, the Broederbond articulated an Afrikaner nationalism and emphasized issues to some extent different to those emphasized by their Cape counterparts. In the Transvaal the content was explicitly anti-British, anti-monopoly capitalism, anti-Semitic, and bemoaned the suppression of the small white Afrikaner man by large English dominated economic and commercial interests. Moreover, they were suspicious of their Cape colleague's flirtations with imperialists tendencies. However, here too, the 'rebellie' and the execution of its leadership struck a chord with local Afrikaners (as it did country wide). It was, at any rate, the Helpmekaar (mutual aid) initiative which laid the basis for the convergence of views and actions between the southern and northern branches of the National Party, and that in turn, paved the way for the Volk Economic Congress of 1939. The Helpmekaar project was initially conceived as a fundraising drive to support families and pay the fines of those imprisoned for their part in the 'rebellie'. The success of this drive and, in particular, the mass response of Afrikaners to this call is widely seen as the real inspiration for the other Afrikaner projects, including SANLAM.

There is, however, no evidence to support a view that the northern provinces were able to act on this inspiration as energetically and imaginatively as did the Cape Nationalists. The most notable initiative to emerge from the north was the formation of Volkskas Bank in Pretoria. Volkskas (literally, People's trust bank) faced great hostility from the established commercial (English owned) banks, but its eventual success was, in large measure, due to nationalist propaganda work, conducted among all Afrikaner social classes by leading Broeders in the mid-1930s. Among these leaders can be counted I.M. Lombard; J.J. Basson and Dr. A. Hertzog, their mobilization drive was particularly effective in the rural areas, so that by 1939, Volkskas had eighteen branches (mainly in the platteland), and its paid-up share capital rose from 1, 500 British Pound Sterling (BPS) in 1937 to 37,000 BPS in 1940 (ibid). Of course, Volkskas Bank has gone through a great deal of changes over the decades, but today's ABSA one of the top four banking institutions in South Africa has its roots in this initiative. Another initiative in the north was the Uniewinkel, a small cooperative formed in Pretoria in 1935 and a similar cooperative store, Sonop (sun rise), was formed in Bloemfontein also in 1937 (O'Meara, 1983: 103). There were thus important differences between the north and south both with respect to their interpretation of Afrikaner nationalism but, crucially, with respect to their capacity for economic activity. It is fair to assume that the different class basis of the two regions does, to some extent, account for some of the differences.

Nonetheless, it was in the 1939 Afrikaner People's Economic Congress that the Cape and Transvaal ideological tendencies were systematically woven together into a coherent strategy. There were two aspects to this strategy. Firstly, the mobilization of an alliance of Afrikaner class forces that would serve as a reliable source of capital for the advancement of Afrikaner capitalist interests. Secondly, this economic mobilization would form the basis for political mobilization of a multi-class Afrikaner constituency behind the National Party. Essentially, therefore, there was going to be an active process of class formation, in line with the broader economic interests of the Volk. Concomitantly, the process would involve tampering the race-based, cheap labour capitalist regime of accumulation in ways that would further the elites' agenda. The Nationalist Party was thus seen as representing the political voice and political expression of the nationalist cause and its vehicle to state power. The Economic Congress made a number of important resolutions directed towards the advancement of Afrikaner interests. Among these was the formation of the Afrikaanse Handels Institute (Chamber of Commerce) to provide a common platform for the sharing of perspectives and strategic thinking between different Afrikaner business leaders and aspirant entrepreneurs. The Economiese Instituut (Economic Institute) was created to supervise and coordinate the economic upliftment of emergent Afrikaner entrepreneurs, while the Reddingsdaadbond (Rescue Mission) was created to raise funds for investment in 'national' Afrikaner enterprises (Welsh, 1974:259). Another challenge arising from the Congress discussions related to the plight of Afrikaner workers. This group was considered important for two reasons. Firstly, any success of Afrikaner industrial and commercial interests would crucially depend upon the presence of a reliable market for Afrikaner products. Secondly, there was a view that the rapid 'Anglicisation' of Afrikaner workers by 'foreign' dominated trade unions would undermine their nationalist sentiment, and hence their loyalty to Afrikaner economic growth. There were thus deep concerns among the Afrikaner elite about the intrusion and impact of foreign ideological influences among Afrikaner workers. Indeed, a furious and protracted struggle was mounted against foreign inspired notions of class struggle in favour of mutual cooperation between workers and employers.

In this connection, an Afrikaner Staff Association – (Die Spoorbond) was formed in the railways, to preach Afrikaner nationalism. Significantly, Die Spoorbond was set up in opposition to other existing trade unions that were considered to be under the influence of foreigners. Moreover, Solly Sachs, a leading trade unionist at the time, found it interesting that the real activists behind this campaign to halt the mobilisation and organisation of Afrikaans speaking workers by 'foreign class organisations' were actually: "Afrikaans professors, lawyers, farmers, financiers and ministers from the Dutch Reformed Churches, and not workers" (1957: 135).

To be sure, this objection of the nationalist elite to the unionization of the Afrikaans speaking workers was attributable to several factors. In the first instance, the nationalist economic development project was essentially and fundamentally a petty bourgeois led project, designed to achieve their bourgeois objectives and aspirations. As to be expected, there was an aversion towards a class conscious and by implication anti-capitalist Afrikaner working class. Secondly, trade unions in the 'right' hands, could provide much needed political and economic possibilities. At a political level, Christian Nationalist Trade Unions could be used for their voting power in the installation of an Afrikaner-friendly government. At an economic level, Afrikaner workers could constitute the consumer markets needed for Afrikaner economic advancement. Trade-offs for such support would lie in promises for job security and superiority over black workers in the work place. It is therefore in this context that many of the labour repressive measures aimed at blacks, and the benefit of Afrikaner workers should be located. This element, too, adds much explanatory weight to the apartheid state's Afrikaner nationalist and racially exclusive character. The next section shines the spotlight specifically on the apartheid state's repressive character and the various responses the repression elicited internally and externally.

Repressive Character

To succeed in pursuing and reproducing the capital accumulation strategy, the South African state has always required an extremely repressive character. The repression and the resultant mass response to it played a critical role in shaping the character and role of the apartheid state. This, in turn, draws attention to two aspects of the apartheid state – the administrative and coercive apparatuses in the establishment and maintenance of state power.

Thus, a discussion of this mobilization, the factors that triggered it, and their impact on the nature of the apartheid state, would seem an important prerequisite to understanding that state. The National Party came to power in 1948 promising to stem the oorstroming and the swart gevaar (black danger).

The South African Bureau of Racial Affairs (SABRA), a Broederbond/ Nationalist Party think tank on racial affairs formed in 1947, provided a swift resolution to both problems. SABRA argued that as the proportion of blacks in the cities increased, and they were allowed to come and go freely into such cities, so would their bargaining power increase in the work place and their political demands in society (SABRA, 1952:11). The solution was therefore to strictly control the flow of blacks into the cities, and instead to pursue a policy of separate development. At the same time, Afrikaner farmers were in desperate need of cheap black labour, which they were fast losing to the better paying manufacturing sector in the cities. At yet another level, Afrikaners were concerned by the under-cutting of their pay by black workers in skilled and semi-skilled positions, that had traditionally been their exclusive preserve. Moreover, the prospect of competing on equal terms with blacks for the same jobs, did not sit comfortably with their nationalist sensibilities. Responding to these needs had the effect of greatly increasing the size and scope of the apartheid state's bureaucracy. In particular, the social engineering this demanded meant that the scope of state involvement in the labour market and the economy more broadly was greatly enhanced. In a compelling study of the implementation of the influx control measures in South Africa, Deborah Posel (1991) showed how the Native Affairs Department (NAD) became "a state within a state, creating its own sub-departments of labour and housing" (1991:7). The growth of the NAD was in turn consistent with the scope of its work, which included the formation of Labour Bureaux, whose tasks were two fold. In the first place, they provided a means of channeling black labour from reserves to the farming sector. Thus by 1960, the Department of Bantu Administration not only claimed that it had considerable success in checking the illegal influx of blacks into 'white' areas, but also that: "the greatest contribution in supplying agricultural labour was drawn from the urban areas and not the Bantu areas (UG, 1960:23).

Secondly, the Labour Bureaux were to perpetuate migratory labour, by systematically restricting the terms under which blacks could remain in the urban areas. For instance, under section 10 (1) and (b) of the Urban Areas Act, " a Bantu may reside in an urban area if he has resided there since birth…has been employed continuously with one employer for more than ten years, or has resided continuously and lawfully in the area for more than fifteen years.." (cited in Guelke, 1974: 105). Over and above this, in terms of the Native Laws Amendment Act of 1952, the number of Labour Bureaux were increased, and scattered all over the country (in both the urban and rural areas) so that by 1960, there were six hundred Labour Bureaux (Beinart, 2001:158). This meant a big bureaucracy and an expanded role for the state. Indeed, the need to control black labour and to suppress their political aspirations, led Greensberg (1987) to the following observation: "By managing [labour] markets in particular, the apartheid state assumes direct responsibility for market results, conflict and inequality" (1987: 129).

The point Greenberg is speaking to here is perfectly captured in the House of Assembly debates on the Native Laws Amendment White Paper. In that debate, the United Party (known to represent mining and industrial interests), expressed various reservations about the removal of black labour from the cities to the farms. Indeed, this was seen as a gross interference with production (labour) costs of these industries and the labour market. In this connection, Van der Byl argued: "one of our principles in this country was that the Native has the right to offer or sell his work in a market most advantageous to him. I feel as far as possible that we should regulate the flow of labour without compulsion" (in HAD, 1952: col. 559-69).

Another UP Member of Parliament, Brook, made the following contribution to the matter at hand: "I think that my friends in industry feel that the law is a little too stringent to be satisfactory from the point of view of industry and its labour requirements: (in HAD, 1952: col.1289).

At the heart of these contributions are objections to what mining and industrial capital essentially saw as state involvement in the production activities of these sectors, which, in manufacturing in particular, were attracting labour both because of comparatively high levels of wages offered and the working and leaving conditions promised by life in the urban centres. The farming sector could simply never afford to compete with this. Accordingly, state policy is seen again intervening on behalf of one or the other fraction of capital, in this instance, agricultural capital, in order to lower production costs and generally to create prosperity in a sector crucial to state reproduction requirements. However, in order to be effective, the state's policies on the distribution of labour to the farms needed an additional number of laws and provisions. To this end, the Natives (Abolition of Passes and Coordination of Documents) Act was passed in 1952, precisely to coordinate the identification, fingerprinting, and more effective control of the status of every black person in 'white' South Africa. Moreover, this law helped to unify the process of black identification and registration across all provinces in the country. These aspects of apartheid policy and implementation thus crucially conditioned the character and role of the state, particularly with respect to size and scope of involvement in all aspects of the social and economic life of society. Related to this and equally important in shaping state form and character, was the mass response and mobilization that these policies elicited among those aggrieved by them, internally and externally. Such responses in turn, had a major impact on the growth and increasing role of the coercive structures of the state in South African social life.

Mass Action

State policies and their brutal implementation triggered extremely high levels of militancy and active resistance from the black majority and other opponents of the system of apartheid. Among other acts of resistance, in August 1956, the Federation of South African Women organized a protest march supported by 20 000 women to the Union Buildings in Pretoria, in protest against pass laws. Specifically, the protest drew attention to the extension of these laws to black women (Simons and Simons, 1983). The Azikhwelwa bus boycotts in 1957, on the other hand, drew specific attention to the low levels of black wages compared to their white counterparts. For three months, residents in Alexandra (a black township a few miles north of Johannesburg) simply refused to use busses after a price hike, on the grounds that black wages were lagging far behind increases in the cost of leaving (Van der Horst, 1976: 115). These laws also triggered the famous defiance campaign, which saw the mobilization of all racial groups of South Africa against the humiliation and indignities of the apartheid system. The defiance campaign advocated the defiance of all racial laws, which included separate amenities, the carrying of passes and repressive labour laws (Mandela, 1995: 108). The leaders of the campaign were moreover, encouraged to publicly burn their passes (seen as the prime symbol of apartheid oppression) as a sign of defiance, while encouraging those affected by the laws to do likewise.

The state responded to these largely peaceful demonstrations and protests by resorting to violence and naked repression. For instance, 156 prominent leaders of the defiance campaign of all races were charged with treason. Scores were banned, arrested and put under house arrest, many more were forced into exile or sentenced to long prison terms. On the labour front, the state sought to thwart any mobilization of black workers and the infamous Suppression of Communism Act of 1950 largely saw to this. Prime Minister D.F Malan had long held the view that black workers: "are incited by the unrestricted influx which has been occurring…Everything indicates that the position is becoming graver" (cited in Posel, 1991:76).

Not only did the Suppression of Communism Act target genuine communist and the Communist Party of South Africa, but it also gave the Justice Minister the power to name and ban all those individuals and organisations he thought engaged in communist activities or the furtherance of communist ideals (Benson, 1966: 135). In this regard, trade union leaders were especially targeted. Indeed, under the provisions of this Act, more than four hundred trade union leaders and activists were banned for their union membership and activities (Crankshaw, 1990: 511). Among these, was General Secretary of the Amalgamated Union of Building Trade Workers (AUBTW), Piet Huyster, whose union was known for its insistence on mobilizing workers on a no-racial basis (ibid). The definition of a communist in terms of the Act was so wide that virtually everyone opposing state policies was affected (Act No. 44, 1950). Ordinary anti-apartheid community protests were treated with the same brutality and state violence.

In this connection the Sharpeville massacre stands out. In that anti-pass law demonstration by local residents in Sharpeville, a township north-east of Johannesburg, 69 people were killed by police and many more wounded (Bunting, 1986). The anti-apartheid struggle was thus shaping the nature and character of the state in important ways - it led to more than just the swelling of the bureaucratic capacity of the state, but also to the increased involvement of the coercive apparatuses of the state in the implementation of the apartheid system. Crucially, this went far beyond the army, police and security services but included the judiciary as well (Wolpe, 1988: 63). In this regard, the hitherto guaranteed power and autonomy of the judiciary from other state organs had to undergo significant changes as a consequence of pressures imposed on the state by struggles mounted by the oppressed black majority. This degree of judicial autonomy was demonstrated for instance in the 1950s when the Appellate Division of the court was able to declare legislation which sought to "deprive coloured people of the right to vote in a common voters roll in parliamentary elections, to be unconstitutional. Another example relates to the refusal of the courts to disbar Nelson Mandela, who was convicted for sedition, on the grounds that his disgraceful conduct made him unfit to practice as a lawyer. The Supreme Court, however, overruled the trial court, on the grounds that, the actions for which Mandela had been found guilty were undertaken for a legitimate cause (ibid).

However, following the intensification of apartheid policies, repression and the resulting mass resistance, such judicial autonomy was effectively closed down, and a coalescence emerged between state policies and the role of the judiciary. The significance of this issue lies in the fact that it draws attention to a more fundamental issue, namely, the impact of apartheid social formation (and the contradictions in engendered) in shaping and changing the role of other state institutions, notably the judiciary. At yet another level, the Sharpeville massacre had occasioned a crisis of confidence in the apartheid state leading foreign investors, the local business community and other observers to re-think their support and associations with the regime. The negative sentiment in turn, caused untold nervousness among foreign investors who started taking capital out of the country, thereby effecting a huge balance of payments crisis. Of significance, above all else, was the response of the apartheid state to this situation, in an attempt to stem capital flight and restore confidence. The state was quick to impose strict import controls and policies to reduce capital outflows. The state was thus compelled into actively intervening in the economy as a direct consequence of mass mobilization, which itself triggered responses in other spheres, including intervention in the finance markets. This, too, even if in a limited way, constitutes an important explanatory variable in understanding the changing character of the state in pursuit of apartheid. This variable receives added significance when viewed against the fact that until the late 1970s, the South African economy had been characterized by a massive state sector and active state involvement in the economy, in response to various threats, including sanctions.

The lull engendered by the effective silencing of all credible opposition to state policies in the 1950s and 1960s through, inter alia, mass arrests and convictions, banning of individuals and organisations and the flight of scores into exile, did not last beyond the early 1970s. Indeed, the early 1970s saw the revival of black anti-apartheid mobilization, and hence further intensification of the role of repression, which was greatly enhanced by the state's accumulation crisis in this period. This was therefore not unrelated to the growing inability of the South African economy to generate the revenue and employment opportunities necessary to drive growth and economic development. What is more, the race-based capitalist accumulation strategy was struggling to reproduce itself.

The resurgence of black protest in the 1970s, supported by an acute accumulation crisis, forced the apartheid state on the defensive. This accumulation crisis was described by Gelb (1991) as manifesting itself in a variety of ways, including a stagnation in output growth, inflation entrenched at over 13% per annum, a weak currency, a permanent decline in foreign exchange reserves, massive and growing unemployment with no net creation of new jobs in the manufacturing sector throughout the 1980s and a low personal savings ratio (1991: 1). This period, moreover, saw the unprecedented centralization of state power under military and security structures. In response to what the state viewed as a 'Total Onslaught' – ostensibly from internal black opponents supported by international communist allies, a 'Total Strategy' was unveiled, with the State Security Council (SSC) assuming a key decision-making role within the state. The SSC was chaired by the Prime Minister and also included senior representatives from the police, the military and the security services. It dealt with crucial policies such as state security and public safety, but it also dealt with matters way outside the purview of the military and security services notably, foreign policy, economic affairs and constitutional matters. This structure was therefore in actual fact: "responsible for the initiation of all strategic policies and in addition, it coordinates and supervises the work of virtually all departments" (ibid). However, the Security Intelligence and State Security Council Act, 1972 (Act 64), even more explicitly situated the role of the South African state within a broadly military/security context. This law defines the functions of the SSC thus:

(a) at the request of the Prime Minister, to advise the government with regard to formulation of national policy and strategy in relation to the security of the Republic, and the manner in which such policy or strategy shall be implemented and executed; a policy to combat any particular threat to the security of the Republic. (b) to determine intelligence priorities: (Act 64: 1972). The 'Total Strategy' was thus seen as necessitating the centralization of state power and its firm location within the security establishment. This is a crucial element and provides important definitional clarity in understanding the nature and character of the apartheid state. Indeed, the policy actors and leading state actors are best placed to unpack the philosophical and strategic significance of this drift towards repression and centralization. In this regard, Lt. General A.S. Van Deventer, Secretary of the State Security Council had this to say on the matter:

The philosophy upon which the organisation is based, is that the Republic is confronted by a multi-dimensional threat- multi-dimensional in the sense that the Republic's enemies attack the constitutional, economic, social and the security bases in accordance with a coordinated plan or strategy... Hence the underlying theme in the management of national security is joint state management involving not only the security services and the intelligence services but also all other government departments and organisations (1983:11). Piet Koornhof, Minister of Cooperation and Development likewise made the point:

The war being waged against South Africa can only be combatted by the coordinated use of the means at this country's disposal. A plan of action in terms of which it will be possible to use all available means in a coordinated manner, is therefore necessary to ensure that this country can ward off this onslaught (House of Assembly, 1982: cols.308-10).

The economic role of the SSC was not as wide-ranging as say, that of the South Korean Economic Planning Board, or the Economic Development Board in Singapore, but there is nonetheless evidence of important economic and industrial activity. On the pretext of ensuring security, the SSC's activities were crucial in enhancing South Africa's economic and industrial development activities, including navigating pressures occasioned by economic sanctions or the threat thereof. In this connection, the uranium enrichment plant at Pelindaba was used to develop nuclear war heads, while the nuclear reactor at Koeberg was designed to produce plutonium for the country's increased capacity to develop nuclear weapons (CIIR, 1986: 18). Moreover, the inclusion of key industrialists and the secondment of the deputy chief of Barlow Rand to head the state's parastatal, Armaments Development and Production Corporation (ARMSCOR), also significantly helped the SSC' strategy of "bringing together both military and industrial interests" (CIIR, 1986: 19). Through ARMSCOR and the State Security Council's Defense Advisory Council, an industrial development strategy was put in place, that led to the rapid consolidation of industrial plants and factories (ibid). This strategy was, moreover, formulated, implemented and monitored directly and actively by the SSC. To consolidate corporate support and to keep business onside, the state also institutionalized its relationship with this section of society via marketing and industrial councils. Parallels with South Korean and Taiwanese economic development planning structures and state-making processes are unavoidable. Unavoidable too, is the East Asian parallel with respect to 'war-making' or the threat of war in accelerating and driving economic growth. In Japan the trigger was the threat and fear of foreign invasion, in South Korea and Taiwan, it was the fear of China and communism. The perceived threats for the Afrikaner elites, as shown, were in earlier periods, English commercial domination and later on oorstroming communism and the anti-apartheid movement.

This is yet another important variable in the definition of the character and role of the apartheid state. This element was inspired and necessitated by the intensification of the anti-apartheid struggles led by the national liberation movement in South Africa. The mass reaction of the victims of apartheid repression and the international solidarity the liberation movement enjoyed contributed significantly in shaping the character of the state, by imposing on it a defensive and hence a repressive dimension. However, equally significant in accounting for the role of the apartheid state is the international dimension. All states are situated within a complex geo-political and economic context, something that plays a crucial role in shaping and conditioning their form and character. Thus, the apartheid state was a product (in part at least) of the pressures on, and opportunities provided by the international socio-economic and political conjuncture. The international dimension matters in understanding the character and content of the apartheid state.

The International Dimension

In the wake of the state repression of the 1960s and in particular as a consequence of the publicity generated by the Sharpeville massacre and later on, the life sentences imposed on leading figures of the liberation movement notably, Nelson Mandela, "South Africa became the moral outcast of the international order- in much the same way that Turkey had finally become the Pariah of the European state system after the Armenian massacre of 1886" (Mayall, 1988: 305). However, the Situation elicited contradictory and at times extremely confusing messages from the international community, and especially its western allies. There were several reasons for this. First, apartheid policies and the internal anti-apartheid conflict reached their peak at a time in world history when Keynesianism was also at its peak – states had greater latitude and independence "than at any moment since the foundations of the modern state were laid at Westphalia in 1648" (O'Meara, 1996: 48). The West, in particular, was thus loathe to get involved in South Africa's jealously guarded internal policies.

The second issue relates to trade and economics. South Africa was the West's major supplier of a number of strategic minerals, including gold, metals and the platinum group, chromium and manganese ores. The only other alternative supplier of the same products would have been the Soviet Union. In addition to this, there was the matter of South Africa's geo-strategic position in the cold war, geographically, it commanded the sea route between the Atlantic and Indian Oceans, while strategically, South Africa fell within the broad anti-Soviet alliance of states. This route gave the West access to a significant proportion of its oil imports, 65 per cent in the case of Western Europe and 28 per cent in the case of the United States of America (Mayall, 1988: 321). Therefore, taking punitive action against Pretoria had to take this reality into consideration. Foreign policy debates within the United States and British state structures are revealing in this regard. The United States' Secretary of State's Advisory Committee on South Africa in January 1987 reported:

> "Having viewed the strategic minerals issue through the prisms of several competing schools of thought in the policy community, we are agreed that a minerals cut-off (either by sanctions or breakdown of the South African economy) would have an undeniable impact on the United States. In

some cases, we could be forced to increase imports from the Soviet Union" (1987: 4)

In Britain too, this matter exercised the minds of policy actors and similar concerns were raised by the House of Commons Sixth Report from the Foreign Affairs Committee, South Africa:

> ...it remains, and must remain, a priority for British alliance policy, that whatever future system of government South Africa chooses for itself, South Africa should remain firmly outside the Soviet sphere of influence and should continue to be allied, if possible more closely, to the defense interests of North America and Western Europe (cited in Mayall, 1988:311).

Fully aware of this strategic dilemma for the West, Pretoria sought to intelligently navigate the international environment in ways that continued to advance its broad strategic agenda and maintained the regime of accumulation. State policies could thus be pursued without fearing international action against South Africa, principally because of the country's strategic position within the bi-polar world system. The international dimension and the role and place of the apartheid state in the global division of labour is thus another crucial variable in understanding the character and policy choices of the state elite. The global context, the pressures, expectations and opportunities it provided for the effective and relatively unchallenged implementation of the state's apartheid policies, is also a crucial variable through which to explore the nature of the apartheid state. As Minister of Defense, P.W. Botha showed a well-grounded grasp of these opportunities:

> During the past two years there have been far-reaching political, economic and military developments in both the global and regional contexts, with direct implications for the Republic of South Africa...The mineral resources of the Republic are of the most importance to the west. In addition, our country has asserted ourselves on the side of the free world in two world wars. (Botha, 1977).

Since the 1960s, the apartheid regime has skilfully manipulated strategic opinion using the international order. This bought the state a lot of time and material support, thereby consolidating state capacity internally. Such therefore, was the role of the international order in shaping the form of the apartheid state. The re-organisation of the state in response to the so-called 'Total Onslaught' and the 'identification' of external and internal 'enemies' had its origins precisely in this context. In one respect, this re-organisation gave the state unprecedented autonomy to pursue policies deemed to be crucial in the execution of the 'Total Strategy', justified as it was on the grounds of internal security and economic development. So, much like the East Asian developmental state experiments, the South African state-making processes also shows that the war and the threat of war greatly enhances room to manoeuvre and the capability of state elites to construct developmental state types. Thus, for the apartheid state and state elites, possible communist encirclement was used as an important condition for buying international legitimacy for the apartheid developmental agenda, however racist and oppressive towards the majority of the population.

So far this chapter has sought to draw attention to a number of essentially political variables (internal and external), through which the role and character of the apartheid state must be viewed. This include the need, in the literature, for a better appreciation of the role of the Afrikaner elites in class formation, state-making and re-defining the accumulation strategy in line with their aspirations. Moreover, I have sought to advance the view that in different ways, all these aspects combined and conspired to give the apartheid state its particular character and role. The significance of this approach lies in its advocacy of a more complex framework in studying the apartheid state. Therefore, race and class are important but hardly sufficient variables if one seeks a fuller and more rounded account of the apartheid state. This section has sought to problematize the debate about the nature of the apartheid state and to place its evolution in its proper historical and global context. Also, this section raises the importance of the global context in exploring the post-apartheid state's capacity and the possibilities this provide for accelerated state action for economic development. It also raises questions about the role and influence of key social groups and individual actors in conditioning and at times, limiting state-action – again something to be considered in later chapters. Furthermore, this section poses important questions for political science with respect to methodology. Specifically, it raises the need for the deployment of methods capable of processing and explaining the complex and dynamic inter-play of structural and agential issues in the current global conjuncture. In summary, therefore, this section has sought to raise the absolute necessity of locating the apartheid state (and indeed, the post-apartheid state), its character, threats and possibilities within a "…complex, evolving, interdependent and indeterminate totality" of political variables (O'Meara, 1996: 47). The next section more directly advances the main argument in this chapter namely, that the apartheid state was an active and often pervasive interventionist agent in the socio-economic development of its chosen constituency.

The Apartheid State's Intervention and the literature

Just as the character and content of the apartheid state are highly contested aspects of the South African debate in the literature, so too, is the extent and role of state intervention in conditioning the economy in favour of sectional interests. The utility of the material reviewed in this section resides in the fact that it not only emphasizes the fact of pervasive state intervention in favour of sectional interests but it also does this on the basis of concrete historical evidence. To this end, it allows for critical engagement with this evidence where it concerns the actual socio-economic benefits to the different Afrikaner social groups. As ever, though, this work, too, is uneven in its rigour and depth of analysis and deductive abilities. Nevertheless, there is sufficient basis to identify and underline state interventionism for fractional interests and economic growth.

The utility of Francis Wilson's (1971) intervention lies more in its historical comprehensiveness and empirical rigour than in the author's systematic conception of the socio-political and developmental function of the apartheid state interventionism. Indeed, Wilson shared the view that state involvement in bolstering Afrikaner farmers was so insistent that: " the principle of greater price stability for farm products has been confused with the social aim of keeping farming incomes more in line with urban incomes: (1971: 144).

Nonetheless, in an otherwise rigorous analysis of the political economy of the agricultural sector in South Africa before and after 1948, Wilson identified a number of important discontinuities. These discontinuities related to the apartheid state's response to agriculture's three main problems since the inter-war period – labour shortages, the pricing of agricultural goods, and insufficient capital in the sector. To deal with these problem areas, the apartheid state identified four areas of direct state intervention in order to stimulate growth and development in that sector.

The first point of intervention was with respect to the pricing problem. The state moved swiftly to ensure that the 1937 Marketing Act which was used by the Smuts government to hold food prices down during the inter-war and post-war periods, were used to pursue a new socio-economic agenda. The control boards provided for by this legislation were consciously and deliberately made up of the farmers themselves. This intervention saw immediate improvements in agricultural prices: within three years the price of the average bag of maize was raised from 21s.3d to 30s (Wilson, 1971: 144). For many farmers, this constituted almost a doubling of net profits. This incentive, in turn, stimulated rapid production increases throughout the sector (ibid). Thus, the overhaul of the control boards and the deployment onto the boards of farmers' representatives themselves, coupled with deliberate bolstering of favoured products, through price controls was one key strategy of state intervention.

The second area of intervention was in the labour supply front. To this end, the state set up numerous Labour Bureaux in line with the provisions of the Native Laws and Amendment Act of 1952, to facilitate the effective distribution of black labour to white farms. The Natives (Abolition of Passes and Coordination of Documents) Act of 1952 and the Group Areas Act of 1953, also conspired to further intensify state control over the mobility of blacks, their working and living conditions. In addition to this, were the state's plans to resolve the labour shortages in white farms by using convict labour, principally derived from pass convictions. Wilson has shown how the state initiated a programme to build prisons in close proximity to those farm areas most affected by labour shortages and how farmers were encouraged to take out shares in this scheme. In this way, partner farmers were guaranteed a reliable supply of convict labour at ridiculously low costs (ibid: 147). Thirteen Prisons were thus built in the Western Cape to cater for wine farmers, nine in the eastern Transvaal to meet the needs of maize and wheat farmers. In Welkom, a prison was built in response to the development of a gold mine in the area, this had apparently drawn labour away from farmers. In all, by 1966, twenty-three such prisons had been erected accommodating a total of 6,000 long term prisoners. So, the state initiated a prison-building programme, not only to hold the victims of the recently passed control measures, but also to systematically channel these in the direction of Afrikaner farmers (ibid).

The third area of state intervention was in the field of education, to tackle the low levels of skills and training among Afrikaner farmers in particular. According to 1960 estimates, no less than 79 per cent of white farmers had less than ten years of schooling. In response, the state set up farming colleges and research institutes in order to enskill and equip farmers for the challenges of the mechanized and scientific farming age, that the state sought to transform the sector into. The Veterinary Scientific Institute at Onderstepoort was an important example in this regard. At the same time, farm schools were also encouraged to better equip black labourers to manage the mechanization and commercialization of the sector. The farm schools also helped to improve [Afrikaans] language skills, so instructions could be easily followed.

The fourth area of intervention was with respect to agricultural credit and the formation of insurance schemes and tax concessions for farmers. This led to considerable fixed capital investment in the sector, coming in the form of irrigation schemes, dams and other farming improvement schemes and implements. A Department of Agriculture Report noted that the total value, at constant prices, of implements rose by approximately 80 per cent between 1948 and 1959 (RSA, 1962). Figure 2.1 below also illustrates the phenomenal increase in implements from the 1948 period – an increase that had a great deal to do with direct state involvement.

Figure 2.1

Mechanization (Index of numbers sold in 1946 = 100)2

Year	Contractors	Combined harvesters
1926	6	N/A
1937	30	34
1946	100	100
1955	431	519
1960	587	594

Source: Wilson (1971)

The indices of total output in white farms underline the absolute centrality of apartheid state intervention in Afrikaner prosperity in the agricultural sector. Figure 2.2 below shows the rapid improvements of output in white owned farms once the apartheid state initiated its interventionist programs.

Figure: 2.2

Output on White-owned farms: 1936/9 – 1956/9 = 100)1

	1936/9	1946/9	1956/9
Maize	100	101	155
Wheat	100	120	194
Potatoes	100	152	185
Groundnuts	100	485	1,378
Fruit	100	123	253
Sugar	100	103	198
Total Crop	100	123	193

Source: Wilson (1971)

The above provide comprehensive evidence of active apartheid state intervention in shaping the agricultural sector into a modern, mechanized and prosperous economic sector in South Africa. Concerned mainly to condemn the market 'distortions' this process entailed, Wilson failed to make the vital connection between this process and the state's socio-economic agenda for the Afrikaners, and the farmers in this instant. Wilson thus failed to make the obvious analytical deduction clearly screaming for attention namely, that the interventionist tendencies of the apartheid state were by design. And so too, was 'getting the prices wrong'. Helpfully, though, the answers are scattered prominently in Wilson's comprehensive historical and empirical data. After all, in East Asia too, developmental elites intervened extensively and got prices wrong in order to drive growth and development in selected sectors and industries.

Jones and Muller's account (1992) had similar strengths and weaknesses. In analysing the banking and financial services before and after 1948, they made the following comment:

> one is left with the feeling from the bank records, that South Africa fell behind in the 1950s and that the economy was not performing as well as it might have done. It seems likely that this was the result of political factors distorting economic development (1992:205).

Not only is there no evidence to support what was ideologically loaded speculation, but more remarkably, these authors failed to identify the developmental motives clearly implicit in their own investigation of the growth of the Afrikaner owned Volkskas Bank and the increasing importance of the Land Bank after 1948. Volkskas, which was only registered in 1942 as a commercial bank, was greatly stimulated by the expansion of its market share after 1948, principally because most state accounts were transferred to it. The accounts in question, as Jones and Muller pointed out, were not only confined to: "central government, provincial government and municipalities, but also the accounts of large state corporations, such as the railways, ISCOR (the state owned steel corporation, SECOM (the Electricity Supply Commission), and the Post and Telephony business. It is therefore hardly surprising that an Afrikaner controlled bank should have grown so quickly" (1992: 206).

The underlying coordinated and very calculated strategy of the apartheid state to empower and bolster the capacity of Afrikaner business in the financial sector escaped analytical scrutiny and is unaccounted for. This systematic nurturing and support of small Afrikaner finance capital is not located properly, within the Afrikaner growth and development agenda, the details of which were clearly outlined in the Volks Kongres, these developmental motives were instead dismissed as 'national socialism'. Indeed, Jones concluded: "the national socialism of the National Party of Malan, Strydom and Verwoed [resulted] in excessive regulation and endless interference by politicians, especially in the field of monetary policy. In South Africa, the Reserve Bank though not nationalized has in practice been a tool of successive Finance Ministers" (1992: 3).

Missing from this analysis is the strategic direction of the National Party's 'national socialism', its strategic beneficiaries and crucially, its overall impact on equity and economic growth in the period under consideration.

Verhoef (1992), in her comparative study of Volkskas' performance relative to the other more established banks, did not take the debate much further either. While recognizing the massive role of the apartheid state in boosting Volkskas' market share and advances relative to the established commercial banks, Verhoef still ascribed the bank's phenomenal performance after 1948 to two factors: "its appeal to Afrikaners to invest their money with their own institution, its acquisition of Trans-Oranje hire purchase company (1992:137).

Direct state action to bolster Volkskas is either seen as insignificant, co-incidental or dismissed as Afrikaners investing in their own institution. Verhoef concedes the role of state intervention in a single sentence, before launching into a detailed and laborious account of the role of diversification in explaining the bank's rapid growth. The role of the state is thus treated as a small, once-off intervention, which requires no serious analytical attention. Nevertheless, Verhoef provides crucial comparative data, which shows a phenomenal increase in the market share and total advances of Volkskas, a relatively new bank with no proven track record in an extremely cutthroat and competitive sector. These advances make sense only when placed within the context of pervasive state support, coupled with the diversification Verhoef alludes to in her study. Figure 2.3 illustrates the assets and annual growth rate of Volkskas relative to its established competitors.

Figure 2.3

The assets of Volkskas and all the commercial banks 1947-81(R'000)

Year	Volkskas total assets	Assets of all commercial banks	Volkskas assets as %
1947	26,171	823,490	3.17
1957	126,995	1,227,300	10.3
1967	486,230	2,708,500	17.9
1977	1,913,000	9,795,000	19.5
1981	3,634,000	19,487,000	18.6

Annual Growth Rate %
1947 – 81 Volkskas =15.62 ....all commercial banks = 9.75
Source: Verhoef (1992)

Deborah Posel (1999), in a study of the apartheid civil service, makes a bolder assessment of the socio-economic and developmental functions of the state's interventionist role. For Posel, the construction of a large, more assertive and ambitious civil service after 1948, must be placed within the context of the apartheid state's interventionist and modernization role. Indeed, according to Posel, the pervasive interventionism was going to be a critical determining factor in attaining social, political, cultural and economic development for the key Afrikaner social groups (1999: 103). An important step in this direction was transforming and Afrikanerising the civil service in such a way that it was properly constituted as an agent of broader socio-economic transformation. In this regard, two important points of intervention for the apartheid state were identified.

The first involved the deliberate and conscious deployment of Afrikaners in all key sectors of the civil service. Related to this, was the systematic purging of 'liberal minded' English-speakers from such positions (1999: 104). Indeed, on both counts remarkable progress was made within a relatively short space of time. An important indicator of the growth of the civil service is the growth in the number of government departments. On the eve of the 1948 general elections, there were 26 departments, but by 1970, this figure had increased by 41 (ibid). The biggest among these was the Department of Native Affairs, which was rapidly transformed from a small under-resourced department into the vanguard of apartheid policy-making, a 'state within a state'. Another crucial indicator of rapid growth in the size of the civil service is the number of public servants, the growth between 1939 and 1958 was 114 per cent, with an additional 53 per cent by 1967 (ibid). And yet another aspect of systematic Afrikanerisation of the civil service involved the purging of English speakers from what were considered strategically important positions, including the Treasury, Inland Revenue, Customs and Excise, the police and military services. Indeed, by 1974, English-speakers accounted for only 20 per cent of senior staff in state departments, and were much less in 1976, when only seven out of 146 posts were held by people with English surnames (ibid).

The second area of intervention related to the education and training of the new recruits, many of whom, according to Posel, were not sufficiently qualified for their positions. To attend to this problem, arrangements were made with Afrikaans universities for the designation of courses and programs tailor-made for the state's new skilling shortages. Although this intervention failed to stem the massive skill shortages (occasioned by unprecedented levels of 'cadre deployment'), the point here is to demonstrate the extent of state involvement in the transformation of the civil service. And above all, it underlines the determined efforts by the state at affirming Afrikaners, thereby improving their human development and socio-economic status. Posel's investigation also shows an important variation from say, the Japanese developmental state case, where Johnson (1982), has shown the importance of merit and competence in the deployment of people to the bureaucracy.

Posel's study thus provides a more useful basis for understanding the interventionist role of the apartheid state and its single-minded determination to use state resources for the developmental benefit of Afrikaners. The study, moreover, provides critical lessons about the significance of skilled and well-trained cadres if a process of transforming state institutions and the civil service is to follow the desired direction.

The active role of the state in the transformation of the civil service was more than 'a jobs for pals' arrangement instead, it was rooted in a deep understanding of the role of that structure as a transformative and developmental instrument. At the same time, it was going to be a crucially important agent in keeping black political aspirations in check. To be sure:

> ..the Afrikanerisation of the civil service had everything to do with consolidating the nationalists' hold on power. Afrikaner strategists were acutely aware of the capacity of senior and middle-level bureaucrats to frustrate the policy initiatives of even the most popular administration: (O'Meara, 1996: 61). And, with this understanding in mind: "all departments were politicized. While the rhythm of this process varied between ministries, it did lead to a considerable centralisation of ministerial control over the state bureaucracy" (ibid: 63).

The significance of the above interventions on the apartheid civil service lies in the fact that what is passed off as arbitrary state action in the previous approaches, is here recognized for the deliberate policy of socio-economic development for Afrikaners that it was.

In this connection, Lazar (1987) also advanced the view that the apartheid state deliberately and consciously sought to respond to the socio-economic challenges confronting different sections of the 'nationalist alliance'. Indeed, English speaking civil servants were purged to create jobs for Afrikaners, while financial capitalists, small traders, workers and farmers all received massive direct and indirect state assistance (1987:38). For the farming sector, consistent state intervention in the sector led to rapid economic development, modernization and mechanization of the sector. Lazar observed that: "By 1960, a relatively small number of powerful farmers and 'land capitalists' controlled a sizeable proportion of South African agriculture" (1987:109).

The growth in the agricultural production and the general mechanization of the sector was in the final analysis attributable to pervasive state intervention. It is in this context that the 50 per cent rise in the physical volume of agricultural production between 1948 and 1960 should be located (ibid:99). Lazar's conclusion seem to support the contention that neither the free market system, nor the enterprise and industriousness of Afrikaners farmers, fully account for the rapid growth of that sector between 1948 and the early 1960s at least. Indeed, any attempt to account for this growth outside the interventionist and developmentalist role of the apartheid state is invariably limited, and takes away from a more informed understanding of South African economic and state-making history.

Conclusion

The role and character of the apartheid state is traceable to Afrikaner history and experience in South Africa, including the Great Trek and the the Anglo-Boer war. The different strands of Afrikaner nationalism espoused by the relatively well-off southerners and the more extreme versions espoused by the northerners, were welded together in the Afrikaner Economic Conference. Out of this conference emerged a more sophisticated form of Afrikaner nationalism that was embedded in economic growth and prosperity and ultimately, Afrikaner political dominance in South Africa. To arrive at that point, however, there had to be, as we have seen, a determined process at class formation and deliberate tinkering with the economic framework (accumulation strategy), in ways that reflected the new socio-economic agenda. In other words, the broadly capitalist social formation had to have unmistakable Afrikaner nationalist and developmentalist imprints. Because developmental states are not there for the taking, a determined Afrikaner leadership elite (Broederbond) was the moving spirit behind ideology, strategies and policies of the apartheid state.

On the one hand, the apartheid state was repressive and oppressive in relation to blacks, who were seen as a 'threat' to the political future of the Afrikaner Volk. On the other hand, the state sought to intervene extensively in the economy in order to advance Afrikaner commercial and economic interests. This was meant to challenge both British dominance in the economy, but also to uplift the socio-economic status of Afrikaners in South Africa. These aspirations gave rise to a particular state type – a janus-faced state that articulated a thoroughly distorted and racially defined form of developmental statism, but developmental statism nonetheless. My concern in the foregoing pages has been to spotlight the role of politics and ideas in shaping that state type. Though partial, distorted and racially backward, it seems to me that there is a case for suggesting that the apartheid state, in historically determined circumstances, fashioned a form of developmental state. The apartheid state experience, moreover, provides important political inferences for current processes of state construction and economic development in South Africa.

The first inference relates to the absolute necessity of systematic state action in the process of economic development and the redressing of imbalances (whether race, gender class, creed etc). In other words, as was the case with the Afrikaners (and the developmental states in South Korea and Taiwan, for fundamental change to happen, there must be a grand idea or a big idea. Part of the effort must surely be to temper with the inherited regime or strategy of accumulation (race-based neo-liberalism) that was designed to fulfill a racial capitalist agenda. One cannot expect the same accumulation strategy that furthered apartheid capitalism, of its own accord, to suddenly serve the interests of the majority. So, the first port of call is to attend to what is essentially a BAD IDEA, transform it into an economic framework that serves a new and qualitatively different social and economic agenda. Crucially, the successes of such state action should be grounded on a project that takes on board the interests of all (and not just one) social classes in society. Therefore, ideas matter in developmental state-making. A second and related inference relates to the importance of capacity, both as it relates to skill and expertise, but especially as it relates to the state's economic resource capacity. State economic intervention like that instigated by the South Koreans, the Taiwanese and, indeed, the apartheid state, show the value of state command over vast economic and financial resources, in order to enhance the state's effectiveness and its developmental impact. Of course, history (especially in the global south) is littered with examples of such state capacity and resources being mismanaged and leading to non-developmental outcomes. The key to effective developmental state-making resides in the presence of a developmental leadership with both the capacity and ideological determination to push through a comprehensive developmental agenda. Thirdly, the apartheid state experience shows the unsustainability of a project based on the violations of human rights and oppression of important sectors of society. Such a strategy invariably brings forth adverse internal and external conditions, thereby choking-off the capacity of state developmentalism. Evans (1995) has also concluded that the future of developmental states lie in more inclusive and people-centred processes of development – a processes he termed 'embedded developmentalism'. In the current conjuncture in South Africa's political and economic reality, attention seem to be called to the need for state action that is grounded on a sensitive appreciation of both international-al and internal political dynamics. This chapter above all, provides a good basis for a fuller engagement with the developmental state concept broadly and in particular, its relevance to current South African socio-economic and developmental dynamics. This exploration of the apartheid state shows the primacy and significance of politics in developmental state-making and that there is developmental state precedence of sorts in South Africa's state history. The developmental state type being explored in this project is therefore not entirely new to South African state history. The next chapter is concerned to briefly reflect on the legacies of apartheid. It is a chapter that is essentially devoted to underlining the magnitude of the challenge inherited by the new state actors and to show how enduring some of the legacies have been, even a whole generation after the formal end of legal apartheid. And how, fur-thermore, the chosen policy framework may not only be inadequate but bad for the socio-economic challenges confronting South Africa. What is called for and what may be missing in the equation is a set of new ideas, a policy framework based on an intelligent state-led process, along the developmen-tal state approach.

3

Apartheid Legacies: Continuities, Discontinuities and Change?

Introduction

The last chapter was devoted to exploring the apartheid state's interventionist and developmentalist function in favour of various Afrikaner social classes. Specifically, the purpose was to show that racial oppression and economic exploitation of blacks only partly explained and defined the character of that state. A fuller explanation of the evolution, workings and operations of the apartheid state, I have sought to argue, resides in an understanding of the primacy not only of politics and political processes, but crucially, of ideas. In other words, all developmental state-making projects have, invariably, been accompanied by the presence of a developmental elite, armed with a big idea (developmental ideology). Typically, the big idea consists in a fundamental structural overhaul of the inherited economic strategy, in pursuit of a new socio-economic agenda with new and necessarily different 'winners and losers'. For, it can only be fundamental change if the power dynamic underpinning such change including economic and property relations are themselves fundamentally altered. So, in its own limited ways, the apartheid state exhibited important developmentalist state characteristic features. Staying with the same themes (the primacy of politics and significance of the ideational) in state-making in general and developmental state-making in particular, I show in this chapter how, failure to pay due attention and give the necessary prominence to these two variables can undermine the best laid plans. Specifically, this chapter shows how failure to temper with politics and ideas has, in the South African context, given prominence to [apartheid capitalist] continuities at the expense of the much expected [post-apartheid] discontinuities and change(COSATU, 2012). Thus, the focus is on shining the spotlight on the legacies of the apartheid system on the broader South African economy and some of the most pressing and seemingly stubborn social challenges namely, poverty, unemployment and inequality.

The central argument in this chapter is that notwithstanding far-reaching and epoch-making changes in the post-apartheid period, twenty-two years down the line, much remains unresolved. In other words, there are indeed, important discontinuities in that the political and policy landscape is undeniably different. The chapter however, shows that, thanks to a fundamentally flawed economic transition prospectus, including property relations and the regime of accumulation and capital formation, the continuities overwhelm the discontinuities in fundamental ways. In other words, the fundamental structure and economic framework of the past hundred years remains, in many fundamental ways, stubbornly in place. Under normal circumstances, of course, there is nothing wrong with this prospectus. After all, it chimes with much of what the IMF and World Bank are prescribing for growth and development throughout the world, even as the world economy is struggling to recover from a devastating global recession. The problem is that there has never really been anything normal about the South African situation, the post-apartheid inheritance presented a deeply unequal society ravaged by racially defined poverty, unemployment, a stagnant economy and a massive socio-economic deficit. A business as usual or one-size-fits-all approach was never going to respond to the complex socio-economic problems confronting the country. Certainly not the neo-liberal package whose inadequacies and failures are only too abundantly apparent (Piketty, 2014). The persistence of this flawed framework, has set the scene for the entrenchment of a pipeline of policy failure (economic growth, social development, employment creation and much more besides), in post-apartheid South Africa. This persistence and endurance of apartheid capitalist continuities, I argue, is in the first and last instance, traceable to the neo-liberal underpinnings of the post-apartheid transformation agenda. Accordingly, the chapter shines the spotlight on the most pressing socio-economic challenges confronting South African society, and use these to assess continuity and discontinuity. The first section explores the economic arena, the second section deals with poverty issues, the third section looks at inequality and the fourth section discusses the labour market structure. These variables are all inextricably interlinked and in many respects mutually reinforcing, they are treated separately here merely for explanatory rigour.

Apartheid Inheritance: The Economy

On assuming Office in April 1994, the new ANC government inherited an economy already in serious decline (Nattrass, 1990; Gelb, 1991). In fact, the South African economy had been experiencing a serious downturn since the 1970s, reversing the growth that had characterized its performance in the 1950s and 1960s, when, along with Japan, South Korea and Brazil, South Africa's growth rate was one of the highest in the world (SARB). Moreover, the distribution of economic power, as is to be expected, largely reflected the overwhelming dominance of white interests, with extremely limited economic power in the hands of the black majority (Lester et al, 2000: 241). In 1994, for instance, 91 per cent of business franchises were owned by whites, compared to only 9 per cent in the hands of black South Africans (du Toit, 1998). These were all patterns the ANC had committed itself to reversing, in favour of equity, redress, affirmative action and equality of opportunities for all (ANC, 1994). Economists generally agree that the ANC inherited an economy in serious decline and as ever, expectations for a radical break with past accumulation and distribution patterns were high.

Gelb (1991), guided by a 'regulation approach', sought to advance the view that South Africa went through three key economic stages between 1960 and 1991. For Gelb, the period between 1960 and 1970 represented what he called a 'stable accumulation regime', while 1970 to 1975 was characterized as a 'transitional phase', and then the crisis or 'unstable regime of accumulation' set in from 1975 and persisted through the 1990s (1989:3). This latter stage represented a crisis in the South African economy because: "the cyclical fluctuations have become significantly more volatile and unstable, when compared with the earlier period of long-run 'boom', and it is this feature which is most closely associated with the decline in the rate of long-run growth" (1991:6).

Moreover, Gelb has pointed to a range of statistical data to illustrate and justify his claim that South Africa experienced an acute economic crisis from the mid-1970s. These included the following factors:

- The rate of inflation, as measured by the Consumer Price Index, rose above 10 per cent in 1974 and has remained there since.

- The private sector investment co-efficient (the ratio of real net fixed investment by private corporations to GNP) averaged 8 per cent per annum, over the period 1946 to 1974, but dropped to 4 per cent per annum during 1975 to 1988.

- The aggregate investment co-efficient – the ratio of gross fixed domestic investment to GDP- declined from around 29 per cent in 1972-4 to around 19 per cent in 1986-7.

- The level of personal savings dropped, as a proportion of disposable income, from about 11 per cent in 1975 to just over 3 per cent in 1987.

- Job creation dropped from 157 000 per annum between 1960 and 1974, to 57 000 per annum between 1974 and 1985 (ibid).

Thus, by all accounts and measures, by the time of the transition in South Africa, the apartheid state's regime of accumulation had indeed, run into a deep-seated crisis.

If crisis is to be understood as the unworkability of the current regime of accumulation or the inability of the current strategy of accumulation to reproduce itself, then the expectations for fundamental economic overhaul must be justified. However, with a lot of help from the IMF, World Bank and other international advisors, the apartheid state's response to this crisis was to adopt stringent neo-liberal policies (De Klerk, 1999, Thatcher, 2002). A plan was set in motion to liberalise the economy, deregulate and privatize many of the state owned institutions. The negotiations process unfolded in the midst of this fundamental transformation of the South African economy from a fundamentally state-centred to a neo-liberal economy. Thus, depending on one's perspective, this was either a poisoned chalice for the ANC or an unprecedented opportunity to pursue a far-reaching Keynesian inspired development growth path. For it would seem that economic performance (or lack thereof) was conspiring to gift the new state actors' policy and ideological ammunition aplenty, for justifying a radical and desperately needed change in accumulation strategy and the structure of the South African economy. Nevertheless, Gelb's contention of an economic decline from around the mid- 1970s accords with the South African Reserve Bank's (SARB) statistical information for various years between 1950 and 1992. Figure 3.1, below depicts a picture of almost uninterrupted decline in the GDP rate.

Figure: 3.1

Average Annual growth rate of gross domestic product (1985 constant prices) {TC/14}

YEAR	GDP GROWTH RATE
1950-9	4.7
1960-9	5.6
1970-9	3.0
1980-9	1.6
1990	-0.6
1991	-0.7
1992	-2.2

Source: SARB, various years

The above table also shows that the economy has declined since the 1970s and has experienced negative growth since 1990.

The same trend is evident on the job-creation front. The statistics show a massive increase in employment in the 1960s, followed by a progressive decline in the 1970s, and a particularly acute decline from the 1980s onward. Figure 3.2 illustrate the point.

Figure 3.2

Comparative Employment Statistics

	Formal Employment		Economically Active Population	
Period	000s	% growth pa	000s	% growth with pa
1950s	86.2	2.1	126.1	2.5
1960s	151.2	2.9	180.0	2.7
1970s	139.6	2.1	256.0	2.9
1980s	50.8	0.7	323.0	2.8
1990s	148.4	1.9	376.7	2.7

Source: SARB, various years

Figure 3.2 shows the relative stability of the growth rate of the economically active population over the years, and the fall in the rate of growth of employment compared with the aggregate increase of the economically active population. Another indicator of economic performance is the extent of the country's reliance on foreign inputs. Although foreign inputs are, in general, crucial for generating growth, over-reliance on such investment may, at the same time, be interpreted as exposing a lack of internally generated economic activity, including infrastructural, manufacturing and investments in research and development. Without such internal inputs, the chances for technological capacity, innovation and the creation of comparative advantage are vastly decreased. In this connection, figure 3.3 below shows how the South African economy was crippled precisely by its over-reliance on foreign inputs.

Once international investments were curtailed as a consequence of the international recession in the 1970s and the anti-apartheid economic sanctions and disinvestment in the 1980s, a yet to be reversed spiral of economic decline set in (Terreblanche, 1992).

Figure 3.3

Foreign capital flows and economic performance

	Foreign Financing of Gross Domestic Investment (Average%)	**Real Gross Domestic Product (average annual % change)**	**Real Gross Domestic Fixed Investment (average annual %change)**
1946-76	13.5	4.6	6.5
1977-84	3.3	2.7	1.5
1985-90	-12.7	1.0	2.9

Source: Terreblanche (1992)

What the above data do not show is that domestic savings also fell from an average of 23.5 per cent of GDP in the 1980s to 17 per cent in 1993 (IBCA, 1994: 320). The mining sector, which has always been the bedrock of the South African economy, was experiencing serious problems by the early 1990s. For instance, the International Labour organisation's (ILO) 1996 report showed that the South African mining sector lost 30 per cent of its jobs between 1987 and 1995. More specifically, employment in gold and coal mines shrank by 35 per cent and 47 per cent respectively (ILO, 1996: 279). This was mainly a consequence of global economic fluctuations, which in turn adversely affected the gold price and, by implication, the South African economy as a whole. Crucially, however, this was also a function of a lack of diversity in the economy and over-reliance on a minerals-energy complex (MEC) (Fine, 2010). The poor performance of the manufacturing sector did not help things either. All these factors contributed to a very negative economic inheritance for the new ruling elite. At the same time, however, the economic inheritance also laid bare the inherent frailties and inadequacies of the ideas behind that economic framework. Thereby throwing up immense possibilities for change and a fundamental overhaul of an economic framework that was deeply flawed and clearly inadequate to meet the needs of the new social order. In later chapters I show that following intense internal ideological shadow-boxing within the ANC-led alliance, since the early 1990s, those who favoured the retention of the broad structural framework of the inherited economic trajectory triumphed. And in so doing, firmly entrenched the ideological approach that was to foreshadow and underpin much of the change process of the past twenty-two years. Unsurprisingly, the politics and ideas of the inherited economic system loom large in all aspects of a transition that has been severely truncated by unfulfilled internal pressure and expectations. In a word, the continuities continue largely unabated twenty-two years down the line. And this is not unrelated, as the rest of this chapter explicitly demonstrate, to the neo-liberal ideological framework and the politics it spawned in post-apartheid South Africa.

Economy, Politics and Ideology

Chapters five and six go into some detail in exploring the politics and interests that characterized, facilitated and explain the ideological compromise that underpin the South African transition. The purpose of this section is however, less ambitious and that is to underline economic continuities in post-apartheid South Africa. It is, by now, common cause that post-apartheid growth rates have overall been dismal. The numbers are particularly miserable when viewed against the backdrop of the massive socio-economic deficit, equity, redress and redistributive challenge that confronted the new South Africa twenty-two years ago. The economic policy and implementation response to the challenge needed to be comprehensive, robust and pointed. Figure 3.4 below tell a grim story of sluggish and inadequate growth.

Table: South African Real Annual Economic Growth 1990- 2015

Year	Growth Rate
1990 -1994	0.0%
1994 – 2000	2.8%
2000 -2004	3.5%
2004 -2008	5.0%
2008 -2010	0.7%
2013	1.9%
2014	N/A
2015	1.4%

Source: IMF,2015

Moreover, the IMF's 2015 Staff Visit statement concluded that the prognosis moving forward is no better. Not only is the growth and jobs outlook for 2015/2016 lackluster, growth is projected at 2 per cent in the same period, assuming electricity problems, policy uncertainty, fiscal risks (to do with the performance and management of state-owned enterprises) and other structural problems do not deteriorate even further (IMF. 2015). The IMF Executive Board has just concluded its 2016 Article IV Consultation with South Africa, held in July 2015. This consultation came shortly after the country's new Finance Minister was compelled to mobilise the widest range of stakeholders, persuade them of the pressing urgency of avoiding a ratings agency down-grade to 'junk status'. This delegation had to meet international financial institutions around the world, to convince them of the country's commitment to prudence and playing by the rules of the game. This is despite the fact that the South African state had been pursuing this path since 1994. True, there were serious impediments to growth that included poor financial management, poor political leadership (the Finance Minister had just been unceremoniously replaced with devastating consequences for investments and the financial markets). As the forthcoming sections of this chapter will show, the education system remained very poor and the skills production processes remained generally at odds with the growth needs of the country. Corruption and state capture of key institutions by vested interests (with inappropriate relations with the head of state and other political figures), were all factors in the country's poor economic performance and sluggish growth. A number of state owned enterprises were very badly run and continued to drain the fiscus (South African Airways, South African Broadcasting Corporation, PRASA, ESKOM and several others besides).

All of these maladies were largely internally generated and could, with effective ethical and meritocratic leadership easily be attended to. However, the big elephant in the room remained the 'deep-rooted structural problems'. After all, with the Fund's tutelage, the South African government had been restructuring the economy for the better part of twenty-two years. How much more restructuring was the Fund calling for and in what direction? Almost all aspects of the economy including agriculture, education provision, water services, were delivered according to the Fund and Bank templates of commodification, commercialization and marketization. Nevertheless, the Fund revised growth projections to 0.1 per cent in 2016, with a weak (1.1 per cent) projected for 2017 (IMF press release: 16/322). The outlook is generally miserable in the outer years, with unemployment rates expected to rise moving forward (ibid). It seems to me that the failure of a variety of developmental plans (answering to Fund/Bank logic), to stem the ever deepening scourge of structural unemployment, inequality and low growth, has been pointing an accusatory finger to more than just the list of issues identified by the Fund's Executive Board. It seems the biggest challenge is that of squarely confronting the very logic, ideological and policy assumptions of such plans. Perhaps, another way is called for.

Agricultural Sector

The role of land reform and the agricultural sector more generally is always crucial in countries that seek (as did post-apartheid South Africa) to turn their socio-economic fortunes around, and embark on a growth path underpinned by economic growth, reconstruction and development. This sector provided an important challenge for the post-apartheid ruling elite, as the iniquitous land distribution was one of the key reasons for continued black unemployment, poverty and inequality (Pheko,1999). Thus, initiating a thoroughgoing land redistribution programme, and transforming the sector in such a way that it benefitted the majority of the population, remained a central challenge (De Klerk, 1991: 198). Moreover, the significance of the agricultural sector lay in the fact that it not only provided a firm basis for the development and transformation of the rural economy, but also served to stimulate "the level and distribution of activity in the economy as a whole" (ibid).

The Racial Structure of the Sector

Of the 11 per cent of arable land in South Africa, 73 per cent was white owned, while only 27 per cent was in areas designated for blacks (COSATU,

1992:56). Added significance is given to this data when viewed against the racial population distribution of the country at the time. In 1992, blacks constituted 86 per cent of the entire population, while whites were equal to only 13 per cent of the population. This made agricultural production and land distribution in South Africa thoroughly unequal, with 80 per cent of the farm produce coming from only 20 per cent of the farmers (ibid). The majority of black farmers were located in the Bantustans, which were not seen as part of South Africa. While data for these 'self-governing and independent states' is virtually non-existent, Jones and Muller (1992) nevertheless estimated the contribution of Bantustans to total agricultural output at around 5 per cent. Merle Lipton (1986) attributed the near absence of black participation in South Africa's agricultural market to overcrowding in Bantustans and to the lack of adequate government support. Moreover, Lipton has argued that by 1973: "the [apartheid] state was still spending twice as much on the 90, 000 rich white farmers, who had decades of favourable treatment behind them, as it spent on over half a million poor African farmers" (Lipton, 1986: 104-5).

This, combined with the generally poor social and economic conditions in Bantustans, meant that economic incentives were weighted against blacks (ibid). Therefore, a crucial element in South Africa's agricultural inheritance was precisely this racially iniquitous structure and resource distribution in the sector.

Agricultural Performance

It is generally accepted that South African agriculture, which had with the rest of the economy benefitted from the boom of the 1960s, started to experience serious problems from around the early 1980s (De Klerk, 1991; Jones and Muller, 1992; COSATU, 1992). The total agricultural debt burden increased from 11. 8 per cent in 1975 to 25.9 per cent in 1988. Furthermore, the output in this sector in 1990 was equal to 6 per cent of the economy's total output, having dropped consistently from 9 per cent in 1965 (COSATU, 1992:56). This, in turn, led to an estimated 30 per cent drop in employment in this sector, over the same period (SAIRR,1992:396). A number of factors had conspired to trigger this downturn, including but not limited to:

Drought

The prolonged drought of 1982-5 affected both arable and pastoral farmers negatively. Farmers without cash reserves were particularly hard hit, as the immediate impact was on their liquidity. The State President's Economic Advisory Council estimated that the drought of 1984 and 1985 was directly responsible for at least 22 per cent of the agricultural sector's debt burden (cited in De Klerk, 1991: 208).

Interest Rates

At least 31 per cent of the increase in the agricultural debt burden in the period 1980-1985 was due to interest rate movements (ibid:209). High interest rates on repayment of loans therefore contributed significantly not only to the escalation of the debt burden, but also to the general instability of the agricultural sector as a whole. In light of these difficulties and uncertainties, many farmers have felt it more prudent to continue borrowing, thereby entangling themselves deeper into debt (and using their farms as collateral), rather than lose their businesses (ibid). In the long run, this state of affairs led only to more uncertainties and liquidity problems for the farming community.

Terms of Trade

The most enduring cause of deterioration in farm finances has been the adverse movement in agricultural terms of trade. The Economic Advisory Council's 1986 report also observed that the terms of trade contributed in large measure to the phenomenal increase in the farming debt between 1980 and 1985. The report estimated that 47 per cent of farmers' debt was due to fairly consistent negative movements in agricultural terms of trade (RSA, 1986). Analysing the same subject, De Klerk came to the conclusion that "… the rate of growth of the domestic farm output can be expected to slow down for much of the 1990s" (1991:213). Agriculture thus posed a critical challenge for post-apartheid South Africa and a large part of the challenge had to do with correcting the racially defined inequalities in the sector especially, land distribution and support. So, the scene was set for the post-apartheid elites to attend to what was a fairly well defined problem, what is the state of affairs twenty-two years on?

Post-apartheid agricultural performance

The performance of the agricultural sector in post-apartheid South Africa has been largely underwhelming. And this is despite the Agricultural White Paper's 1995 promise of:

> A highly efficient and economically viable market-directed farming sector characterized by a wide range of farm sizes, which will be regarded as the

economic and social pivot of rural South Africa and which will influence the rest of the economy (South African Government, 1995).

Of course, the irony and futility of seeking to effect radical transformative land and agrarian reform to address three hundred years of land dispossession, via a 'market directed' approach seem to have been completely lost to the authors and supporters of this document. Sadly, however, twenty-two years down the line, there is no discernible evidence of a qualitative shift from this fundamentally flawed policy prospectus, and unsurprisingly, the impact on land and agrarian reform has been pitiful.

Between 1993 and 1997, the average annual GDP growth rate in agriculture was one per cent per annum, while the rest of the economy grew at an average 3.7 Per cent in the same period. Furthermore, the agricultural sector contributes 2.3 per cent to the country's total GDP, down from 4.3 per cent in the early 1990's. Thus, from absorbing more than ten per cent of the labour force in 1990, the South African agricultural sector currently absorbs less than three per cent of the labour force (Stats SA, 2014). Commercial farms, highly mechanized and a key source of revenue and exports, have always been the epitome of South African agriculture. In the early 1990s, there were 60, 000 tax paying commercial farming units, in 2013 this number had declined to 40, 000 (Bernstein, 2013: 26). Cousins (2014) has shown that by 2013, the state had spent a total of R10 billion for the settlement of 79,696 land claims (this involved some 1,44 million hectares of land).

There was an additional R6 billion spent on cash compensation, because the land could not be restored (the majority of these were in urban settings). Even in this instance, only 59, 758 of the 79, 696 claims have been finalized, due to budgetary constraints. Minister of Land Reform and Agriculture, Gugile Nkwinti has suggested that even where land had been successfully handed over to new owners, 90 per cent of the associated land reform projects had collapsed (Nkwinti, 2013). Land reform and agrarian researchers on their part attributed such failure to inadequate post-settlement support, undercapitalization and conflict within large groups of claimants (Aliber et al, 2013).

By all measures then, there has been an almost uninterrupted decline in agricultural performance in the past twenty-two years. There are several reasons for this. The most obvious reasons reside in flawed policy choices, poor implementation and lack of support and follow-through. Poor implementation of land reform, in ways that would dynamise the sector and lead to access, equity and growth for all, has led to a negligible impact on the lives of the poor and financially disenfranchised (Cousins, 2014). Instead of the thirty per cent of the land that was promised for redistribution in the first five years of democracy, less than ten per cent of the land has been redistributed twenty-two years later (RDP, 1995; Aliber et al, 2013). The second and arguably, most pressing reason for the poor performance of the agricultural sector has to do with ideology and by extension policy choices arising from the ideological framework. At the heart of the problem is the insistence of the new leadership on 'market-directed or assisted' reform in agriculture, including the ill-conceived decision to subject the sector to harsh and poorly sequenced trade liberalization policies (Cousins, 2014: 378). As if this was not bad enough, any prospects of growth and development were further choked off by the lowering of tariffs even below the bound rates agreed to in the Marrakech Agreement of 1994. This was ostensibly to win the confidence and buy goodwill from the international trading community (Hirsch, 2005).

Apart from the adverse impact these policy choices had on agricultural performance, they also had devastating socio-economic effects on the poorest sections of South African society. Deregulation meant that price controls for bread, maize meal and dairy products were abolished so that retail prices for these products were set by market forces. As to be expected, this led to product price decline and food price inflation. Internal economic policy debate within the ruling ANC-led alliance in the late 1980s and early 1990s, had already shown the foolishness of following one-size-fits-all neo-liberal prescriptions in attending to South Africa's problems. So, too, did the debates expose the short-sightedness of Soviet style command planning mechanisms, hence the popularity of a middle road of sorts dubbed 'a mixed economy' (MERG, 1993). Nevertheless, as in the economy as a whole, the texture, speed and content of land and agricultural reform were underpinned by the neo-liberal perspective. Which in turn, gave rise to a deeply flawed and ineffectual policy pipeline. In the end, the ideological and policy framework adopted would seem to have been neither efficient, affordable nor impactful. It is for this reason that Ashman, Fine, Padayachee and Sender (2014) concluded that at the heart of the poor performance of South Africa's post-apartheid agricultural sector, is the ideologically driven and unilateral removal of state support for agriculture(2014:72). As a consequence of such investment neglect and lack of support for farms, the Producer Support Estimate: "has declined substantially and is now at a very low level (3 per cent), well below the OECD average of 20 per cent" (ibid). And for this very reason, middle and upper middle income developing countries have consistently increased their support for agriculture, and thereby boast a far more superior export growth than South Africa. As part of the apartheid state's hurried liberalization efforts, the old agricultural marketing councils were also abolished. In the last chapter I have shown how effective these were in institutionalizing state-agricultural business relations.

Similar structures were used by East Asian states to direct, implement and allow for policy input from key agricultural and sector stakeholders. It does seem to me that part of the explanation for South Africa's policy failure in agriculture has to do with the absence of structured sectoral institutions between state and various sectors of the economy.

South Korea, Taiwan, China, Japan and other East Asian states stand out as examples of successful agricultural and agrarian reform. In 1965, about 41 per cent of South Korean households were officially estimated to be living below the poverty line. This figure was dramatically reduced to 23 per cent by 1970 and 12 per cent by 1978 (Koo, 1984:1030). In Taiwan, too, the developmental state's intervention in the agricultural sector, was such that resources (seed, implements, pricing structure, access to markets) were distributed in ways completely defied the market mechanism (Amsden, 1978:341). This led to growth and relative equity in the countryside. Ranis (1978) has shown that although the Taiwanese Gini Coeficient was around 0.7 in the 1950s, this figure had improved to below 0.3 by 1972, and continued improving further thereafter. Thus, both in South Korea and Taiwan, the impact of and outcomes of a policy overhaul in agriculture (and the broader economy) was discernible within the first ten years of implementation. This is the hallmark of developmental state-making. It impacts not only high levels of economic growth and development (as it should), but its efficacy is also demonstrated in radically improved human development indicators, within the first ten years of implantation. The significance of getting the agricultural sector right resides in the fact that it can and does lay the basis for high level industrial and manufacturing growth. This is because, according to French public policy guru, Paul Sabatier, the effectiveness of any public policy should tell and be ready for evaluation after ten years of implementation (Sabatier, 1993).

Thus, South Africa's poor handling of land and agrarian reform is not only hurting millions of rural and landless poor (invariably black) people, but it also constitutes a lost opportunity for dealing with unemployment, poverty and sluggish agricultural performance. In large measure, the continuities loom larger than the discontinuities and the desperately called for change.

Manufacturing Sector: The inheritance

The South African manufacturing sector has always depended on imports of capital goods for its survival and continued expansion. These imports were attained through foreign exchange which was in turn dependent on the stability of the price of gold (the main export product since 1920), and other primary products (Black,1991:161). Another structural feature of the sector related to South Africa's highly skewed income distribution, which produced an unequal and racially determined pattern of demand. On the one hand, this served to limit the development of a broad mass based market, while on the other, it has led to the expansion of a substantial market for expensive consumer durables (Blacks and Stanwix, 1987; COSATU, 1992). Indeed, by the early 1990s, there was limited local demand for locally manufactured goods, and the sector found itself unable to penetrate the overseas export markets (Marais, 2001:103). Figure 3.5 below, clearly illustrates the gradual decline in the performance of the manufacturing sector since the early 1970s. Of particular interest, is that between 1980 and 1990, the total manufacturing output increased by just 0.1 per cent.

Figure 3.5

Gross Domestic Product and Manufacturing growth 1946-1990, Average rate of growth per annum.

Year	Manufacturing output (%)	Manufacturing employment (%)	Total GDP (%)
1946-1950	9.1	6.6	4.7
1950-1955	7.5	3.0	4.8
1955-1960	4.5	0.9	4.0
1960-1965	9.9	6.8	6.0
1965-1970	7.4	3.2	5.4
1970-1975	6.0	4.1	4.0
1975-1980	4.1	1.5	3.4
1980-1985	-1.2	-1.0	1.1
1985-1990	N/A	N/A	N/A

Source: SARB various years, COSATU (1992)

The crisis in manufacturing could, moreover, be illuminated by isolating three key areas as follows:

Job Creation

A COSATU report on this aspect of manufacturing performance revealed that between 1980 and 1990 output increased by a mere 0.1 per cent. In

1980, manufacturing employment comprised 28 per cent of total non-agricultural employment, while by 1990 this proportion had declined to 26 per cent (ibid:45). The significance of manufacturing data is accentuated when it is recognized that this sector was the largest contributor to output and employment in the South African economy. This clearly had important implications for employment trends and employment creation in the economy as a whole. The inability of this sector to create jobs was in part related to its inability to produce value added manufactured goods for export purposes. Related to this was the sector's inability to attract sufficient investments and foreign exchange for expansion and job creation purposes (Joffe, Kaplan and Lewis, 1993: 93). As shown in fig. 3.6, real manufacturing value added started to dwindle from around the mid-1970s.

Figure 3.6

Average growth rate GDP and manufacturing value added factor cost(1985 constant prices)

	GDP Growth Rate (%)	MVA Growth Rate (%)
1950-9	4.7	6.1
1960-9	5.6	8.8
1970-9	3.0	4.9
1980-9	1.6	0.4
1990	-0.6	-1.3
1991	-0.7	-2.4
1992	-2.2	-3.2

Source: SARB, various years

These limitations have thus contributed to the frustration of any job creation possibilities in the manufacturing sector.

Gross Domestic Fixed Investments by manufacturing has also declined (in real terms) by approximately 50 per cent between 1980 and 1990 (Samson, 2000:9). South Africa's manufacturing sector could thus be characterized as a good example of capital-intensive production that did not support job creation (ibid). The pattern of capital and labour use followed in South Africa's manufacturing sector was, according to Fourie (1997), typical of industrialised economies that do not experience the same unemployment and skill development challenges confronting South Africa. Fourie attributed this lack of employment creation in the sector to a variety of causes including the usage of inappropriate technology from industrialised countries, the scarcity of skilled workers, and the preference of imported consumer goods (1997:368).

Capital Goods Production

The South African manufacturing sector was notorious for its inability to produce machinery and other capital goods which were essential for the sector's vibrancy and self-sufficiency. Instead, the preference was to obtain these from abroad, thereby making the manufacturing sector a considerable net user of foreign exchange. This meant that every unit of output produced by the manufacturing sector used up more foreign exchange than it earned (Joffe et al, 1993:94). Stainless steel aptly illustrates this point. Although South Africa was one of the world's foremost producers of steel, it is remarkable that stainless steel itself was not manufactured in South Africa (COSATU, 1992: 61). Instead, steel was exported in raw form, with no value added, and turned into stainless steel abroad. This would then be imported into the country (much more expensively) in the form of machinery and equipment, the life blood of South Africa's manufacturing processes (Van Holdt, 1991:22).

Were South Africa to establish its own stainless steel plants, this would open up the possibility of developing a large stainless steel products sector. This, of course, is on the assumption that pro-domestic growth trade policies were adopted. Such diversification and creative use of comparative advantage would moreover, be an important job creation measure, as well as a crucial growth area for the sector in general (ibid). These were but some of the possible areas of intervention for the new policy-makers, if the economy was to be turned around into a high growth and job creating economy.

Manufacturing for Exports

The inability of the manufacturing sector to sell what output it did produce successfully in international markets, lent a striking quality to the country's trade profile, rendering it more dependent upon gold exports and other primary exports than was the case a decade earlier (Black,1991: 61). This profile did not compare well with other middle income developing economies notably: Brazil, Mexico and Argentina which, together in 1991, had an import coefficient of approximately 10 per cent, against South Africa's 24 per cent (ibid). Also, between 1960 and 1989, the proportion of non-gold goods exported as primary raw materials increased from 29 per cent to 42 per cent and processed raw materials registered an increase from 40 per cent to 46 per cent (Hirsch, 1991). In the same period, exports of finished goods fell from a share of 16 per cent of non-gold exports to 6 per cent (ibid). Such therefore, was the inheritance of the ANC government in the manufacturing sector

Room to Maneuver

As daunting as the manufacturing legacies were, the sector also presented some positive aspects on which the new policy actors could build in order to turn the economy around. The first was a generally positive international good will towards South Africa and its prospects moving forward. This, combined with the 'Mandela dividend', provided the new government and the private sector with enormous room to impose a thoroughgoing redress, growth and developmental project. The end of the disinvestment and sanctions campaigns only served to add to the scope for change. Second, at 22 per cent of GDP in 1994, the country's external debt burden was regarded as small for a developing country, this gave policy makers further scope to increase the debt load in the direction of economic transformation, reconstruction and development (ILO, 1996:31). Thirdly, a large state sector inherited from the apartheid regime (some 47 per cent of the country's total fixed economic assets) provided the new state elite with a formidable arsenal to alter economic and power relations, through a state-led developmental process. Specifically, it would give them considerable scope and leverage in determining, setting the terms, and strategically controlling and directing further investment flows. Therefore, the massive economic infrastructure and skilled (predominantly white) human capital also augured well for the country's developmental future. The possibility of a state elite committed to social transformation and economic redress for the majority was also an important factor in favour of the country's future, especially when the ANC's Reconstruction and Development Programme, envisaged a leading and enabling role for government in guiding the economy and the market, including a reversal of some past privatization (RDP, 1994).

Post-Apartheid: manufacturing performance

The South African manufacturing sector is perhaps the most disappointing of all economic sectors, given the centrality of this sector in industrial growth, foreign exchange and the general diversification of the entire economy. This sector's performance has remained stagnant, from constituting 19 per cent of total output in 1994, it was marginally below this figure at 17 per cent of real GDP in 2012 (Bhorat et al, 2014). These poor growth levels mean that manufacturing in the post-apartheid economy has remained an inadequate contributor to job creation and GDP. The World Bank has calculated that average manufacturing contribution to middle income countries should be at 21,2 per cent share of GDP, while for upper middle countries, the figure should be at 22. 5 per cent (World Bank, 2013). This compares poorly with South Africa's 17 per cent.

From a developmental state-making view point, of course, the absence of a dynamic job-generating and competitive manufacturing sector bodes ill for South Africa's growth and development prospects. After all, East Asian developmental state success was predicated on agrarian reform, which was in turn, used as stepping stone for massive expansion of manufacturing and diversification of the whole economy. At the heart of manufacturing's poor performance are bad policy choices, informed by a flawed ideological frame-work which in turn was inspired, it would seem, by the 'tyranny of the status quo' (Friedman, 1962). The neo-liberal economist, Milton Friedman, was lamenting inertia among economists, their inability to think outside of the box even when circumstances call for such innovation and creativity, he put it thus:

> Only a crisis – actual or perceived – produces real change. When that crisis occurs the actions that are taken depend on the ideas that are lying around (cf: Pally, 2012: 9).

As I show in more detail in the remaining chapters, both the post-apartheid and pre-developmental state intellectual environments were awash with 'ideas lying around', which of these were adopted by the elites concerned was a matter of ideology, choice and intentional action. Trade policy choices and South Africa's insertion into the World Trade Organisation (WTO) and the intense internal contestation within the new ruling elite, provide some explanation for the continued sluggishness in the sector. Indeed, where some saw room for manoeuvre and opportunities, key policy makers saw impediments to competitiveness of the country's manufacturing sector. In this regard, Asham, Fine, Padayachee and Sender (2014) have shown that the stated reasons for the adoption of conservative, non-developmental macro-economic policies were ostensibly to attract foreign direct investment and avoid the punitive reaction of the markets in the event of the adoption of more developmentalist policies. However, the past twenty-two years have shown a different reality at the heart of which has been the dismal failure of these policies to facilitate the effective attraction of long-term investment (2014: 69). But more ominously, they have facilitated the rapid detachment of South African capital from the South African economy, while also paving the way for increased financialisation (at the expense of manufacturing expansion and investment), a phenomenon that accounts for the strain the economy is under (ibid). Furthermore, this detachment was facilitated and entrenched through post-apartheid policy leaders' ideologically inspired obsession with a flawed economic policy prospectus. Off-shore listing and complicated transfer practices, facilitated by exchange control liberalization, led to illegal and legal flight of billions of Rands worth of revenue and investments. Fine (2012) puts the figure of illegal capital flight at around 20 per cent of GDP in 2007. While mining company Lonmin (best known for its role in the events that triggered the Marikana massacre), has been accused of diverting more than R1.2 billion in illicit financial outflows, tax base erosion and profit shifting (Hansard, 2015).

These days, what private investment does come South Africa's way is mainly in the speculative and non-productive and non-developmental finance sectors of the economy. And finance is, incidentally, the fastest growing and most active sector of the South African economy, thereby closing off any real prospect of private sector led developmental initiatives (certainly not in the scale called for by the economic needs of the country). What is remarkable about these developments is less the fact that they are happening, after all, current global reality places great responsibility on state actors and policy makers to be creative and dynamic in how such internal and global challenges are managed. What is remarkable and even shocking, is South African President Zuma's response to a variety of questions about the role and place of the state in navigating complex internal and global economic forces. Instead of setting out a state led developmental plan designed to counter or at least ameliorate the worst effects of the negative internal and external economic forces engulfing the country, the president responded thus: " some of the trade issues are determined by the World Trade Organisation (WTO) and other international organisations that determine how trade should go between countries.....How trade moves in the world is determined by market forces. You can't be a country that moves on its own, while the world move in a particular direction" (Hansard, 2015).

This was in response to a question about whether government was considering intervening in stemming the impending job losses and possible collapse of South African steel companies as a result of cheap Chinese steel imports flooding the South African market. On a question about the widespread illicit financial flows, the president is of the view that: "Government does not interfere with business or the private sector, otherwise we would be chasing everybody.... we can't do anything about business decisions, we don't run private companies, we run government". Of course, these are deeply ideological answers that allow for inferences to be made about the state's ideological outlook on a range of factors not excluding the role and place of the state in the economy, market, finance and trade policies. Nonetheless, all of these factors were to foreshadow what promises to be a gloom prognosis for manufacturing performance in particular and the wider (especially) productive economic sectors of the economy.

Exports in South Africa's manufacturing Sector

Hausman and Klinger have shown that although South Africa has been the biggest economy on the African continent until recently, Egyptian and Moroccan manufacturers were higher than South Africa's (2006:4). While Kaplan (2015) has shown that South African manufacturing is also performing poorly in comparison to other BRICS partners, both in terms of total exports and in particular, for manufactured exports (2015: 246). What makes this significant is that in the mid-1990s, the status among BRICS partner countries was largely similar. Figure 3.7 below depicts the comparative performance (in trade value) of BRICS countries between 1995 and 2010.

**Manufacturing exports, trade value, Brics, 1995-2010
(current $ US millions) (% change**

	1995	2000	2005	2010	1995-2010)
Brazil	24,703	31,987	62,534	72,467	193
China	125,168	219,841	700,075	1,476,007	1,979
India	23,277	32,970	71,319	140,471	503
Russia	23,061	24,323	45,278	58,696	154
SA	12,200	14,149	26,435	33,169	171

Source: Comtrade

True, the table shows a steady increase in manufacturing exports, what it does not show is that export per capita is only slightly higher than was the case in 1960 (Hausman and Klinger; IMF, 2015). South Africa does not perform any better with respect to its share of high technology manufactured exports, South Africa is well below other BRICS countries in this regard (Kaplan, 2015:249). Figure:3.8 below shows that South Africa's share of high technology exports in total manufactured exports was higher than Brazil's in 1994. Things have been on an uninterrupted down-ward spiral since reaching its peak in 1998.

High technology exports as a share of manufactured exports, BRICS (1994-2010)

	1994	1998	2002	2006	2010
Brazil	4,6	9,41	16,52	12,08	11,21
Russia	-	11,98	19,16	7,78	8,85
India	4,78	5,62	6,24	6,07	7,18
China	8,29	15,36	23,67	30,51	27,51
SA	4,88	8,75	5,16	6,46	4,28

Source: World Development Indicators

Value Added as a Share of GDP

South Africa's manufacturing value added as a share of GDP declined from 21 per cent in 1995 to 14 per cent in 2010, this decline has yet to be contained (Kaplan, 2015).

Change in Economic Profile

An interesting dimension of the post-apartheid economy is the change from a dominant role and performance of the non-renewable sectors to the dominance of a globally competitive financial and business sector. This has essentially cemented South Africa's financialisation at the expense of manufacturing growth generation and employment creation (World Economic Forum, 2013). Thus, on the one hand, the South African economy is dominated by a highly sophisticated, globally competitive financial sector, on the down-side, the export profile is predominantly natural resource and capital intensive based (Bhorat et al, 2014).

Employment Absorption

South African manufacturing has yet to return to the levels of 1989 – 1990, in terms of job creation and retention. The sector's capacity to create and sustain employment has been badly compromised by the dramatic fall of the ratio of jobs to value added since the early 1990s (Black and Gerwel, 2014: 25). Therefore, poor manufacturing performance has contributed significantly to the unsustainably high unemployment rates in South Africa. True, the number of households living in poverty has declined and this is thanks, in large measure, to the aggressive expansion of social grant recipients. According to the IMF (2015), there is a direct causal relationship between

South Africa's failure to take the necessary steps towards risk mitigation and attending to the pressing structural changes, especially in investment and the manufacturing sector (2015:11).

As a consequence, the IMF's Staff Visit of June 23, 2015, make very grim projections for South Africa's overall economic performance in the next several quarters. Figure 3.9 below is a summary of the Fund's Assessment of South Africa's growth prospects.

Economic Indicators

National Income and Prices (annual percentage change unless otherwise indicates)

	2011	2012	2013	2014	2015	2016
Real GDP	3,2	2,2	2,2	1,5	2,0	2,1
Real GDP per capita	1,7	0,7	0,6	-0,1	0,4	0,5
Real domestic demand Gross govt debt	5,1	3,8	2,7	1,1	1,7	1,9
Gross govt. debt	37,6	40,5	43,3	54,5	47,0	47,5

Source: IMF, 2015

It is significant to note that the poor performance of post-apartheid manufacturing sector (including its inability to create jobs and generate demand) is not unrelated to the flawed economic strategy adopted at this time. An economic policy largely guided by the 'free' hand of the market has seen finance and financial markets gradually eclipsing the productive economy and, as expected, undermining employment creation, demand and the country's consumption base. A complete overhaul of this flawed strategy is called for, to stem the perennial fragility of the South African economy.

Poverty and Inequality

A 2014 ground-breaking OECD research report confirmed something many left theorists, heterodox economists and developmental state writers have been saying for the past thirty years or so. And this is that there is a direct correlation between income inequality and economic growth, in both the developing and developed countries (OECD, 2014). The research further shows that the most direct policy instrument to significantly reduce inequality is redistribution, another policy question long resolved by left thinking economists, developmental economists and social scientists. Yet another notable development has been the publication of Thomas Piketty's (2014) book on the history and causes of inequality. Like the OECD report, Piketty's book shines the spotlight firmly on the role of ideology and politics in driving a global process characterized by inequality and inegalitarianism. This at a time when researchers are increasingly converging on the reality that lower inequality is highly correlated with faster growth and that more equality in income distribution is associated with longer growth spells (Berg and Ostry, 2011). However, more than thirty years of neo-liberal policy implementation globally has shown that there is congruence and mutual reinforcement between these policies and equity. Instead, research around the so-called top one per cent shows the opposite. The wealth gap between the top one per cent and the rest of humanity has grown to shocking levels in the past thirty years and what is more, the only way to halt this schism, the existence side by side, of abject poverty and outrageous opulence – is through re-imagining the global structure of accumulation, wealth creation and distribution. At the heart of such re-imagination has to be increased levels of egalitarianism. In the South African context, this thinking is contained in much of the ANC's earlier economic perspectives (MERG, RDP, Freedom Charter etc). This section briefly sets out the apartheid inheritance in as far as poverty and inequality are concerned, and then assesses the state of affairs a generation into a democratic system. Of course, as we move further and further away from 1994, commentators and analysts are understandably loathe of tracing current problems of inequality, poverty and unemployment to South Africa's apartheid past. Whilst there is merit in the argument that post-apartheid leaders and policy-makers are going to have to take responsibility for ill-conceived policy responses, there is absolutely no doubt that there are deep-seated structural constraints – that have their genesis in the racial capitalist social structure. True, two decades is sufficient for the new leadership and policy elites to have, at the very least, accurately diagnosed the problem – its structural and ideological underpinnings. Nonetheless, for analytical and explanatory rigour – historical context is an unavoidable and critical point of departure.

The Apartheid Inheritance

The post-apartheid leadership elite inherited a deeply unequal country, one characterized by racialised poverty and unemployment. Contrary to what so many of today's television and radio economists and political analysts would have the world believe, these maladies were never transient problems to be easily swept away by the implementation of 'prudent' policies. This inheritance is, instead, deeply structural and is reinforced by global financial interests. In other words, unless there are determined efforts to fundamentally overhaul the structural and ideological underpinnings of these challenges, the grand policy interventions (ASGISA, NGP, NDP etc.) will continue to have only partial and tentative success. In the final analysis, if the object is to overthrow racialised inequality, poverty and structural unemployment, then plans and strategies must be designed to squarely confront the institutional arrangements, structures, politics and the power relations that produce and reproduce poverty, inequality and unemployment. In the South African context, these social problems have their genesis and continued existence to an accumulation strategy that has persisted (save for some tactical modifications in the late 1940s, again in the mid to late 1980s and of course, in the mid-1990s and beyond). Built into this regime of accumulation is an institutionalized and systematic exclusion-inclusion matrix, which affects economic participation, ownership structures, employment and educational opportunities and much more besides. To be sure, it has been the expectation of the immense majority of South Africans and the promise of the post-apartheid leadership elite that these social and economic challenges would be addressed, leading to growth, development, equality and prosperity for all. What has been the experience two decades later?

Ownership Structure

Post-apartheid South Africa, as indicated above, is in very many respects a different and better place than apartheid South Africa, especially for the immense majority of black people in that country. Indeed, the work of a team led by (Finn, Leibbrandt and Woolard, 2013), endeavors to disaggregate the notion of poverty, this they do by focusing specific attention to the Multi-dimensional Poverty Index (MPI) in South Africa since 1993. The utility of the MPI is that it is able to factor in aspects that a normal, money-metric poverty measure, is unable to capture as accurately. Thus, the MPI captures aspects of human well-being like: education, health-care, living standards, nutrition, sanitation, water and energy, child mortality and other variables (ibid:2). This work shows that there has been a considerable decline of this kind of poverty since the new political dispensation. The picture, however, with respect to what is commonly referred to as money-metric measure, is less straight-forward. It is to these measures that echoes of continuity between the past and present seem to be most palpable. The most telling indication of this continuity is to be found in the ownership structure ir.cluding asset and wealth concentration. The Johannesburg Stock Exchange is the largest stock market in Africa and the sixth largest in the developing world (Hassan,

2014:165). Current research suggests that the JSE, measured by the ratio of market capitalization to GDP is around 190 per cent (ibid). Thus, the JSE is a significant indicator of the structure of asset and wealth ownership and control. In this regard, it is consequential that the Johannesburg Stock Exchange holds that black South Africans own around 23 per cent of shares in the more than 400 firms listed there (Newton-King, 2015). Government (and specifically the Presidency) on the other hand, has strenuously contested this figure. In his State of the Nation Address, Zuma maintained that the methodology deployed by the Johannesburg Stock Exchange was misleading, as it failed to distinguish between direct black ownership and control and black ownership and participation via a complex network of mechanisms. These included mandated investments including BEE schemes, pension funds and life policies (Zuma, 2015). Were one to probe beyond these schemes, insists Zuma, then the real tragedy of an untransformed and racially defined ownership structure and asset management and control would emerge. And this is that South African blacks in 2015, still directly own and control less than 3 per cent of the companies at the JSE (ibid). A disturbing and equally unsurprising aspect of the JSE ownership structure, has to do with the fact that the value of foreign shareholding has steadily increased and not decreased in the post-apartheid period. In 2013, the value of foreign shareholding stood at 39 per cent.

This, of course, is not unrelated to post-apartheid South Africa's increased 'financialisation' and the penetration of internationalized interests across South African capital (Ashman et al, 2014). In the context of South African social, political and especially economic history, whatever methodological shortcomings, neither of these figures are encouraging. However, were Zuma's (3 per cent) figure to be accurate, it would represent a shocking indictment against the post-apartheid leadership elites. Above all, it would stand (as does the current Greek tragedy) as yet another signal of the inadequacies and failure of the neo-liberal framework to respond to twenty first century human and economic development needs. More significantly, it would be yet another indication of a fundamentally flawed prospectus and structural framework.

The persistence of a flawed accumulation framework is also discernable in post-apartheid income inequality distribution, where race stubbornly remains a defining factor of inclusion and exclusion. In this connection, Statistics South Africa (StatsSA) has shown that in 2012, the average income of an African headed household was R69 632, 5.5 times less than a household headed by a white South African at R387 011 (StatsSA, 2012b). A StatsSA 2013 survey also shows that despite a variety of policy interventions, South

Africa remains (at a Gini coefficient of 0.655 in late 1993, 0.72 in 2006 to 0.825 using the 2001 Census and stabilizing to around 0.69 in 2012), the most unequal societies in the world, certainly among those that do measure inequality (StatsSA, 2013). Of course, post-apartheid South Africa is not unique in the world as far as income distribution is concerned. Indeed, As Piketty has shown, those in the top ten percent of the income scale, will continue to reap the benefit of the neo-liberal framework, whilst those in the bottom will lose and the lower you are the bigger the loss and exclusion. Therefore, in order to overcome the atrocious levels of income inequality, and to fashion genuine racial harmony, state policy and policy thinkers will have to pause and consider the real culprit in the policy failure. It could very well be the structural framework that is crying out for change.

The desperate need for fundamental change in South Africa's owner-ship structure is also demonstrated by the country's shocking racially defined inequalities in asset ownership and control. Post-apartheid South Africa's poorly conceived and ill-fated land reform programme has had devastating consequences not only for blacks looking for access to agricultural land, but it has had ramifications for land and property (asset) ownership more broadly.

Contrary to the East Asian experiences, where thoroughgoing land re-form programmes led to the redistribution of massive tracts of agricultural and non-agricultural land to millions of previously dispossessed families, South Africa's land reform programme has been muted and largely ineffectu-al. It is also consequential that the land and agricultural reform programmes in both Taiwan and South Korea took under two years to implement. In post-apartheid South Africa, by contrast, property relations and asset own-ership patterns have not changed in any fundamental ways in the last twen-ty-two years. What is more, the continued perpetuation of apartheid spatial planning patterns, means that even those blacks that do own their properties, will not see the appreciation of these assets as do those whose properties are located in more affluent and lucrative parts of the town or city. The World Bank has also demonstrated the link between location and access to econom-ic opportunities in South Africa (World Bank, 2012). The Study concluded that the spatial disadvantages of townships, informal settlements and rural villages, represent a 'continuity' of the structural inequalities against South Africans located in these areas (ibid). Therefore, tinkering with land policies that are structurally and institutionally limited has meant that a potentially huge opportunity to equalize property and asset ownership has been squan-dered for more than two decades.

Another driver of racialised inequality in post-apartheid South Africa is wage inequality. This, of course, has its roots in the 'cheap labour system' introduced by segregationist governments more than a hundred years ago, and given added impetus by apartheid policy planners after 1948. This wage structure, too, has not been altered in any fundamental ways. The endurance of the apartheid wage structure is discernible in StatsSA analysis for 2013, and it shows that while an African family earned a median monthly income of R2 600, the figure for the white population was R10 500 (StatsSA, 2014a). Whereas a great deal of media and analytical attention has understandably focused on the loss of life and police brutality in Marikana, few have paid adequate attention to the sub-human living conditions of miners and the shockingly low salaries of South African mine workers. Whilst the average South African miner earns an annual salary of around R167, 140, the corresponding figure for Australian mineworkers is upwards of R700 000 (NUM, 2011; iminco.net, 2014). Apart from poor salaries, another driver of the Marikana massacre were the poor working and living conditions of workers in the platinum belt. Lonmin Plc, a British owned company, had undertaken, in terms of a 2006 Social and Labour Plan (SLP), to radically improve the workers' conditions by, among other things, constructing 5 500 housing units and modernising the single-sex hostels (Amnesty International, 2016). Despite committing, in line with South Africa's Mineral and Petroleum Resources Development Act and the country's Mining Charter, Lonmin nonetheless failed to live up to these commitments. After all, no pressure or consequences were forthcoming from the South African government, black workers have been slaving under these conditions for more than hundred years. And so too, had the black cheap labour thesis, as I have shown in chapter two. In the absence of support from a progressive government, one with strong ties to the labour movement, workers had little choice but to take matters into their own hands. It is common knowledge now that this challenge to an inequities labour regime led to the cold-blooded massacre of scores of workers on that fateful day in August 2012. Amnesty International's report shows that four years after the massacre and following high-level state-business agreements for improved conditions, not much has changed. And, as expected, very little movement has been forthcoming from the state. The distribution of unemployment too, shows important echoes of the pre-1994 realities, as figure 3.10 below clearly demonstrate.

Unemployment by race

By Population group	Narrow (%)	Expanded (%)
African	27.1	38.5
Coloured	23.0	26.8
Indian/Asian	12.5	17.1
White	7.2	8.4

Source: Stats SA, 2012c

The unemployment problem in post-apartheid South Africa is significant not only because it underlines deep-seated racial inequalities and inequalities with respect to access and opportunities, but is a critical variable in its own right. For one thing, more than any other variable, high and stubborn unemployment rates signify post-apartheid economic failure. For another, and related to the first one, it calls attention to the futility of tinkering with ideologically loaded policies that do nothing but reproduce the current institutional framework. Moreover, research by heterodox thinkers (Wittenberg, 2014; Bhorat et al, 2014; Ashman, 2014) have shown the limited utility of arguments that portray South Africa as having a high wage structure and then go on to attribute this 'fact' to lack of employment creation. This argument overlooks the reality that 50 per cent of black workers earn at the median of R2 600 a month or below (Stats SA, 2014). What stands out from the above is that South Africa is, in very many respects, screaming for fundamental structural change, it is also clear that the ideological framework guiding socio-economic change in the past twenty-two years is itself in need of transformation and change. Another important driver of inequality in South Africa is reputedly the labour market structure of that country, it is to this aspect that the next section briefly turns.

Apartheid Inheritance – The Labour Market

Various research studies have sought to characterize the apartheid labour market in South Africa as racially defined and deeply segmented (Commonwealth Report, 1992; NEPI/NECC Report, 1992; SALDRU, 1993). Specifically, the segmentation was around four, almost distinct, categories namely:

* A Primary labour market

* Subordinate primary market

* Secondary labour market, and

* The informal sector (SALDRU, 1993)

These categories help to underline and contextualize the depth and structural nature of the apartheid inheritance with respect to both the labour market and wage structures. Figure 3.11 below illustrates the point.

Labour market segmentation in South Africa (1994)

	Primary labour market	Subordinate primary market	Secondary market
	Professional and managerial (white)	Formal black employment	Formal but casual black
Economic Activity	High pay formal sector	Formal manu-facturing	Small enterprise/ Agri
Share of potential labour force	20 – 25%	15 – 20%	15 – 20%
Legal protection	High	High, thanks to unionization	Very weak
Skills	High, often su-pervisory	Informal – high	Mostly informal
Unemployment levels	Very low	Relatively low	Very high

Source: Manpower Survey (1996)

The Primary Labour market

The racial capitalist structural framework manifested itself fully and firmly within the inherited labour market and wage structures. As is to be expected, the employees in this labour market segment were predominantly white and the employers were in the main, large corporations operating in key areas of production – especially manufacturing, utilities and financial services. The jobs ranged from technical, professional and managerial jobs, which required post – secondary education and training. The salaries too, were reasonably high, as was job security and opportunities of career and salary progression (Heintz, 1998: 5). Moreover, this segment boasted high levels of legal job security, low unemployment levels and a high rate of unionization for the white manual production workers (ibid). The gender spread was also disproportionately in favour of white males, with a minority of white women occupying high – level positions (NECC,1992: 10). Around twenty per cent of the apartheid labour force fell into this segment (Heintz,1998: 5).

96

The Subordinate Primary market

The employees in this segment were predominantly black and the employers – as ever- were the large corporations both national and international. Compared with conditions in the secondary labour market, both the pay and working conditions were better, since workers here were highly unionized and semi-skilled. The ability to engage in collective bargaining also distinguished workers in this segment from those in the secondary segment. The unionization levels here have seen a dramatic increase in the workforce's (previously non-existent) legal protection. The overwhelming majority in this segment were male, except in the clothing industry, where women were in the majority, including a small number of unionized black women in operational roles (NECC,1992:10).

The Secondary Labour market

The black unskilled and non-unionised workers were concentrated in this segment. The employers were, in the main, small enterprises, which paid low wages, offered limited job protection and made extensive use of casual labour (Heintz,1998:5). The possibility of mobility from this segment to the subordinate primary segment were very low. An important feature of this segment was the disproportionate representation of African women. At least ten to fifteen per cent of the workforce was represented in this labour market segment.

The Informal sector

This segment included people involved in hawking, taxi services, home-based crafts, brewing, petty trading and food preparation among other activities. Around fifteen to twenty per cent of economically active South Africans were involved in the informal labour market (NECC,1992:10). Of course, they were overwhelmingly black (ibid). Although it is difficult to offer accurate data (there are still no reliable datasets from which to make extrapolations), since most enterprises were essentially survival-oriented. Judging by the living conditions (including Human Development Indicators) of those involved in the informal sector, it is safe to assume that pay was generally very low. Indeed, a study conducted by the Human Sciences Research Council (HSRC, 1993), and elaborated in figure 4.11 below shows monthly per capita income levels from the informal sector, were well below the minimum R1 110 – 00 per month demanded by workers in the formal sector at the time. In its study, the HSRC concluded that informal work earned around thirty per cent below 'current formal norms' (1993:159). Job security too, was non-existent and largely determined by luck, skill and business acumen. Given the poor education system, low levels of education and training (among black South Africans) and the high levels of unemployment, there were expectations that post-apartheid policies would focus special attention on the informal sector, as an area with potential to stimulate growth, encourage entrepreneurship and efficiency. Figure 3.12 documents the estimated contributions of different informal occupations.

Figure: 3.12

Contributions of different informal occupation

Occupation	Employment	Annual income (R millions)	Monthly per capita Income (R)
Trade/hawking	965 194	5 145,9	422
Services	249 155	521.1	175
Crafts	602 513	4 405,1	609
Home crafts	326 866	1 106,7	282
Transport	161 360	3 488,5	1 801
Scavenging	163 785	204,5	104
Accommodation	20 289	58,4	240
Other	237 669	1 096,6	384

Source: (SCC, 1990; HSRC, 1993)

Another study conducted jointly by Frankel Max Vinderine Inc, SANLAM, Ernst & Young and the HSRC (1993), forcefully advocated for a state-private sector role in regulating the activities of the informal sector, thereby creating solid linkages between the informal and mainstream economies. The report stated that:

> …in Japan and other successful Asian nations, the concept of down-streaming contracting and service sourcing has played a major role in the industrial development of these economies (1993: 158).

Thus, the key findings of the report included the need for better regulation, training and support for the informal sector. Through 'down-streaming', the idea was to open markets, widen credit access to what was clearly a very vulnerable and disadvantaged group, and to promote capacity building programmes, which would lead to improved efficiency and by extension, improved profit margins.

This succinct synopsis of the workings and operations of the apartheid labour market shows that race, gender and class inequality were deeply embedded in the system and structure of that market. Furthermore, there is evidence that the politics and policies of the apartheid state permeated and made their mark in the labour market, including the reliance of the system on cheap black labour. Above all, the inequalities reflected in the apartheid labour market are a manifestation and consequence of the apartheid elites' big idea. However, what is the status quo twenty-two years after the formal end of apartheid?

The Post-apartheid labour market order

The 1994 political break-through brought forth a number of very important changes to the form and character of the South African labour market. These changes can be summarized succinctly as follows:

De-racialising apartheid labour market segments

To change the complexion of the apartheid labour market segments, the new government embarked on a massive exercise of de-racialisation and expansion of blacks in the public sector. This expansion mostly involved skilled and educated blacks, their deployment in middle and upper middle management positions of state. Apart from radically transforming the racial composition, this intervention instantly catapulted a significant number of blacks firmly onto the top twenty per cent of South Africa's distribution. This group was further bolstered by general de-racialisation of employment opportunities in the private sector, BEE equity sharing arrangements and the lifting of some of the most onerous restrictions for black entrepreneurship.

For the bottom forty per cent of the population, a low hanging fruit has been the massive deployment of social grants. By 2012, more than sixteen million people were recipients of one or other state grant, this is the equivalent of around a third of the population. These two interventions by the state, at the top and bottom of the income distribution, significantly transformed and altered the racial and gender dimensions of the labour market. There were other changes, outside the control and influence of the state.

Feminisation of employment

A critical feature of the post-apartheid labour market is the massive increase in employment opportunities for women, especially black women. Indeed, Bhorat and Mayet (2012), show that women employment grew twice the rate of male employment between 1995 and 2009.

Youth unemployment

All research into employment trends in post-apartheid South Africa suggest that young people (between 16 and 24) are more likely to be unemployment than other age groups. And so, one of the most prominent features of post-apartheid must be the unprecedented levels of unemployment and disengagement of young people from economic activity.

The decline of mining, agriculture and manufacturing

Fluctuations in the gold price and oil price, industrial instability, government policies, the global economic recession together with the ever-increasing importance of finance capital in the national economy, have all conspired to undermine job-creation and expansion in agriculture, mining and manufacturing.

The expansion of Services, retail and casual work

Whereas in the apartheid period mining, manufacturing and agriculture where the main generators of jobs, this trend has significantly changed in the post-apartheid period. The key job generators (in line with a global trend of increased financialisation) are business and financial services, wholesale and retail trade. In turn, around seventy-seven per cent of all jobs created in the services between 1995 and 2009 can be classified as temporary work (casual work), driven by labour brokers.

These changes in the character of the post-apartheid labour market mean, among other things, that more opportunities have opened up for blacks and women. Important efforts have been undertaken to reduce poverty (through the social grants and de-racialisation). However, substantially, the underlying structural inequalities of a racial capitalist framework, driven by cheap black labour remain firmly institutionalized in the post-apartheid labour market. The roots are deep-seated and every bit structural.

Skills mis-match

There is overwhelming consensus in South Africa that inclusive growth and economic development is unlikely to be realized in the context of a poor education system and an ill-conceived skills and training system. For, a growing economy requires constant and regular production of high level quality skills. Post-apartheid South Africa has yet to transform the education system (primary, secondary, vocational, technical and university) into a dynamic, quality and responsive system, that effectively responds to the requirements of the country's growth needs. Therefore, twenty-two years down the line, employers generally have no confidence in the quality and capacity of the graduates produced by the education and training system. Furthermore, the growing numbers of unemployed graduates are attributable to a lack of articulation between the schooling system and the post-schooling system, the post-schooling system and the university system and, in turn the university system and colleges and universities of technology. Crucially, however, the biggest break in communication and articulation is between the entire education and training system and employers (the world of work). This, more than anything else, accounts for the continued production of largely irrelevant skills and qualifications. The structural underpinnings and continuities are clearly evident when considering some of the stubbornest gender and racial dynamics. SALDRU (2012) research shows that being African and female still lowers the probability of finding employment relative to non-African graduates (even for those Africans graduating from historically white institutions) (2012:18). The post-apartheid policy maker's obsession with quantitatively 'ramping up' the number of graduates from vocational training colleges is misconceived, as the fundamental problem is the quality and work readiness of these graduates. At any rate, South Africa's skills problems start much earlier. Access to quality basic education and training has a major impact on the country's capacity to produce relevant skills that are aligned to the growth needs of the country. Therefore, an often missing puzzle in the diagnosis of South Africa's skills and growth problems is the role and significance of quality basic education at primary and secondary level.

Political intrigue and the absence of sold relationship between state and business has seen the Sector Education and Training Authorities (SETAs) also failing to fulfil their fundamental remit – the production of skills and knowledge as required and demanded by the economy. The SETA system, through a levy system, makes approximately R12 billion available for skills training annually. Theoretically, these funds should respond to long term skills needs of all sectors of the South African economy. The SETA funds should also, guide the changing labour market dynamics, constantly make available to the private sector, a ready and highly skilled cadre of potential employees that keep up with the changes in the labour market. Those already in employment should also benefit from these funds for constant improvement of skills and know-how, all in keeping with a complex and constantly innovating labour market. In essence, therefore, this calls for sector authorities that are highly agile and deeply embedded in the sectors in which they are supposed to operate. This includes institutionalized relations with employer bodies. Located as they are at the intersection between state and business, it is imperative that they eschew normal state bureaucratic red tape and be run far more professionally, competently and effectively. The skills, qualifications and competencies of those who head these institutions is thus, consequential. So, too, are the skills and competencies of those who are asked to sit in the boards of these critically important and potentially useful entities. There are instructive lessons elsewhere in the world about how the SETA system can and should be re-imagined in such a way that they are less an additional and costly layer of bureaucracy and more a critical lever in the skills development, job-creation and growth driving matrix, so desperately called for in the post-apartheid South African economy. So, as much as ideas are consequential in promoting growth, so too, is organizational design, institutional arrangements and meritocratic deployment of available skills, in ways that could potentially shake the structural framework.

The Challenge of post-apartheid South Africa's labour market

Research of the post-apartheid labour market indicate that the challenges in the labour market space are multifaceted and layered. At the heart of all the challenges, however, would seem to be the overriding reality that the fundamental structural and institutional basis of the apartheid labour market have yet to be challenged and overturned through pointed and effective public policies. As a consequence, race, gender, class and geography and other social cleavages permeate all aspects of the post-apartheid labour market.

Accordingly, a brief synopsis of the key labour market challenges and characteristic features is instructive:

There has been important transformation in the complexion of the labour market, this is seen in the drastic increase of the black middle and upper-middle class in the intervening period. However, some have suggested that this middle class is not organic and its hold onto this class status is extremely precarious and tentative at best (Netshitenzhe, 2015).

Important inroads have been made in improving the gender profile of the labour force across the board. However, research seems to indicate that both race and gender remain pervasive defining categories for the South African labour market. More specifically, blacks and women are disadvantaged.

The post-apartheid period has seen a phenomenal increase of new entrants into the labour market, especially in the services sector of the economy. Much of this growth (around 35 per cent) has been categorized as 'sales not in stores'. This means that the informal sector has been a huge driver of job-creation in the post-apartheid period. This, of course, raises the additional aspect of formalization, regulation and support of the informal sector.

Almost all job creation growth in the 'formal' economy has been in the tertiary sector notably, retail and finance and other services sub-sectors (including security services). An interesting feature of this growth has been its casual nature, in other words, it has largely been driven by labour brokers, were job security and other benefits are limited or non-existent.

There has been a massive decline in job creation in mining, agriculture and manufacturing, leading to a declining share of GDP in the domestic economy more broadly. This, together with high unemployment rates in the country – 25.7 per cent and 36.7 per cent (expanded unemployment rate), have conspired to drive earnings inequality in post-apartheid South Africa (Stats SA, 2013).

The Structure of the economy is increasingly geared towards higher skilled jobs and this, in the context of a failing education and training system that is struggling to produce (let alone accurately define) required skills. Concomitantly, demand for unskilled and semi-skilled work in the extractive and manufacturing sector has collapsed.

Failing land and agricultural reforms has meant that consumption goods for the poor are largely produced in South Africa's urban centres, thereby foreclosing local economic growth potential. All opportunities for job-creation by stimulating rural economies – through say, agro-processing and other agricultural value-chains are closed off.

Conclusion

The continuities-discontinuities and change dialectic in post-apartheid South Africa makes for interesting and analytically fascinating reading. For one thing, the end of apartheid raised expectations and placed vested interests at the centre of the change process. This rendered the transformation agenda a deeply contested process, with internal and external interests and expectations vying for the right to define the ultimate complexion and content of the post-apartheid settlement. For another, the socio-economic and political contradictions afflicting the country (the South African question) were so deep-seated, multifaceted and complex that no half-measures were likely to suffice. The situation called for an all-out overhaul of the inherited regime of accumulation, and its replacement with an ideological framework and public policy pipe-line that erred on the side of developmental state-making. As it happens, the neo-liberal framework has been maintained and continues to inform the broad policy direction, but with tentative and half-hearted implementation of aspects of radical developmental policies. As to be expected, two decades down the line, the results have been mixed, with the socio-economic framework and regime of accumulation largely conditioning and shaping public policy. And this at a time when social democrats and leftwing parties throughout the globe (Syriza in Greece, Podemos in Spain, Die Linke in Germany etc) are being propelled to the centre stage by communities exhausted by years of economic crisis, austerity, inequality, high employment rates and dismal growth rates. In the United Kingdom, Labour Party supporters have placed their faith in Jeremy Corbyn, an anti-austerity leftwing politician. This is a movement inspired by a desire for alternatives to neo-liberalism, after all, they have experienced it for over three decades and have seen the devastation and destruction it has caused. Should the South African leadership elite not be at the centre of the search for an alternative developmental and ideological vision?

In his famous 'Prison notebooks', Italian intellectual, Antonio Gramsci (1971), refers to the need for 'organic intellectuals' to drive the process of attaining 'cultural hegemony', in order to re-order and re-imagine the current social order. For, once you win the battle of ideas, the rest becomes relatively easier.

This chapter is essentially a journey into the legacies of apartheid, their depth, their structural nature and the developmental opportunities presented by the transformation period. It shows, too, that in the main, the past twenty-two years have been characterized by important changes and improvements in the socio-economic and political conditions of many South Africans. A crucial and truly exciting dynamic of the post-apartheid period, relates to the significant reduction of poverty (especially among the poorest sections of the black majority). It will be gratifying to the new elites too, to report that the labour market and the economic arena have been significantly de-racialized in the intervening period (with blacks featuring in almost all aspects of the economy). Hidden behind these positive statistics, however, is a very grim picture of 'sameness', and even reversals in some important aspects.

The Economic arena

The economic arena has been characterized by policy zig-zag (RDP, GEAR, ASGISA, NGP, NDP), and of course, such policy uncertainly was always going to bode ill in a country with such huge and pressing economic challenges. There has been a distinct lack of sure-footedness in the economic policy front. Significant reversals in growth and job-generation capacity of key sectors and industries (manufacturing, agriculture, mining) have severely limited the developmental prospects and vibrancy of the post-apartheid economy. Of course, South Africa's conservative trade policies have not really helped the situation much, as these have all but closed off any room for the state to manoeuvre. Post-apartheid liberal trade and finance policies have opened the door for much investment into the South African economy. However, much of this has, in large measure, been speculative also referred to as 'hot' investments, as against investment of the productive type (that leads to growth and development). Furthermore, the trade policies have made capital flight (both of the illegal and legal variety) easier, thereby costing the state billions worth of revenue. All forecasts, measures and estimates suggest that the prospects of growth and by extension, developmental state-making are severely limited in the current policy environment. There is also no indication that a re-think in ideology and policies is on the cards at this time.

Poverty and inequality

There is much to be celebrated in the government's efforts at tackling the worst effects of poverty in the country. Apart from the massive role played by state grant interventions, there is also evidence that by 2010, the number of blacks who had joined the top ten per cent of the income bracket had risen by almost 70 per cent (SALDRU, 2014). This is a huge leap by any measure. So, the policy impact is discernible both at the top and bottom of the income brackets. Inequality, by contrast, is a completely different matter. Research demonstrates that the inherited cleavages (race, gender, class and geography) remain stubbornly intact. White South Africans continue to be in the majority of earners in the top 10 per cent of the income distribution – 56 per cent (ibid). Thus, despite some commendable changes and improvements in the conditions of blacks in post-apartheid South Africa, more than 80 per cent of them continued to live well below the 1995 pcY threshold (SALDRU, 2014: 19). A common fallacy is to see what have essentially come to be the defining features of South African social reality, as transient. Inequality and poverty are institutionalized and deeply structural in South Africa, and no amount of social grants is going to sustainably change that. Instead, substantial structural changes are called for. This seems to echo the fundamental argument that the transformation prospectus carries with it, all the contradictions and inequities of the past, and that this prospectus itself is screaming for transformation and overhaul.

Unemployment and the labour market

All statistical information show that in the main, South Africa has fallen far short in creating the number of jobs needed to stem the jobs crisis that was inherited in 1994. What is more, there is evidence that (thanks to the collapse of the job-generating capacity of manufacturing, mining and agriculture), unemployment numbers have skyrocketed in the intervening twenty-two years. Where there has been formal sector job creation (financial services, security services, wholesale, retail and the informal sectors), these have largely been casual jobs driven by labour brokers.

Unemployment is a defining characteristic feature of South Africa's economic failure, it is not transient, it is systemic and institutionalized in the structure and workings of the country's chosen trajectory. The chapter also shows that the labour market has seen many positive subjective changes, and these are reflected in the improved participation of blacks, women and the disabled in almost all segments of the labour market. What has not disappeared after twenty-two years, however, is the segmentation and stratification of that labour market. Compounding the situation (and a testament to the structural nature of the problem), is the disarticulation in skills production processes and economic [growth] requirements. Furthermore, the changes in the labour market have also meant a dearth in demand for unskilled labour and increasing demand for more skilled labour (a scarce commodity, especially among the black majority). Given the inadequacies of the education and training system, this too, is proving extremely difficult to overcome.

Overall, it would seem that continuities do indeed, overwhelm discontinuities and change in a variety of respects. The next chapter is an introduction of the provenance and key features of the RDP.

CHAPTER

The Reconstruction and Development Programme (RDP)

Introduction

This chapter is divided into three main sections: the first examines the geo-political and strategic context within which the RDP evolved, the second traces the provenance of the RDP, and the third focuses on the key features of the RDP. The chapter concludes by noting both the possibilities and limitations inherent in the geo-political situation and historical evolution of the RDP as a programme capable of promoting state-led development akin to East Asia's. The key question to be explored relates to whether or not the internal political conditions (and the associated contextual realities) of the early 1990s were amenable to the construction of an interventionist developmental state, along East Asian lines. This is achieved by sketching both the broad context within which economic policy evolved in the early 1990s, and the factors and circumstances that contributed in shaping its direction. As the strategic relational approach makes plain, clearly articulating structural factors is critical as it both underlines the overarching forces at work, and establishes the parameters and limits of political action. However, the really important insight of this approach resides in its recognition of the fact that, although structure is crucial in defining the broad parameters of possible outcomes, such structural factors cannot, on their own, account for policy choices and political outcomes and action (Hay, 2002:

129). In other words, while structure can and does influence behaviour, it does not determine it.

And, of course, all political circumstances bring about not only constraints but also opportunities and choices, so there is always room to manoeuvre.

RDP: Geo-Politics and Context

To correctly apprehend the conduct, attitudes and actions of different social actors in respect of the RDP requires, first and foremost, an understanding of the socio-economic and geo-political context within which the RDP itself was born and operated. In this connection, four aspects are of particular relevance.

The Collapse of the Soviet Union

The RDP was conceptualized and born into a world system characterized by major cataclysmic changes and shifts in the global 'balance of power' (Hobsbawm, 1994). Thus, on the strategic level, the African National Congress and its allies confronted challenges vastly different to those successfully navigated by the South Korean and Taiwanese elites in the 1950s, 1960s and 1970s. The East Asian developmental elites, were not only aided by the stand-off between the two super powers, but they actually manipulated that stand-off actively in ways that benefited their developmental projects (Amsden, 1989; Wade, 1990; Evans, 1998). Moreover, the East Asian developmental processes were initiated in a period when state-led economic developmental perspectives were still very much in vogue (World Development Report, 1997: 23).

Such preoccupation with "state intervention, the Marshall Plan, Keynesian demand management and the welfare state" proved particularly attractive to the new elites in the newly de-colonised countries in the developing world (ibid). By 1990, however, when the search for alternative policy approaches began in earnest in South Africa, the Soviet Union was experiencing a rapid process of disintegration, statist theories were on the defensive and the ANC's age-old characterization of the global order as "a transition from capitalism to socialism" could no longer be realistically sustained (ANC, 1985).

To this end, there was no alternative Soviet bloc around which the new South Africa could structure its trade, aid and investment relations. More significantly, there was no cold war for the new state and political elites to manipulate, as did the East Asians in an earlier period. Therefore, the space afforded the Koreans and Taiwanese to almost operate outside the world trading and economic system until they were ready to enter or re-enter on terms favourable to their developmental agenda, was not available to South Africa. Instead, the 1990s and the collapse of the Soviet Union:

> sounded the death knell for a developmental era…governments began to adopt policies designed to reduce the scope of the state's intervention in the economy. States curbed their involvement in production, prices and trade. Market friendly strategies took hold in large parts of the developing world (World Bank, 1997:23).

The International Monetary Fund (IMF) gave a poignant characterization of the 1990s and the options available to policy makers in transition societies like South Africa in that period:

> many countries liberalized their trade during the 1990s and introduced reform programmes to reduce the role of the state in the economy and enhance private sector growth. Policy measures included price liberalization, deregulation and privatization of state enterprises… These policy changes reflected the recognition that reliance on administrative controls had driven much economic activity outside formal channels, depressed exports, contributed to an inefficient structure of domestic production and hampered long run growth (IMF, 2000: 6).

Key examples of countries that have followed this path since the early 1990s include Kenya, Mauritius, Uganda and Zambia (IMF, 1998). Therefore, South Africa's transition kicked off at a time when the international policy and intellectual environment had shifted decisively against state-led developmental processes. This geo-strategic and policy environment thus constituted a critically important variable in shaping the nature of the new South Africa's socio-economic and developmental discourse. The collapse of the Soviet Union coincided with a renewed dominance of neo- classical views on the role of the state. However, for the ANC/SACP alliance, the collapse had more direct significance. For the better part of the last century, the Soviet Union had been the liberation movement's principal mentors and advisors on matters of ideology and strategy. Also, the ANC/SACP's perspectives on the character and role of the post-apartheid state and its socio-economic policies were largely informed by Soviet thinking on these matters (Slovo, 1988).

Therefore, the collapse of the once mighty Soviet Empire led to serious strategic and ideological turmoil within the movement, and such lack of leadership and ideological cohesion played an important part in undermining South Africa's developmental state prospects. Therefore, this development too, was to significantly impact the character and content of the South African transition, especially were issues of trade, investment, price, industrial policy and the role of the state were concerned. This is not to suggest there was no left or anti-neoliberal voices, for there were many. The point is that leadership and ideological cohesion around a common left perspective was dealt a heavy blow by the confusion engendered by the Soviet collapse.

The Neo-liberal Discourse

The neo-liberal paradigm is traceable to the end of the long growth phase sustained by Keynesian state managed processes in the early to mid-1970s (Amin, 1996; World Development Report, 1997). The end of what Hobsbawm (1994) has described as the 'golden age' of international capitalism was essentially characterized by the end of twenty-five years of sustained post-war growth in the advanced capitalist countries (Amin, 1996: 27). The turn-around was assisted to a significant extent by the 1973 oil crisis which, among other things, led to a serious decline in profitability. In these circumstances, the neo-liberal approach essentially argued for restored profitability through the opening up of new avenues to private accumulation (privatization, deregulation, commercialization and liberalization).

In his review of the meaning of the politics and economics of the 'Washington Consensus', John Williamson (1990) has shown that both the *political Washington* of Congress and senior members of the administration, and the *technocratic Washington* of international financial institutions, share a common neo-liberal perspective on economic development (1990: 7). This approach can be summarized as follows: "…prudent macro-economic policies, outward orientation and free market capitalism" (ibid). However, it was not only with economics that neo-liberalism was concerned, it also had a profoundly political dimension (Leftwich, 1993: 608). At the political level, neo-liberalism posited a functionalist theory which attributed the poor economic development performance of much of the developing world to state interference with the market (ibid). Such interference in turn, undermined individual freedom and free market activity, since there was an over-concentration of political and economic power in the hands of state actors (ibid). And this in spite of the increasing evidence, which had been observed by Myrdal that, "…a major reason for economic stagnation of many developing countries is the absence of a 'hard' state that can override conservative interests in favour of social reforms and transformation" (cited in Chang, 1996:183).

Nevertheless, this aspect of the power and role of the state in economic development was of cardinal importance for the RDP and, indeed, the economic development policy debate generally in South Africa. State involvement in the economy was held to cause rigidities, which put pressure on incentives for innovation and diversification.

Moreover, policies that sought to protect domestic industries against external competition were seen as causing distortions that eventually impoverished the domestic economy. Furthermore, the private sector was regarded as far more efficient than the state in running the economic enterprises. At the same time, freeing the economy from state regulation (and rent-seeking) was thought to be the best way of attracting often desperately needed foreign investment, and of ensuring international competitiveness. According to this approach, therefore, state policies involving the restriction of the entry of foreign direct investment were considered foolish and self-defeating (Williamson, 1990: 15).

Related to this was the increasing role and influence of International Financial Institutions (IFI) like the World Bank and the IMF, in elaborating economic policies for countries in the developing world. This role became particularly pronounced from the early 1980s, when many developing countries had accumulated massive debt burdens and desperate for bail-outs (Habib and Padayachee: 2000:15). The acceptance of IMF/World Bank market-centred policies by state elites in the developing world was important if only to maintain credit-worthiness and access to foreign exchange. Indeed, as more and more developing countries depended on the Fund and Bank for loans and resources, the power of these states to shape their economies on terms other than those prescribed by these institutions decreased significantly (Bond: interview, 30 October, 2002). Former Malaysian Prime Minister, Dr. Mahathir Mohamed came to the same conclusion, Mohamed argued: "the problem with the countries of the South is that they are fragmented mainly because they are placed under obligation to the people who have lent them money, given them aid or to whom they are obliged" (cited in: *The Hindu*, 5 February, 2001)

The World Bank, for its part, stood firm in its anti-statist policy with regard to economic development. Indeed, despite the massive evidence crediting state leadership and intervention in the economy with East Asian success, the Bank was adamant the 'Asian miracle' was essentially attributable to the adherence to neo-liberal policies (Johnson, 1987; Cumings, 1991; Evans, 1995; Leftwich, 1996). To this end, the Bank Report on the East Asian miracle stated:

> Mainly the answer lies in fundamentally sound market-oriented policies… Financial markets generally had low distortions and limited subsidies… Market forces guided resources into activities that were consistent with comparative advantage (World Bank, 1993: 325).

Perturbed by what they viewed as a gross misrepresentation and revision of their region's economic history and the factual inaccuracies in the Bank's Report, the Japanese government commissioned a study on the East Asian miracle in order to resolve the explanatory confusion occasioned by the Bank's Report. The point is that there was a profound and unapologetic ideological onslaught visited on the indebted developing countries, led by the Bank and the Fund. For despite their stated policies that they would not be influenced by the political character of the country requesting credit, there is evidence in abundance that both institutions actively imposed their ideological views with respect to the desirability of states and markets in developing economies.

Thus, the predominance of a neo-liberal orthodoxy was another aspect shaping the thinking of policy-makers in South Africa in the period under consideration. To be sure, in the case of South Africa, the Fund and the Bank were determined to have their say on the complexion, texture and substance of the post-apartheid economic order, as Khan (2000) has shown:

> After the changes announced by the De Klerk government in the early 1990s, the IMF along with the World Bank, began to increase its visibility in South Africa, with increasing numbers of, and more broad based visits, including contacts with academics, labour movement and NGOs. It was clear at this stage that the IMF was concerned with the economic policies that would be followed by the new government (2000: 7).

Equally instructive were Margaret Thatcher's reflections on her meeting with Nelson Mandela in May 1990:

> I warmed to him. But also found him very outdated in his attitudes, stuck in a kind of socialist time-warp., not least in economic thinking....it was a disadvantage in the first few months of his freedom because he tended to repeat these out-dated platitudes which in turn confirmed his followers in their exaggerated expectations. I pointed out the harm which all his talk of nationalization could do to foreign investment and the economy in general (1993: 533).

Lord Robin Renwick, British Ambassador to South Africa between 1987-1991, shared with me the details of a three-hour meeting between Mandela and Thatcher. According to Renwick, there was a vigorous exchange especially regarding the ANC's 'barmy ideas about economic policy', and Thatcher "insisted on giving him [Mandela] a course on Economics 101" (Interview:7 April, 2003). There is, thus, a preponderance of evidence that the advocacy and lobbying work done by the Bank, Fund and others was quickly taken to heart by some sections of the leadership elite. For instance, in 1993, Tito Mboweni, ANC Chief Economist, in a major policy somersault on developmental policy, state leadership and nationalization in the ANC, insisted: "we want their [IMF/World Bank] overall stamp of approval, the kind of working relationship that will send a signal to private investors that we are pursuing policies that are not unsustainable" (*Financial Times*, 11 June 1993)

Policies designed to send signals to foreign investors – notably privatization, commercialization, liberalization and a reduced role for the state – rarely sit comfortably with radical developmentalist policies. For these policies invariably involve a strong and leading role for the state, a measure of nationalization of key economic assets, redistribution, regulation of trade and the financial sector, to suit the requirements of the new developmentalist agenda. Moreover, they sit uncomfortably with (often pressing redistributionist requirements) such as spending on housing, quality health care for all, a quality education and training system and basic services. Above all, anti-state policies seemed, at the time at least, to contradict the spirit of the Freedom Charter and subsequent programmatic documents of the ANC notably, the Harare Resolutions and their final product' Making Democracy Work' (MERG, 1993). Yet another contextual issue relevant to the RDP and the economic development policy debate in South Africa was the role and place of the negotiations process *vis-à-vis* the economic policy process.

Negotiations

One of the key negotiators on the ANC side traced the pressure to negotiate on South Africa's major political protagonist thus:

> …the apartheid power bloc was no longer able to continue ruling in the old way and was genuinely seeking some break with the past. At the same time, we [the ANC] were clearly not dealing with a defeated enemy and early revolutionary seizure of power by the liberation movement could not be realistically posed (Slovo: 1992: 36).

Slovo would further concede that some of the ANC's inputs during the negotiations process had been 'too ad hoc' (ibid). Since the ANC had for decades posited the notion of a 'seizure of state power' as the only feasible route to South African freedom, the possibility of a negotiated settlement and how to approach it in practical terms, left the movement extremely disorientated and wrong-footed. No detailed strategic and organizational plan was in place to anticipate the massive organizational pressures that come with a prolonged negotiations process. Former South African President, F.W De Klerk emphasized that the timing of his historic announcement (designed to normalize the political environment) was calculated precisely to catch the ANC off-guard. De Klerk would later observe in this biography: "We were ready to start work as soon as Nelson Mandela was released. The ANC, however, was not. Our package of 2 February 1990 caught them completely off-guard, they had to stall for more time" (1999: 176). The impact of this imposition of an alternative route to power and the real possibility of this materializing much sooner than the leadership could ever have anticipated, on economic policy formulation was particularly telling. Two factors attest to this. First, the constitutional negotiations engaged the bulk of the senior leadership of the ANC for much of the period between 1990 and the 1994 democratic elections. As a consequence, economic policy development received much less attention from the leadership than did the search for a political settlement (CICP, 1993). Indeed, key economic decision-makers in the ANC were, in the main, non-executive members (NEC) notably, Trevor Manuel, Tito Mboweni, Max Sisulu. It would seem that, once the process of dialogue between the National Party (NP) government and the ANC took root, the entire National Executive Committee of the ANC became immersed in the process (Groote Schuur Minute, 1990). According to this minute, the two sides were required to constitute themselves into various Working Groups focusing on the resolution of a variety of issues including the release of political prisoners, ending violence and making constitutional changes among other things (ibid). Interestingly, there was no Working Group set up to focus on a future economic dispensation. Figure 4.1 shows some of the key NEC members of the ANC sucked in the negotiations process for a new political dispensation but neglecting economic policy:

Working Group 1	Joe Modise, Jacob Zuma, Penuel Maduna; Kadar Asmal
Working Group 2	Cyril Ramaphosa, Mohamed Valli Moosa, Frene Ginwala, Arthur Chackleson
Working Group 3	Thabo Mbeki, Joe Nhlanhla, Joel Netshitenzhe, Dullah Omar
Working Group 4	Alfred Nzo, Mathews Phosa, Barbara Masekela, Pius Langa
Working Group 5	Pallo Jordan, Zola Skweyiya, Lucill Meyer, George Bizos

Source: Rantele (1998: 174).

Working Group One was responsible for creating conditions for free political activity and the role of the international community in the transition. Working Group Two was concerned with constitutional principles, while Working

Group Three was concerned with transitional arrangements more broadly, Working Group Four concentrated on the future of homelands and Working Group Five had the responsibility of looking into the implementation of all resolutions from other Working Groups (De Klerk, 1999: 235).

These were only the official representatives in the Working Groups.

Many more top members of the ANC leadership were attached to the negotiation process in one way or the other (Rantele, 1998:175). Aside from the senior leadership, however, the process also required that provincial and local ANC leaders be engaged in the process. A fax attached to the Groote Schuur Minute, from a Brigadier R.P. McIntyer to the ANC Head Office, sent on the 23 October 1990, further illustrates the point, and it states:

1. In accordance with paragraph 5 of the Groote Schuur Minute, the Minister of Law and Order, Mr. Adrian Vlok and Mr. Jacob Zuma, Information Chief of the ANC, met to discuss the creation of efficient channels of communication between the government and the ANC.

2. After an in-depth discussion it was agreed that:
   - Liaison Committees be established on a regional level and also on a district level or local level, depending on the need. The object of the committees is to maintain regular contact between the South African Police and the ANC.
   - Both SA Police and the ANC will as soon as possible, provide one another with the names and addresses and telephone numbers of persons they appointed as Liaison Officers on the different levels so that the system can become operative by 30 October, 1990

3. The object of the exchange of names of liaison persons is to ensure a line of two-tier communication. Up to date the SAP has received only 29 names of the ANC liaison persons.

4. Please furnish the SAP with the rest of the names of your liaison persons so as to ensure the efficient functioning of the channels of communication (Groote Schuur Minute, 1990: attachment).

The above signifies the range and depth of input required from the ANC by the process at all levels and in different spheres. It also demonstrates the lack of preparedness of the recently unbanned (and relatively unsettled) ANC to cope with the demands on its human resources. Well, on the other hand, it could very well underline the continued mistrust by ANC cadres of the South African Police. Not only were many ANC members still in prisons across the country, in exile and in hiding, so the idea of exposing oneself as an ANC member, share your address and phone numbers, must have been unsettling for some of those called on by their movement to do so. After all, no one new for a fact how the negotiation process would eventuate. At any rate, the constitutional and political negotiations were not the only activity that exercised the ANC at this juncture. The process also largely overlapped with the ANC's internal process of elaborating its economic policies, although this aspect enjoyed comparatively less prominence in the leadership's list of priorities. This view was echoed by a survey conducted by the University of Stellenbosch on elite attitudes. The political leadership of the main political parties, asked in 1991 to list three priority areas for the next five years, responded as follows:

Figure:4.2
First Policy Priority by Political Party support in %

Party	Economic Development	Social Development	Political Development
CP	53	4	43
NP	74	5	19
DP	61	6	32
Indian parties	82	9	14
IFP	77	6	16
ANC/SACP	35	14	50
PAC	40	2	49

Source: Centre for International and Comparative Politics, University of Stellenbosch, 1993

Though much could be extrapolated from the survey results, my concern for now is to underline the importance attached by different political parties to economic and political development as priority. The survey essentially confirmed the preoccupation of the senior leadership of the ANC with the political and constitutional processes to the relative neglect of economic policy issues.

This is significant in light of our earlier discussion regarding the importance of big economic development ideas among all developmental state elites and the prioritization of economic development as the overriding *raison detre*. It is significant, too, that the National Party and the Inkatha freedom Party attached far more significance to the complexion of a post-apartheid economic dispensation than did the party of liberation. Talks and research concerning the elaboration of the movement's economic policy position were, instead, assigned to a lower level of leadership within the

ANC alliance (Stewart, 1997: 5). This, in turn, raises two considerations for the RDP and ANC economic policy-making during this period. First, in the early stages, the strong developmentalist outlook of ANC policy proposals was in keeping with the movement's Freedom Charter on the role of the state and redistribution. Secondly, and crucially, once the political and constitutional break-through was reached at the negotiation table, all the compromises and the give and take, had to be incorporated into and reflected in the economic policy positions espoused by the ANC. Moderation was thus necessitated in a range of policy areas, including the economy and civil service transformation (see Interim Constitution, 1994). Chapter sixteen of the Interim Constitution aptly summarized the spirit of compromise and restraint that was envisaged:

> This Constitution provides a historic bridge between the past and deeply divided society characterized by strife, conflict, untold suffering and injustice, and a future founded on the recognition of human rights, democracy and peaceful co-existence... (1994: 81).

Furthermore, Joe Slovo, in his proposal for compromise on the part of the ANC, clearly confronted the 'exaggerated expectations' of the vast majority of South Africans, on the eve of the compromise settlement:

> ..the immediate outcome of the negotiating process will inevitably be less than perfect when measured against our long term liberation objectives....a degree of compromise will be unavoidable (1992: 37).

This recognition of the inevitability of compromise arguably also constitutes an important consideration for understanding the ambiguities and ambivalence of the RDP, especially on economic policy. Indeed, any attempt at developmental state-making would have to contend with these realities. In particular, two factors aptly underscore the extent of compromise and its impact on the character of the post-apartheid socio-economic and political deal. The first of these factors is the $ 840 million IMF loan facility to South Africa's Transitional Executive Authority (TEC), under the Compensation and Contingency Financing Facility (*IMF Survey* 10th January, 1994). The details of this transaction is discussed in more detail in chapter six, for now the point I wish to underscore is that that transaction and the ANC' acquiescence thereto, represented an early indication of the big economic development idea the country was likely to follow. The second factor which is crucial to any explanation of the growth path ultimately followed by the South African elites, concerns the GATT arrangement endorsed by the ANC/NP coalition in 1993. In an interview with *Global Dialogue* (1999), Trade and Industry

Minister, Alec Erwin would later concede that important obstacles were built into South Africa's negotiated package. According to Erwin:

> South Korea in particular, but also Malaysia and other East Asian economies, were able to achieve quiet rapid industrialization through very interventionist methods…. However, a country such as South Africa which started its economic reform in the 1990s, was prevented from using such interventionist methods by WTO rules (*Global Dialogue*: April, 1999).

While this is not the place to engage with the merits of Erwin's argument, it is clear that the leading lights of the ANC in the economic policy sphere had no intention of engaging with the structural and institutional constraints confronted by the transition. There seem to have been an acceptance of the constraints, despite the frenzied internal discussions within the alliance about the merits of concluding these transactions. So, it was not from lack of wiser counsel, the decision to pursue a neo-liberal path was very much an intentional and well-informed one (see Alan Hirsch, 2005).

Such is the broad institutional and structural context within which the content and politics of the RDP should be situated. This section serves to underline the important role played by structural issues in conditioning and shaping the character of the socio-economic and political settlement that finally emerged in South Africa. This analysis also lays the foundation for the exploration of agency in later chapters.

Provenance and History of the RDP

The Reconstruction and Development Programme was, in effect, the ANC's election manifesto during South Africa's first democratic elections held on the 27th April 1994. Having swept into power with 61% of the vote, the ANC held out the RDP as the new government's central socio-economic and developmental programme, enjoying support from all key social actors in the country. However, the history of the RDP originates much earlier than 1994, and (certainly its earlier versions) had its core intellectual sources in earlier ANC documents and programmes. The authors of the RDP saw the document as a policy elaboration of the Freedom Charter, adopted by the ANC and its allies in 1955 (ANC, 1994: 2). Like the RDP, the Freedom Charter was a product of extensive consultation between the ANC and its allies at the Congress of the People (Mandela, 1956). And, like the Freedom Charter, the RDP was largely inspired by Keynesian influences, especially with respect to the significance of the role of the state in redressing socio-economic imbalances (Turok, 2014). Indeed, the Freedom Charter benefitted from, and was highly influenced by, statist approaches as reflected in post-war planning and the general intellectual and practical ascendancy of Keynesian policies during the post-war reconstruction period (ibid). This influence is apparent in both documents: the Freedom Charter and the ANC alliance's version of the RDP. For instance, the Charter states:

> The national wealth of our country, the heritage of South Africans, shall be restored to the people; mineral wealth beneath the soil, the banks and monopoly industry shall be transferred to the ownership of the people as a whole (1955).

Years later (1969), and in response to accusations from a variety of sources that it was a socialist blueprint, the ANC, in its conference held in Morogoro, Tanzania, sought to elaborate on this clause of the Charter. This was not a call for socialism, the conference declared; instead, it was an appeal for state leadership in redressing apartheid imbalances in the economic sphere. Furthermore:

> At the moment, there are vast monopolies whose existence affect the livelihood of large numbers of our people and whose ownership is in the hands of Europeans only. It is necessary for monopolies which virtually affect the well-being of our people, such as mines, sugar and wine industries, to be transferred to public ownership so that they can be used to uplift all the people (ANC, 1969).

The RDP, too, insisted on demand-led growth, which benefit the disadvantaged and be based largely on infrastructural investments led by the state. The RDP declared that:

> Reconstruction and development will be achieved through the leading and enabling role of the state…. The state will…eliminate poverty, low wages and extreme inequalities in wages and wealth generated by the apartheid system, meet basic needs, and thus ensure that every South African has a decent living standard and economic security [it will] address economic imbalances and uneven development within and between South Africa's regions (ANC, 1994: 78-9).

Thus, both documents seemed to emphasise the significance of the role of the state in redress and redistribution. Parallels could be drawn in this respect with the perspectives of List and Gerschenkron discussed in the foregoing chapters. Although there is merit in Blumenfield's (1997) charge that, analytically and ideologically, the RDP, like the Freedom Charter, was in some respects ambiguous, it nonetheless contained an unmistakable Listian and Keynesian developmental perspective. This appeal to a statist developmentalist model can be further illustrated by the more extensive examination of the history of the RDP. The RDP emerged as a consequence of several processes designed to evolve an economic development programme for the ANC. Key in this evolution was the work of the Macro-Economic Research Group.

The Macro-Economic Research Group Process (MERG)

The MERG process itself was initiated by the ANC following a conference held in Harare, Zimbabwe, in March 1990. The conference resolved to set up a policy research institute "....to provide the democratic movement in South Africa with the necessary research capacity to formulate economic policy" (NIEP, 1993: 2). However, given the urgency attached to the matter by the ANC's Department of Economic Policy (DEP), it was resolved that the establishment of a fully-fledged institute be preceded by an interim arrangement (ibid).

British economist, Ben Fine and his colleagues in the MERG were therefore well aware of the fact that the "MERG Report was commissioned at the highest level of the ANC leadership to prepare an alternative to neo-liberal economic policies" (Interview with Ben Fine, London, 16/12/2002). The interim arrangement involved the mobilization of ANC-allied economists mainly from five universities that would constitute the initial bases of the project (Western Cape, Durban Westville, Forte Hare, Natal and Wits). To broaden the group's capacity, academics based overseas were also brought into the process notably, John Sender, Ben Fine and Stephen Gelb. A statement of intent, operationalizing the Macro Economic Research Group, was signed by the ANC and participating universities on the 23rd November 1991 in Johannesburg (NIEP, 1993:3). The statement stipulated the following objectives for MERG:

- Strengthen the economic capacity of the ANC/COSATU and other components of the democratic movement by undertaking research into issues, trends and objectives identified as relevant by the democratic movement.

- Facilitate the development of economic policy research capacity of the participating universities.

- Construct a macro-economic framework and model to facilitate the development and testing of policy options and recommendations.

- Undertake policy research into priority areas for urgent attention and other short-term priorities dictated by the needs of the ANC and other components of the democratic movement.

- Set up the legal and administrative infrastructure for the National Institute for Economic Policy (NIEP) (ibid).

An advisor for the Bank of China and long-time ANC economist, Vella Pillay, was appointed as coordinator of the group. The efforts of this group were published in September 1993 in a book entitled 'Making Democracy Work'. The RDP base document encapsulated many of the central propositions of the MERG report, examples can be found in various aspects of the report, including the role of the state and the financial sector.

On the Role of the State

The MERG report advocated a strong and un-apologetic role for the post-apartheid state in redressing apartheid imbalances and driving growth and development for an inclusive economy. The Report stated:

> No country could achieve the extensive redistribution to benefit the poor which South Africa needs, without state orchestration and implementation (1993: 266).

Moreover, the late Dr. Vella Pillay, delivering the Oliver Tambo memorial lecture in November 1993, elaborated the Group's findings on the role of the state more sharply:

> Our research conclusions suggest that the South African Reserve Bank should be subordinated to the government such as to allow monetary, interests and exchange rate policies and the flow and direction of credit in the economy to be consistent with the democratic state's policies in the areas of public sector expenditure and taxation, in trade, industrial diversification and development (Pillay, 1993).

On the same subject, the RDP emphasized that:

> Reconstruction and development will be achieved through the leading role of the state (ANC, 1994:78).

On the Financial Sector

Contrary to the dominant trends of the 1990s in economic policy formulation, towards deregulation and privatization, the MERG Report remained steadfast in its interventionist and regulationist approaches. For the authors

121

firmly believed that the massive social and economic deficit inherited by the new elites could never be redressed within the neo-liberal framework. Indeed:

> MERG recommends that the state policy should favour nationalization if any of the four largest banks require lender of last resort support. A new broad framework of regulation is required to promote good practice by banks in the process of economic transformation. Regulations will be put forward prohibiting discrimination on the grounds of status related to race or gender (1993: 259).

The base document also demonstrated, to some extent, its MERG origins on the issue of financial control:

> The democratic government must therefore consider increasing the public sector in strategic areas through for example nationalization, purchasing of shareholding in companies, establishing new corporations or joint ventures with the private sector (ANC, 1994: 80).

Thus, although there was clearly a relationship between the MERG Report and aspects of the RDP, a closer examination of the RDP reveals that there were also important deviations. These appear mainly with respect to the emphasis and clarity of the message on state-led economic developmentalism and equity. Patrick Bond has suggested that MERG researchers like Vella Pillay and Ben Fine "were driving the policy process towards a direction considered too Keynesian by the DEP members like Tito Mboweni and Trevor Manuel, their approaches were calling for too much state intervention including nationalization of the Reserve Bank" (Interview: 30 October, 2002). Indeed, by the time the final report was presented in 1993, ANC [leadership] thinking on economic policy had taken a fundamental rightward shift.

Unsurprisingly, all the quotations taken from the MERG Report, above, could equally have come from the ANC/COSATU economic conference that conceived the MERG. Some of the resolutions of that conference bear an unmistakable relationship with the MERG Report. For instance, on the role of the state, the conference resolved as follows:

> within the context of a mixed economy, the democratic non-racial state would assume the leading role in the reconstruction of the economy in order to facilitate the realization of its developmental objectives (*Sechaba*, 1990: 18).

On exchange controls, it argued:

The non-racial democratic state would pursue control measures in order to retain domestic savings within the country and to prevent destabilizing capital flows (ibid).

On Nationalisation and ownership, the view was that:

The non-racial democratic state would retain existing nationalized industries and would be prepared, as a matter of fundamental policy, to re-nationalise privatized assets. Furthermore, it would set up new corporations.... (*Sechaba*, 1990: 20).

Nonetheless, an analysis of the MERG proposals suggests that "Making Democracy Work" presented the ANC and South Africa with the first real opportunity to proceed along a state-led developmentalist path in the 1990s. Certainly, the adoption of its key proposals on the role of the state, redistribution, industrial and monetary and trade policies, would have come very close to the developmentalist state strategies associated with East Asian economic success. For this was meant to be the ANC elites own Big Idea for fundamental social transformation and economic development. All developmental elites have had radical developmentalist 'big ideas' around which new societies are created. These ideas have generally radically altered the economic framework and regime of accumulation – in other words, they have generally sought to shatter the old framework including the instigation of processes of class formation and economic restructuring. In the case of South Africa, it was not to be, and there are several reasons for the ANC elites' decision to disown the MERG Report. One of the key authors of the report, Professor Ben Fine, made the following remarks:

One point that is symbolic, was our argument that the Reserve Bank should be accountable to the new state. Trevor Manuel said we should not even discuss this issue, let alone take a position against the Reserve Bank's independence, he saw this as unnecessarily provocative. That was highly indicative of a sharp change in the ANC policy stance (Interview: 16 December, 2002).

For yet another author of the MERG Report, the disowning of the Report had to do with the fact that it had become too radical, too statist and would essentially sit very uncomfortable with the political compromises reached at the Kempton Park negotiations. Indeed, for John Sender (who was also economic advisor to COSATU's Alec Erwin):

At the political level a range of ideas were being made to accommodate the old regime and international capital...The debate was always put in stark terms, either we have bloodshed, acceleration of killings and death on the streets, or we do a deal, we compromise. And I suppose in economic terms, either we have a mass investment strike, capital flight or we do a deal (Interview: 16 December, 2002).

These were some of the factors that explain what Ben Fine has referred to as the denunciation of the MERG Report at the highest level, the very same level that initiated the process with great fanfare and expectations a few years earlier. As expected, this left most of the left thinking and Keynesian inspired participants in the MERG report including the late Vella Pillay and Ben Fine deeply frustrated and disappointed not only in how the Report was handled but more ominously, what economic framework and strategies lay ahead for post-apartheid South Africa. This early disappointment however, did not stop COSATU' economic policy processes from forging on, trying to win back some ground in what was clearly becoming a deeply fractious and contested economic policy arena. It is COSATU's persistence that saw the production of the first RDP base document.

The Reconstruction Accord

More directly, the provenance of the RDP is to be found in COSATU's formulation of a 'Reconstruction Accord', a mandate from its March 1992 Economic Policy Conference held in Johannesburg. The idea behind such a conference itself was inspired by a number of factors. One of these was inspired by COSATU's participation in the two sessions of CODESA (multi-party talks held in December 1991 and again in May 1992), and this alerted the labour leadership to two crucially important factors. First, was the relative insignificance of labour and labour matters in the political and constitutional negotiations process, and the almost complete obscurity of economic policy issues on the agenda of the talks. Secondly, and related to the first, COSATU's campaign against what they viewed as an unrepresentative budget confirmed the vulnerability of labour (the working class) and the existential crisis the federation itself might face in the new dispensation. COSATU had no alternative economic policy blue print, nor did they have a clearly defined pact with which to bargain with a future ANC government. The 1992 economic policy conference mandated the leadership urgently to draft a Reconstruction Accord, to deal precisely with these concerns. The resulting document would then constitute the basis of the federation's engagement in the negotiations process, and in particular, with a post-apartheid democratic government (Work in Progress, 1992: 28). The first draft was released by the Head Office on the 11th January 1993 for comment by the different affiliates. The comments in turn, led to the circulation of two additional drafts in March and May respectively. Meanwhile, the ANC/COSATU/SACP alliance resolved that, instead of an accord, the three alliance partners should use the COSATU document as a basis for the formulation of a Reconstruction and Development Programme, that would guide the new government's work. Thus, the fourth and fifth drafts were the products of a much broader alliance effort. Moreover, the character of the document that was being crafted had changed from an accord between state and labour to an alliance plan for socio-economic transformation and economic development. The South African Communist Party's Jeremy Cronin said at the time:

> Unity within and around the ANC is not going to work if it is built purely on sentiment and mythology, on nostalgia for old times. It needs to be built around a programmatic perspective that is itself the product of a broad based, plural movement (*Work In Progress,* 1993:17)

At COSATU's Special Congress held in September 1993, the delegates were confronted with and asked to deliberate on a substantially amended fourth draft of the document. Congress nonetheless, adopted the document with the proviso that the following aspects (which had been removed resulting in a much more watered-down version), were re-inserted and unambiguously emphasized in the final product:

- The nationalization of strategic sectors, these included Eskom, public transport, the Post-Office, Telkom, State Forests, Iscor, Roads, Health and Education.

- The commitment (in the latest version) to a strong form of macro-economic stability not be used to block real reallocation of resources.

- That the final document returns the meeting of basic needs back to the top of the document (it had been relegated to the end).

- That the need and commitment to an industrial policy be spelt out clearly (WIP, 1993; SALB, 1993).

Congress thus instructed the Central Executive Committee (CEC) to work on a fifth draft which would cater for the concerns and reservations of the delegates. What is commonly known as the base document is therefore the sixth draft of a lengthy process of consultation and engagement within the ANC-led alliance. This document was in turn, adopted by an alliance 'Conference on Reconstruction and Strategy' in January 1994 in Johannesburg, three months before the first non-racial elections. The document was subsequently formally adopted by the leaders of the principal participants in its crafting. The following organisations were thus its key architects:

Nelson Mandela	African National Congress (ANC): President
John Gomomo	Congress of South African Trade Unions (COSATU): President
Joe Slovo	South African Communist Party (SACP): Chairperson
Lechesa Tsenoli	SA National Civic Organisation (SANCO): President
George Mashamba	National Education Coordinating Committee (NECC): President

(ANC, 1994)

At the close of COSATU's Special Congress in September 1993, outgoing General Secretary (and future RDP Minister), Jay Naidoo summarized the Federation's understanding of the RDP thus:

> The RDP will be a tool by which we will be able to manage expectations and find the means of unlocking the resources in the country. It is intended to be a realistic programme which provides the basis for engagement (ANC, 1993).

In the spirit of the original Reconstruction Accord, therefore, COSATU saw the RDP as a programme against which the new government' performance and responsiveness to people's needs could be assessed by the Federation. For COSATU, therefore, the new government needed to be kept accountable and the accord was the instrument to measure and monitor its performance and responsiveness to labour's needs and expectations. For the ANC, according to former National Executive Committee Member, Phillip Dexter:

> ...the idea behind the RDP was that although you had the Freedom Charter prior to 1994, there was a sense that you needed a coherent set of policies on reconstruction and development. It was really an articulation and elaboration of the Freedom Charter (Interview, 21 March, 2002).

Thus, for Dexter, the RDP was about concretely translating into government policy the demands set out in the Freedom Charter (ibid). In this context, the contribution of the ANC to COSATU's initial Reconstruction Accord was to give it a broader socio-political flavour, which went well beyond narrow worker concerns. However, what is also clear in these early engagements on the country's new economic policy blue print, is that this was a deeply contested ideological and policy space.

This section has underscored the initial stages of the battle for ideological hegemony within the ANC-led alliance. This battle was fought by those in the movement who sought and were desperate, as John Sender put it, ' to do a deal' and those who sought to uphold the historic commitment of the ANC to a redistributive state-led development perspective. The contest was most glaringly demonstrated in the side-lining of the MERG Report in 1993 (Fine, 2002), only for the key principles underlying the Report to resurface later that year through COSATU's efforts. At the same time, this section has underscored the depth of a state developmentalist perspective within the ANC alliance, from the Freedom Charter to the MERG Report. In other words, the intellectual and ideological origins of the RDP had an important developnentalist thrust. Some (although not all) of these developmentalist elements survived in the final RDP document. The next section briefly outlines the key features of the base document in order to lay the foundation for a consideration of the conflicting interests it embodied, and the extent of its consistency with the developmental state approach.

Key Features of the RDP

This section provides a summary of the key features of the RDP, focusing in particular on its developmentalist aspects.

Meeting Basic Needs

Meeting the basic needs of the majority of the population who constituted the main victims of the apartheid system was a central pillar of the RDP, that is why COSATU delegates were disturbed by the sudden relegation of this section of the document to the end. The Basic Needs section was redistributionist in content and based on clear targets:

- Creating opportunities for all South Africans to develop tc their full potential.

- Boosting production and household income through job-creation, productivity and efficiency, and creating opportunities for all to sustain themselves through productive activity.

- Improving living conditions through better access to basic physical and social services, health care, and education and training for urban and rural communities.

- Establishing a[social] security system and other safety nets to protect the poor, the disabled, the elderly and other vulnerable groups (ANC, 1994: 15-6).

Furthermore, the document's redistributionist substance is expressed through its emphasis on linking reconstruction and development. This, it was hoped, would "…lead to growth in all parts of the economy, greater equity through redistribution and sustainability" (ibid: 15). Meeting Basic Needs more specifically refers to the provision of a variety of goods and services, energy and electrification; telecommunications; transport; nutrition, health care; social security and social welfare (ANC, 1994:16). Predominantly rural South Korea and Taiwan initiated 'basic needs' (extensive land redistribution) strategies to accelerate their development projects, while at the same time, ensuring equity (Ranis, 1978; Lee, 1978; Koo, 1984; Deyo, 1987; Jenkins, 1991; Pempel, 1999; Kohli, 1999). Indeed, in the South Korean and Taiwanese context, the state's attack on poverty and landlessness was crucial in providing these states "…extraordinary leverage to reshape the behaviour of industrial elites and led these same governments to see their political survival as depending on rapid industrial growth" (Evans, 1998: 80).

Developing Human Resources

The RDP placed great emphasis on educating and training those previously denied access to such training by the apartheid system. To this end, the RDP sought:

> ….an integrated system of education and training that provide equal opportunities to all irrespective of race, colour, sex, class, language, age, religion, geographic location, political or other opinion. It must address the development of knowledge and skills that can be used to produce high-quality goods and services in such a way as to enable us to develop our cultures, our society and our economy (ANC, 1994: 60).

Concretely, the fragmented, racist and unequal apartheid system was to be transformed into a single education and training system with equal opportunities for all South Africans. Furthermore, curriculum change would be geared towards preparing students at all levels of the system for the challenge of reconstruction and development. In other words, education and training would be much more closely linked to the country's labour market and economic development requirements. The programme, moreover, committed the government both to the provision of a ten-year period of free and compulsory education for all children, and to ensuring that by the year 2000, the teacher-pupil ratio would have moved from the apartheid average of 1:50 for black schools to well below 1: 40 (1994: 64). Additionally, the programme promised a system of lifelong learning, targeted specifically at adult learners, to enhance further education skills development (1994: 63).

Ha-Joon Chang and Kozul-Wright (1998), in their work on South Korea, have identified a similar obsession of the elites in East Asian developmental states to transform their human resource structures in such a way that they met the developmental challenges of growing economies (1998: 26). On the same subject, Rhys Jenkins has commented that "..throughout the 1960s and 1970s, even among late industrializing countries, South Korea stood out in terms of many indices of education" (1992: 117). Therefore, the RDP's commitments to education and training had important parallels with the East Asian contexts.

Building the Economy

This sub-section of the base document is scathing in its characterization of the legacies of apartheid in the economy. Indeed, the very first sentence laments the deep-seated structural crisis afflicting the economy and calls for its fundamental reconstruction (1994: 75). At the same time, it was acknowledged that:

> Successive minority governments and business have tried to promote growth by encouraging local production of manufacturing goods which were previously imported. This policy led to the emergence of a significant manufacturing sector in our country (ibid).

Thus, to revive growth and development, while building on the foundations of the 'significant manufacturing sector' bequeathed on the new government by the apartheid state elites, the RDP rejected rigid ideological strategies. Therefore, neither commandist central planning, nor strategies based on the belief in the unfettered free market system would be favoured. Instead, the state was to be given a leading role in driving the process of economic growth and development, informed by the concrete realities obtaining in post-apartheid society. This would include the expansion of the country's technological capacity "…to ensure that as part of the restructuring of industry, South Africa emerges as a significant exporter of manufacturing goods" (1994:87).

The impact of South Africa's acceptance of the General Agreement on Tariff and Trade in 1993 is clearly felt in the RDP's sharp departure from say, the MERG Report's insistence on the protection of strategic sectors. Instead, the RDP could only manage the following:

> The democratic state must simplify the tariff structure and begin a process of reducing protection in ways that minimise disruption to employment and to sensitive socio-economic areas (1994: 90).

This absence of a robust statement in the RDP on trade regulation is thus attributable, in part, to the provisions of the GATT agreement, which among other things, meant that demand side measures like direct producer subsidies, which worked by raising producer prices to compensate for lack of competitiveness, were no longer an option. Nonetheless, the RDP placed great emphasis on the need for state control over those sectors of the economy it considered to be strategic to the country's economic development and reconstruction. In this connection, the process of commercialization and privatisation started by the apartheid government in the mid-1980s, was viewed with suspicion. Referring to this privatization process, the RDP stated:

> the democratic government will reverse privatization programmes that are contrary to the public interest (1994: 91). And in particular:

> we must seek the return of private mineral rights to the democratic government.... our principal objective is to transform mining and mineral-processing industries to serve all our people. We can achieve this goal through a variety of government interventions, incentives and disincentives (ibid:99).

The RDP also called for the regulation of the financial sector, in order to deal with a situation whereby South Africa' financial assets had become centralized in the hands of a few large financial institutions (1994: 110). To correct this anomaly (at least in the view of the authors), the RDP called for the establishment of a housing bank to provide access to those historically marginalized by the formal banking sector. The democratic government was also charged with the task of facilitating the establishment of Community Banks of various types (ibid). In addition, the Reserve Bank was to be made accountable to the broader goals of development and maintenance of the currency, while the "Act of governing the Reserve Bank [had] to ensure a Board of Directors that can better serve society as a whole" (1994" 112). This formulation was of course a significant departure from the MERG approach, as discussed earlier. True, there were important shifts from the original approach of the MERG and indeed from the approaches followed by the East Asian Newly Industrialising Countries (NICs) of the 1960s and 1970s. These shifts are clearly discernable in the RDP's dealings with financial management and the role and status of the Reserve Bank in the broader process of economic growth and development. However, the developmentalist thrust of the programme was still largely in place. After all, it was not only on the basis of pronouncements that the developmentalist impact of the RDP would be judged, but rather on the basis of the impact of its implementation. So, although tensions were brewing within the ANC alliance around some of these matters, there was generally hope that things would turn around.

Land Reform

Chapter three deals extensively with the legacies apartheid as far as the land question is concerned. It also shows the continuities or endurance of that legacy (twenty-two years after democracy) and thus the need for 'another way'. South Korea and Taiwan have implemented comprehensive land redistribution programmes, with far-reaching socio-economic benefits for these societies. These benefits have included the fostering of economic citizenship in the country-side, the stimulation of the rural economies and the consolidation of the agricultural sector, even as there are moves to drive industry, technological development and other sectors. Above all, however, the key contribution of land reform in East Asia has been relative equity, stability and drastically reduced unemployment rates. The authors of the RDP were also well aware of the significance of land reform in South Africa's evolution towards growth and development. For this reason, the RDP called for the implementation of land reform policies akin to those initiated by South Korea and Taiwan, including redistribution through restitution, expropriation with and without compensation (depending on the circumstances) (ANC, 1994: 20-21). The author's appreciation of the importance and the need for a speedy and effective resolution of the land question is apparent:

> The RDP must implement a fundamental land reform programme. The land policy must ensure security of tenure for all South Africans, regardless of land-holding. It must remove all forms of discrimination in women's access to land (ANC:20).

The issue of expropriation and returning the land to actual tillers or those who work it, is also addressed very directly by the RDP thus:

> The redistribution programme should use land already on sale and land acquired by corrupt means from the apartheid state.... Where applicable, it will expropriate land and pay compensation as the Constitution stipulates. All legal provisions which may impede planning and affordability of a land reform programme must be reviewed and if necessary revised (ibid).

Therefore, the RDP document promised a far-reaching land reform programme, whose implementation would certainly have dented land hunger, poverty, inequality and unemployment in South Africa. Such land reform would also go a long way in facilitating rural economic development, with important spin-offs for economic growth and development in the country more broadly (Lipton, 1974: 270). As the case was in South Korea and Taiwan, a strong agricultural and land reform process could serve as a spring board for accelerated manufacturing growth. And, for this reason too, The

131

RDP, in many different ways constituted a critically important plank on which a developmentalist state type process could be built.

Implementing the RDP

The RDP envisaged thoroughgoing state leadership in monitoring, coordination and implementation of its programmes. In this regard, it stated:

> The RDP will require the establishment of effective RDP structures within national, provincial and local governments. These structures must monitor the implementation of the RDP, including the elaboration of planning frameworks and coordination between departments and tiers of government

And further:

> While not displacing the line functions of other government departments, the structures will require powers of coordination and an appropriate budget (1994: 138).

Thus, the state's process of driving RDP implementation was envisioned as predicated on the presence of effective institutional arrangements, and the thorough transformation of existing institutions. Some of the institutional changes that were put in place to facilitate effective RDP implementation are dealt with in the remainder of this section.

Institutional arrangements

The RDP envisaged the creation of an RDP national coordinating body based in the Office of the President:

> A prime function of the structures will be to overcome tendencies for fragmentation of different departments while not displacing the line functions of other departments, the structures will require real powers of coordination and an appropriate budget (ANC,1994:138).

The RDP White Paper itself stated:

> The President is leading the transformation and renewal of our society, and is responsible for the overall coordination of the RDP (2.2.2).

RDP Politics within the State

To properly understand the operations of agential factors in the rise and fall of the RDP requires an approach to politics that takes account of both politics inside the state (institutional arrangements) and politics between state and civil society. This section looks at RDP politics inside the state, and lays the foundation for an examination of RDP politics at a different level in the next chapter. The two levels are both distinct and intimately related, examining them separately can serve to tease out and illuminate the roles and activities of key agents in a given *strategically selective context* (Hay, 2002: 131).

Key Institutional Changes

The RDP was institutionally and operationally located in the President's Office. Former COSATU General Secretary, Jay Naidoo was appointed Minister in charge of RDP implementation. In addition, a special RDP Cabinet Committee was set up comprising Ministers responsible for policy formulation and implementation of the RDP (RDP White Paper, 1994: 2.2.3). This Committee was coordinated by the RDP Minister and was accountable to the Cabinet through the Deputy President (ibid). The RDP Minister's planning, research, and policy formulation capacity was significantly boosted through the inclusion onto his portfolio the Central Economic Advisory Services (CEAS), Central Statistical Services CSS) and the National Productivity Institute (NPI) (RDP White Paper, 1994: 2.2.11). The broad task of the Cabinet Committee together with the planning agencies included, *interalia*:

- Assisting the RDP Minister in formulating policies and strategies
- Setting goals, targets and priorities for RDP implementation.
- Developing an institutional framework for the RDP, which included mechanisms to monitor performance and evaluation of overall progress.
- Establishing a poverty monitoring and transformation management system.
- Augmenting all the state's planning and developmental functions and centralizing this in the RDP Office (ibid).

To this end, President Mandela, in his 'first hundred days' in office speech, to parliament, on the 18th August 1994, explained:

> In line with the objectives of the RDP, we will by end of the year, require clear and long term strategies from all government and parastatal institutions on mechanisms to shift their operations to meet the requirements of reconstruction and development (Hansard, 1994,col: 1546).

This was in response to an RDP demand, calling on all state structures to prepare five year plans to re-orientate their programmes, improve their efficiency and enhance their use of resources in such a way as to position themselves for RDP implementation (RDP White Paper, 2.5.1). It was hoped that such planning would lead to synchronisation between the RDP Office's own five-year plan and those of the different line departments. In terms of the RDP five-year plan, R2.2 billion would be allocated for the programme in the fiscal year 1994/5, this would increase to R5.6 billion, R7.5 billion in 1996/7, R10 billion in 1997/8 and R12 billion for the fiscal year 1998/9 (Weekly Mail and Guardian, 02 February, 1996). This plan provides clear indications that there were intentions to extend the life of the RDP much further than March 1996. However, the RDP's institutional arrangements led to a number of implementation problems. For instance, it was difficult for the RDP Minister to monitor and expedite progress within line departments, which were often slow in implementing RDP programmes and controlled by what were largely recalcitrant civil servants, who lacked both the capacity and expertise to run a programme of the RDP's magnitude (Kraak, 1995: 12).

Although provincial and local RDP structures were still in the early stages of conception when the RDP Office was unceremoniously closed down in early 1996, some provinces had already stumbled onto some institutional framework. According to work conducted by the Johannesburg-based Centre of Policy Studies (1996), Gauteng and Mpumalanga were among the front-runners (in terms of crafting a provincial institutional framework). The process of overhauling the local government system meant that the local RDP structures were delayed until the new local government system was fully in place. For instance, this process was only completed in November 1995 in the Western Cape, leaving very little time before the closure of the RDP National Office in March 1996, for structures to be set up in that province (*The Cape Time*, 19th November, 1995).

Nevertheless, Gauteng Province, with only the broadest guidelines from the National Office, were the first to experiment with an RDP Commission, located in the Premier's Office (Gauteng Government, 1995:1). In line with the national structure, the idea was to align the provincial processes to national processes. At the same time, the provincial leadership sought to underline the centrality of the RDP to the province's economic development programme. The Provincial RDP Commissioner (appointed by the Premier), was an ex-officio executive council member, since the constitution in the province did not provide for more than ten Members of the Executive Committee (MEC) (Centre for Policy Studies, 1996: 13). This lack of executive status, in turn, weakened the position of the Commissioner relative to other fully established provincial ministries. More significantly, the status of the Commissioner meant that the RDP would have no budget of its own, thereby making nonsense of the government's claim that the RDP was the kernel of government programmes (CPS, 1996: 14). In a move demonstrative of the haste and lack of proper planning that preceded the RDP Commission's conception, the post of RDP Commissioner was abolished, and the political responsibility for the Commission and the RDP more broadly was assigned to the MEC for Economic Affairs (ibid). Former Commissioner, Ben Turok, attribute this to political intrigue, a creeping conservatism in economic policy and a hostility to integrated development planning, this driven by a 'silo' mentality and territoriality (Turok, 2014:30). Under its new head, the RDP Commission was charged with elaborating policy formulation and implementation (ibid). A crucial feature of the Gauteng structure is that, unlike the national level, the RDP was 'added' onto an existing ministry and department. Hence, contrary to the claims of the provincial leadership, it was not the central focus and policy loadstar of provincial government.

In contrast to Gauteng, Mpumalanga's RDP institutional arrangements had their origins in the work of a non-statutory RDP Planning Forum, comprising the Mass Democratic Movement (MDM), and allied organisations and individuals. The Forum released a discussion document in June 1994 dealing with possible institutional arrangements for the province, and more broadly, with the question of how the process of implementing the RDP should unfold in Mpumalanga Province (Mpumalanga Government, 1994). Largely informed by the RDP base document, the provincial government went a step further, it identified four stages in the evolution of the RDP in the province. The first stage was devoted to consultation with the broadest possible section of stakeholders in the province, in a bid to give provincial RDP processes popular appeal. The second stage was about planning and policy formulation for the short and medium term, while the third stage was to see the official establishment of the RDP process with clearly defined priorities, structures and functions. The fourth stage was to be the first cycle of planning, programming and budgeting (CPS, 1996: 17). As had been the case at national level, an RDP provincial cabinet committee was established, with an RDP MEC as political head. However, as was the case in Gauteng, the status of this MEC was said to be running foul of the provincial constitution, leading to a situation where the RDP MEC had much less power than his counter parts (ibid). Here, too, there were complications associated with the funding of the RDP function. For that reason, the premature closure of the RDP National Office served in many ways, to save Mpumalanga from a tricky constitutional and implementation crisis.

Financial Control

All international and domestic grant aid received by government, revenues from lottery, gambling and revenue obtained from the sale of 'non-strategic' state assets, were supposed to be directed to the RDP (*RDP Monitor,* November, 1994). Furthermore, the RDP obtained funding through transfers or 'top-slicing' of five per cent from all government departments (*RDP News*, 1995: 3). This arrangement was put in place as part of government's drive to compel departments to think strategically about how they spent their budgets, and to re-prioritise in line with RDP requirements. The five per cent would then be returned to departments on condition that a clearly set out business plan, detailing how funds would be deployed on RDP work, was received and approved by the RDP Minister. The business plans had to satisfy 'basic guidelines for business planning' including the degree of labour intensity of the projects, the job-creation and skill enhancing possibilities of the projects, the degree of focus on the neediest target groups and the extent of support to small and medium enterprise development (Blumenfeld, 1997: 73).

Additional sources of funding included the five per cent levy charged on all South Africans earning R500 000-00per year and over. This was only for the augmentation of the 1994/5 budget. From this, the RDP Ministry received an allocation of 2.8 billion for the first of its operations (Munslow and Fitz-Gerald, 1997:51). In addition, oil reserves stored by the apartheid regime, as a measure to lessen the impact of sanctions, were sold. Some seventy-seven barrels were sold, giving the RDP Minister access to well over R4 billion (*Weekly Mail and Guardian*, 26 September, 1994). By the end of the first year of its existence, the Government of National Unity (GNU) had managed to mobilise a total of R11 billion in foreign aid for the RDP, including R4 billion in grant finance, R4billion in trade credits, R2 billion in concessionary loans and R800 million for parastatals (Sunday Times, 2 October, 1994). Thus, for the fiscal year 1994/5, the GNU had allocated just under 2 per cent of budget, or half a per cent of GDP, while for 1995/6 the plan was to spend three per cent of the budget on the RDP (Naidoo, 1995:5). This, however, did not include the 5 per cent 'top-sliced' from each government department, nor the 22 Presidential Lead projects designed to kick-start the programme (Blumenfeld, 1997:67). According to Ben Turok (1999), these resources gave Naidoo some leverage in propagating RDP principles in how government worked and spent some of the funds at its disposal. (1999:56). Such financial control and power to shape developmental processes (by Ministers in the Presidency) was of course, not altogether unique to South African RDP processes. In South Korea, the Economic Planning Board (EPB) was made responsible for planning and budgeting for economic development immediately after President Park ascended to power. The same agency was placed in charge of price controls, foreign aid, loans and investment and transfer of technology (Luedde-Neurath,1988:95). In Taiwan, too, the Council on International Economic Cooperation and Development (CIECD), was established in 1963 to formulate and coordinate plans and lead negotiations for external financial and technical assistance (Myers, 1986:53). Both structures had tremendous power to shape and drive the developmental processes in the countries concerned. They were located in the President's Office precisely to give them power and prestige, so they were able to oversee and (where necessary) intervene in the work of line departments, to ensure that focus is not lost. Therefore, with the full backing of the President and the leadership elite, structures of this kind have near unlimited scope to deliver on the elite's vision. However, if such support wavers and if there is uncertainty and lack of leadership cohesion and coherence regarding the vision, such a structure could also fail spectacularly.

Personnel Matters

The bulk of the personnel in the RDP Ministry were associated with the labour and Mass Democratic Movement (MDM), these are mostly people who had, in their own policy areas, played an important role in the evolution and definition of the RDP. The down side of this, of course, was that in the main, the RDP office was filled with people with very limited if any government administration experience. Far more serious though, is that by the time of its closure, the RDP National Office was operating with just sixteen senior managers, a grossly inadequate number given the brief of that office. Furthermore, the RDP precisely because of the political background of its senior personnel, had to contend with another key centre of power and economic policy – the National Treasury. According to Tebogo Phadu, former RDP coordinator at the ANC Head Office, the bulk of the personnel at Treasury were largely inherited from the old order. They were part of the negotiations compromise that saw apartheid Finance Minister Derek Keys carried-over to the first Cabinet of the Government of National Unity. The retention of Keys thus set the tone for the country's economic policies and how even the progressive elements were to be implemented (or not implemented). And thus, the RDP (and RDP policy implementation) found itself at the centre of this policy maelstrom, Phadu put it thus:

> The leadership surrounding the Finance Minister were very clear about the ideological position they wanted to push. For them, the priority was attacking the deficit, attracting foreign investment. Development and RDP implementation were to be predicated on these fundamentals (Interview,22 August,2002).

Therefore, Treasury was seen as serving as a countervailing force to an RDP Office that was perceived to be run by people holding radical developmentalist perspectives. Since the politics and ideological orientation of Keys and his largely unchanged Ministry and Ministry officials were known to the ANC leadership, Phadu despairingly declared: "This appointment of Keys signaled the beginnings of a process by our leadership to empty the RDP of its progressive content. It also subordinated RDP implementation to market demands" (ibid).

Furthermore, the ideological thinking at Treasury was bound to come into conflict and essentially undermine the RDP's 'growth through redistribution' approach. Apart from this ideological battle for its survival, Andre Fourie has also observed another battle front for the new RDP Minister. The power of the RDP Minister seemed to cause a great deal of resentment from his cabinet colleagues, a resentment partly fuelled by the fact that they all had to apply to Naidoo, who was their equal in political terms, for funding that belonged to their departments to start with (Interview with Fourie, 2002). Also, although the CEAS, CSS, NPI and the Development Bank of Southern Africa (DBSA) were meant to boost the RDP Ministry's research and policy formulation capacity, the history of these institutions, as servants of the apartheid socio-economic and political order raised important questions of strategy and institutional reform. Indeed, the challenge of institutional reform, especially in and around the RDP office, was not lost to some ANC members. Max Sisulu Member of Parliament (MP), responding to the announcement that the CSS, CEAS, NPI and DBSA would be incorporated into the RDP Ministry, warned:

> The extension of governance to all South Africans requires that institutions that were created to serve a particular political purpose be restructured and reorganised and refocused to serve the interests of a new South Africa and the objectives of the RDP (Hansard, 1994col:3358).

For Sisulu, therefore, behind the need for institutional transformation lay both issues of legitimacy and, crucially, competence to deal with a new and qualitatively different social order (ibid). An additional challenge arising from this was the need for the swift reform of these institutions without, at the same time, losing sight of the urgency of RDP implementation. Thus, both from an RDP perspective and from the perspective of developmental state-making, RDP politics and institutional arrangements were inescapably bound up with the nature of post-apartheid deal-making, compromise and accommodation. This would certainly have foreclosed the construction of institutions like the South Korean (EPB) or the Taiwanese (CIED), both devoted to single-minded implementation of the elite's developmental programme. And, not insignificantly, actors in such institutions were carefully recruited both on merit and on loyalty to the cause of the ruling elite namely, state-led economic development (Myers, 1986; Luedde-Neurath, 1988).

RDP politics within the state were also characterized by important conflicts and battles for the definition and content of the RDP. And, as Fourie (2002) has observed, the RDP and its institutional arrangements also triggered a territorial war between the RDP Minister and his cabinet colleagues. Resistance from line department Ministers in turn, underscored the lack of effective presidential authority and support behind the RDP Minister. For this very reason, Naidoo was viewed by his colleagues not as the man representing the President in implementing the most important programme of government, but instead, as a colleague overplaying his hand, and interfering in areas which he did not, and should not, have control (Phadu, 2002; Fourie, 2002). While not providing an exhaustive account of the RDP, the above examination does capture the key features and should provide sufficient background for an appreciation of the focus of chapters: on the politics of the RDP.

Summary

There was certainly a strong developmentalist thrust in the RDP. However, as I make plain in the foregoing pages, has made plain, developmental states are not there for the taking, their successful construction depends on the satisfaction of a number of essentially political factors, including the presence of a 'developmental elite'. It is also clear that there were a number of deviations from the developmental state approach. For instance, the RDP was institutionally weak, with provinces free to elaborate their own institutional processes subject to only limited direction and leadership from the centre. The RDP Minister was not the Chief Accounting Minister for RDP funding and implementation, a large part of this role belonged to the Minister of Finance. A Minister known to subscribe to conservative neo-liberal economics and did not share the RDP's statist and redistributionist thrust. Lastly, there were the internal inter-ministerial conflicts regarding the powers of the RDP Minister. Indeed, the most vivid expression of the divergence of interests that sought to claim a stake in the RDP was demonstrated by the discussions generated by the draft White Paper. It is, indeed, from this process that the real politics of the RDP can be extrapolated. And that, is the subject of the next chapter.

CHAPTER

The Politics of Reconstruction and Development

Introduction

This chapter focuses attention on the role of key actors (agential factors) in explaining the strategic direction and economic policy followed in 1990s South Africa. It is an analysis that is significantly informed by the concept of 'strategic actors' (Hay, 2002: 128). According to this approach, the socio-economic and political elites always act in carefully calculated ways, in pursuit of definite interests and objectives. This is, therefore, above all else a discussion of the politics of the RDP, and the contribution made by politics and political processes to the character and content of South Africa's current economic policy trajectory. For, as demonstrated in the preceding chapters, the construction of developmental states is fundamentally a political process. Indeed, if the political conditions are not appropriate, then developmental state-making can be extremely illusive.

The politics of the RDP are examined in this chapter from the vantage point of the various organs of civil society and their interactions with the state or state policy as given in the RDP White Paper (1994). The RDP White Paper provides the strategically selective context within which state-society interactions are explored. From this, both the character of the RDP as economic growth and development policy and crucially, its prospects as an instrument for developmental state construction can be derived. More specifically, however, the chapter is devoted to analyzing the actions of various interests and actors, and the extent to which agential action constrained or encouraged the RDP's prospects for constructing a developmental state. This approach also shares important parallels with French policy analyst, Paul Sabatier's approach to the policy making process. According to Sabatier, elite opinions and interests provide the best possible means for understanding policy formulation and change (1993: 30). It is, indeed, the opinions and actions of elites that ultimately explain movement in the policy process (ibid). This analysis thus seeks to unpack and understand the conflict and jostling between various political actors, it also seeks to probe the actions of such actors against and in defense of the institutional and structural contexts in which they operate. The chapter concludes by describing the process of the RDPs collapse – the closure of the RDP Office, and its replacement with a new, different growth strategy – the Growth, Employment and Redistribution macroeconomic strategy (GEAR).

It became clear after the publication of the draft White Paper that the excitement about the broad-based support enjoyed by the RDP was grossly exaggerated. The perception of unanimity originated from the ambivalence of the RDP on the most controversial socio-economic issues, and a poor reading and interpretation of the real detail of the RDP by almost all the stakeholders.

"Capital and opposition parties broadly supported the RDP because they saw it as a platform of engagement to pursue their own agenda. Its broad formulations allowed these forces to embrace it. More importantly, the broad themes of the RDP were popularized by the movement during and after the elections, while the controversial detail was not popularized" Interview with Phadu: 22 August, 2002).

According to Phadu, therefore, once the White Paper elaborated the hitherto little publicized detail and interpretation of the different aspects of the RDP, conflicting interests began to emerge. A careful analysis of the public submissions to the RDP White Paper process suggests that at least two main politico-ideological trends began to emerge, fighting for the heart and soul of the RDP. A broadly anti-statist, anti-redistributionist neo-liberal tendency led by private capital (domestic and international) on the one hand, and a broadly statist, redistributionist and developmentalist tendency led by labour and its left allies on the other. The remaining part of this section is, in essence, a documentary analysis designed to look at how those conflicting interests played themselves out through the RDP White Paper process. First, a brief note on the White Paper process.

The RDP White Paper

The RDP White Paper was meant to be the legislative interpretation of the ANC's RDP document. While it largely reflected the broad thrust of the original base document, the White Paper also contained significant deviations. Blumenfeld (1997) for instance, has commented on the White Paper's more technocratic and market friendly slant, and in particular, its moderation and suppression of 'contentious proposals for nationalization or other forms of interventions' (1997:72). Specifically, the White Paper's shift from the base document's proposals is represented in three key areas.

Fiscal discipline

Whereas the base document saw fiscal discipline as an important tool for achieving the broader goals of redistribution and economic development (ANC, 1990: 90), the White Paper elevated the notion of fiscal discipline to a key principle of the RDP. In the White Paper, fiscal discipline was inserted as a key condition for the success of the programme, thus: "all levels of government must pay attention to affordability given our commitment to fiscal discipline and achievable goals" (White Paper, 1994: 8).

In the White paper, therefore, fiscal discipline ceased to be a necessary aspect of the goals of redistribution and economic development, it became a goal in itself. Another deviation concerned the issues of redistribution.

Redistribution

The base document forcefully asserted the centrality of redistribution for the reconstruction process. It also recognized a dynamic link between redistribution and development, which would be underpinned by equity and redistribution (ANC, 1990:82). Furthermore, the base document explicitly emphasized the centrality of redistribution to the success of the RDP (ANC, 1990: 79). The White Paper for its part omitted redistribution in its linkage of reconstruction and development. Instead, the White Paper made increasing use of the term 'reconciliation' in its dealing with redistribution issues. This emphasis on reconciliation aimed at accommodating the interests of the overwhelmingly white corporate sector and the white populace at large. Thus, economic development and redistribution were to be contingent on sensitivity to white and corporate fears (NIEP, 1999: 2). This would essentially set the scene for capture and subordination of the country's developmental agenda to the interests of local and global capital.

The Role of the State

In spite of its vagueness on the exact role of the state in the economy, the base document can at least always be credited for its forthright assertion of 'a leading role of the state in economic development'. The White Paper saw the role of the state as that of *managing* the transformation process in society, and it went on to promise that such management would include' cutting government expenditure wherever possible'. This, too, was an important shift from the RDP base document. Thus, while the White Paper encapsulated the main thrust of the base document, there were important changes smuggled in, which sought to shift the programme in a neo-liberal direction. Nonetheless, it remained a useful tool both for public engagement and for the restoration of the ANC's long held redistributionist and developmentalist strategies.

Therefore, if the side-lining of the MERG Report was the first indication of an ideological shift from interventionist and redistributionist positions within the ANC-led alliance, then the RDP White Paper was another important step in that direction. These were some of the key differences between the base document and the White Paper. The next section provides a more detailed analysis of the White Paper through the inputs of the key social actors in South African society. For, it is through this jostling of various social and economic interests, that one can gain better insights into the politics of the RDP. Such jostling is typically against each other but also against or in defence of the new political and economic structural and institutional dispensation.

Tendency towards Statism and Redistribution
The COSATU Intervention

The labour federation readily aspired to the construction of some kind of developmental state in their response to the RDP White Paper. After all, they were key architects of the original and earlier drafts of the RDP and a large part of the White Paper process for them was also about winning back as much of the original content as they could. COSATU's submission demonstrated that they had serious reservations with how the White Paper had altered the original documents, in this regard, we focus on five key thematic areas that were of particular concern for the federation:

On Worker's Rights and the Labour Market

With respect to labour market issues, the following amendment and recommendations were made by the COSATU submission:

> The role of a new Labour Relations Act. The role identified in the White Paper is not correct. The LRA's role to promote collective bargaining, regulate disputes, and provide a framework of organizational rights. This would lead to an improved labour relations dispensation in South Africa

In this regard:

> The White Paper should advocate a pro-active labour market policy where the state actively intervenes in the labour market, to promote training, employment creation etc., as well as providing an adequate safety net for those who are injured, become old or sick etc. In the light of the substantial economic restructuring which faces us, the state needs to develop a coherent strategy to deal with the social consequences of restructuring (COSATU, 1994: 4).

On Fiscal Discipline and Public Spending

The federation, consistent with the provisions of the base document, was in favour of fiscal discipline in the way public funds were spent. Such fiscal discipline was, in COSATU's view, not at variance with the RDP's (base document) demand for an expansion in welfare and service delivery by the government to the majority of the population. Instead, fiscal discipline would imply:

> increased public spending and employment in certain areas, while reducing it drastically in others (COSATU, 1994: 2).

Indeed, the duplication and wastage of the apartheid system (notably the many Bantustan administrations) provided ample opportunities for cutbacks and savings on government spending. Of great concern for COSATU was:

> the apparent ideologically-driven approach on this matter, articulated by former Finance Minister and more recently, his successor, Minister Liebenberg, who stated in October 25 that government expenditure would be reduced from 22% of GDP to 17% of GDP over the next five years. This target is based on an immutable law of fiscal discipline, rather than being demonstrated to be able to meet the needs of implementing the RDP (ibid).

This ideologically-driven approach was in turn, perceived by COSATU to have found its way onto the White Paper and constituting a major shift from the base document. With regard to this particular matter, the submission stated:

> The RDP WP does not state clearly enough that cut-backs in the public service will only take place in areas which do not benefit the RDP. Further, it interprets the commitment to fiscal discipline to mean that there will be no increase in employment. This could contradict the need to dramatically increase personnel in key areas of delivery of the RDP (COSATU, 1994: 2).

On the Economy

COSATU was of the view that section 3.2.2 of the White Paper 'omits to mention affirmative action as a key objective, and democratization of economic decision-making as a central element of our economic strategy is omitted in 3.3.1' of the White Paper (COSATU, 1994). The Federation also expressed dissatisfaction with the White Paper's failure to address the 'investment strike' by the South African employers and in particular, the lack of cooperation with respect to job-creation and investment in RDP projects. In this regard, 'government will have to apply both carrot and stick methods to deal with this fundamental obstacle to economic development'. Also:

> Insufficient emphasis is placed on negotiated processes of industrial restructuring, which remove management's exclusive prerogative over strategic decisions, as a critical element of the solution to our structural economic problems. Instead, the focus in the document [WP] is on one-sided monetarist measures (COSATU, 1994:6).

The role of privatization was central in the public debate on economic policy. COSATU viewed this matter as extremely sensitive, requiring absolute clarity. The federation felt that the government's position on privatization was not clearly spelt out in the White Paper and open to different interpretations. Thus it was declared:

> While on the one hand it talks of the central role public enterprises will play in delivering the RDP, on the other hand it talks of the RDP Fund 'benefiting from the sale of state assets'. Sale of useless state assets recently referred to by government, which are of no value to the RDP, such as unused properties here and abroad, don't pose a problem. Government needs to clarify if this is the extent of what is being considered. To remove any doubt that government is considering privatising assets which are an integral part of the RDP (ibid).

146

Furthermore:

> The reserve Bank needs to be restructured to make it accountable to society, and ensure that it is in line with the broad objectives set out by the RDP – and does not remain the captive of an old Thatcherite bureaucracy and the large conglomerates (ibid).

Interests and Conflicts

Several issues of conflict and interests can be extrapolated from COSATU's interaction with the RDP White Paper. The intervention was in the first instance, concerned with defending the 'heart and soul' of the RDP base document. In the main, COSATU's submission sought to expose deviations from the base document and focused on calling for retention of the original content. It was important for COSATU that as much of the progressive content of the base document as possible, be carried onto the government White Paper. Secondly, COSATU was concerned to defend the immediate interests of its members. This comes through in the discussion of the public sector, and the lengthy consideration of the labour market and labour rights. Thirdly, COSATU seemed to be fighting an ideological battle through the submission. There was a perception in the labour movement that a neo-liberal shift was at work in explaining the discontinuities from the base document to the White Paper. The constant swipes at an 'ideologically-driven approach', Thatcherite' and 'monetarist' approaches, support this perception. In particular, the bogeyman for this onslaught were key government actors – Finance Ministers Key and Liebenberg. Indeed, the occupation of such a crucial government portfolio by individuals who not only did not share the government's broad developmentalist vision, but who were also known to subscribe to views that were diametrically opposed to the RDP's statist and redistributionist content, was a source of concern for COSATU. Fourthly, the submission seemed to be fighting a 'war of position' with business and business interests, in support of the interests of labour. This is clear from COSATU's demand for the 'removal of management's exclusive prerogative over strategic decisions'. This also comes across in the federation's preoccupation with a Labour Relations Act that would keep management activities in the labour market in check.

The Mass Democratic Movement

The Mass Democratic Movement (MDM) comprised a range of community-based organisations and other organs of civil society. These organisations were essentially brought together by their support for the Freedom Charter, their non-racial political orientation and opposition to apartheid and importantly, their centrality in elaborating upon the sectoral chapters of the RDP base document. The organisations involved included: The National Education Coordinating Committee (NECC) for the education sector; South African National Civic Organisation (SANCO), the National Land Committee for land issues, among others. The MDM submission was a comprehensive forty-two-pages document, presented under the auspices of the National Institute for Economic Policy (NIEP). Some of their key concerns were as follows:

Redistribution

On this subject, the submission insisted:

> the RDP is about redirecting resources back to the disadvantaged, and in the process, restoring quality of life and personal power to those groups (NIEP/MDM submission on RDP WP). The White Paper's omission of redistribution as a fundamental prerequisite for the success of the RDP was the source of profound disquiet among MDM members, and constituted, in their view, a major departure from the base document's redistributionist path. Indeed, for this group, the RDP needed to accurately capture the collective interests and priorities of the vast majority of South African communities, as this was a *sine qua non* for successful state-led development.

On Health

The submission essentially re-stated and in some instances, elaborated upon the base document's approach to issues such as health care. For instance:

> The RDP approach to health reform must not only take into account the state of existing service delivery infrastructure and changes that could be implemented to ensure improved efficiency, but it must also look towards a model that provides health services equitably, to a minimum level that is acceptable to the whole country (ibid).

On Social Welfare

Here too, the approach was to restate the principles underpinning social welfare in the base document:

> A holistic approach is needed to address poverty as defined in the RDP. The emphasis should be placed on development rather than a hand-out approach and therefore it is important to link social security programmes to

all developmental programmes relocated to the alleviation of poverty. The principles underlying a developmental approach to social security are:

- Accessibility
- Efficiency
- No discrimination
- Accountability
- Equity

On Land Reform

Land reform and land redistribution, it was argued, would be a key indicator of RDP success or failure. To achieve success, the NIEP/MDM submission recommended:

> The government increase the restitution funds from R187 million [proposed by the WP], to R800 million (ibid).

The NIEP/MDM submission was thus unambiguous in its intentions. It sought to restore as much of the original content of the base document as possible.

Interests and Conflicts

The interventions in this submission were essentially focused on maximising benefits for the sectors concerned, be it land redistribution, social welfare, decent health care and quality education. The MDM formations had come to the conclusion (as had COSATU) that the considerations in the original base document, were in critical ways, watered down, and in some cases rendered vague to the point of meaninglessness. For that reason, the MDM submission was thoroughly comprehensive, re-stating in a systematic and detailed way the MDM's stance on all the areas of dispute.

Anti- Statist Neo-liberal Tendency
Business and the White Paper

Business, too, represented strong special interests, which sought to fight for the 'soul' of the RDP in such a way that the final product represented their interests. The South African Chamber of Business (SACOB) like many other social actors in South Africa purported to be in favour of the broad claims of the RDP. It was, however, the publication of the White Paper that brought the document's short comings, in the view of SACOB, into sharp focus. SACOB's annual report carried in the organisation's mouth piece, *Voice of Business*, in December 1994, observed: "there is one matter central to the RDP, about which the business community is concerned, and that is state intervention in the economy" (1994:1).

For the Chamber, therefore, the single most important anomaly in the White Paper was the prominent role accorded to the state in the economy. Following their conference on government policy held in October 1994, SA-COB was able to emerge with a more coherent and systematic response to the RDP, and put forward some concrete proposals. In general terms, SA-COB felt that the White Paper, like the base document, was biased in favour of:

> The requirements of labour in economic development, particularly as it relates to the role of business in that development. In its present form, the White Paper has a prominent labour orientation towards reconstruction and development (SACOB submission, 1994).

On the Role of the State

SACOB felt that the bulk of the anomalies and contradictions in the White Paper were due to the simultaneous pursuit of conflicting philosophies – market and command driven economic strategies. While SACOB as an organisation was not completely hostile to a measure of state involvement to correct some of the most salient distortions of apartheid:

> If intervention is employed in a heavy-handed manner or for securing ideological objectives, the result for the economy would be disastrous. In this respect, it must be clearly recognized that the private sector's profit incentive and indeed, the legitimate self-interest motives of all individuals, must be harnessed intelligently so as to ensure the delivery of benefits to the poor and disadvantaged and, as importantly, to make it possible for individuals to acquire wealth (ibid).

Therefore, for organized business, the White Paper's philosophical and ideological outlook left it open to statist and populist interpretations at the expense of a recognition of the private sector's 'profit incentive'. On this issue, there was a drive for clearly defined policies.

On Investment Policy

SACOB was supportive of the White Paper's commitment to attracting foreign investment, and thereby, enhancing political stability and promoting economic growth. However, what was not spelt out clearly enough in the White Paper was the fact that:

> the conditions necessary for encouraging domestic investment are no different from those designed to attract foreign investment. Those conditions hinge upon sound macro-economic policies that are market driven and free from excessive regulation. In this latter respect, it is of concern that this section implies the possibility of targeted investment areas (SACOB, 1994).

Its institutional weaknesses aside, the RDP strategy of targeted investment areas shared important similarities with the South Korean and Taiwanese cases discussed in and earlier period. This strategy gives state and policy actors extraordinary powers to drive the economy in a targeted and sequenced manner, focusing on growth and development for all. SACOB was nervous about this possibility, specifically: "the issue of targeted industrial sectors [picking winners] presents difficulty in who identifies them and how" (ibid). SACOB was concerned at what they saw as the usurpation of the market's intrinsic self-regulatory function by state actors.

On Trade Policy

While appreciative of the difficult adjustment requirements that would be engendered by South Africa's acceptance of the GATT principles in 1994 (and endorsed by Parliament in 1995), SACOB was nonetheless, pleased with the liberalization of trade policy this implied. And in this respect, they argued:

> As a broad generality, the view of business is that the objective of trade policy should be neutral. That implies that exports and imports should not be discouraged" (ibid).

On Competition Policy

SACOB tempered their acceptance of the need for such a policy with a cautious note:

from experience, SACOB is wary of misguided efforts by bureaucrats to impose regulatory measures for supposed improvement of market structures (SACOB submission, 1994).

Also, sensing the RDP's preoccupation with competition policy may have been in part targeted at the large conglomerates associated with some of SACOB's affiliates, the submission added: "the paranoia concerning their [large conglomerates] curtailment is misplaced, particularly as South Africa' political transformation provides the prospect of investment and capital inflows which enhance competition [for example, economic growth, abolition of exchange control]" (ibid). The main concern here was with regulation and bureaucratic interference as was the case with monetary policy.

On Monetary Policy

SACOB was concerned that the changes envisaged by the RDP White Paper, notably revising and redefining the role and status of the Reserve Bank, would lead to rigidities in the country's financial sector. Moreover:

> Interventions of this nature could seriously undermine the country's banking system with concomitant consequences for the entire economy. In the global context, such intervention could influence South Africa's access to capital flows from external sources. Foreign investors must necessarily consider the perceived soundness of the country's banking system (ibid).

Labour Market Policies

This section of the White Paper was, in SACOB's view, in conflict with the RDP's own objectives, and crucially, with the reality of South Africa's situation, following the government's acceptance of GATT provisions. For SACOB:

> A liberal trade policy will expose South African business to competition from products produced in more flexible labour markets (ibid).

In other words, markets biased towards the interests of labour would be inflexible, and would stand no chance of success in a global context characterized by the rapid movement of capital and investments to the most attractive [flexible] destinations. This would mean that South African goods, which would be relatively more expensive to produce, would not compete favorably with goods produced much more inexpensively, in countries with more flexible labour market policies and keeping with global trade demands. Furthermore:

It is SACOB's opinion that paragraph 3.11 does not address the labour market and human resource development in sufficient detail" (SACOB, 1994) And more generally on economic growth:

SACOB stresses that the attainment of high levels of economic growth and its accompanying employment creation, which is the focus of the RDP, cannot be achieved by rearranging the political and economic system alone. The investment necessary to promote high economic growth levels simply cannot be funded from domestic savings. Large capital inflows will be required and be actively encouraged (ibid).

Here, SACOB was appealing for the relevant section to commit the RDP more explicitly to mobilizing and working for foreign investors to come to South Africa. This, coupled with the GATT principles, would certainly strengthen the hand of business, in as far as orienting the economy unambiguously in a free market direction. This, in turn, would severely weaken the state-centric and labour friendly elements of the RDP. Over and above this, SACOB pointed out what they saw as important contradictions permeating the White Paper:

The White Paper advocates higher wage earnings, but high wage earnings have resulted in job losses in a number of key industries eg. mining

It is in favour of a low interest rate policy to promote investment, but is in favour of an effective monetary policy to control inflation (it cannot have both); and

It is in favour of a small effective state sector, but advocates a greatly increased bureaucratic framework to make the RDP effective

Interests and Conflicts

Like labour, SACOB's first instincts were to emphasise the RDP's labour origins, and in this way lay the foundation for an argument designed to correct that slant towards labour, particularly where it conflicted with business interests. Secondly, a large part of the SACOB intervention was devoted to countering and warning against what was perceived as an ideologically-driven economic policy towards a state-centred approach, as against market-centred policies. These concerns came across in SACOB's dealings with various sections of the White Paper, including competition policy, trade policy, investment policy and monetary and financial policy. Therefore, as with the COSATU submission, there was concern to secure the ideological orientation and underpinnings of the RDP in a business and market friendly direction.

Thirdly, SACOB sought to protect the immediate interests of its members both individually and collectively. On the collective front, SACOB insisted on the importance of encapsulating business' profit motives in defining its role in the country's growth strategy. There was also the direct appeal for the preservation of large conglomerates, in response to the White Paper's perceived hostility towards these entities.

Fourthly, a part of the SACOB submission argues that the White Paper was an essentially contradictory document, open to various interpretations and therefore weak as a policy platform, meant to give clear policy directives. SACOB further committed to continue engaging the government in dialogue to seek a more acceptable solution to the critical issue of the country's economic policy. Business, Anglo-American Chairman Julian Ogilvie Thompson, boasted at the time, had access to government leaders and would "actively engage with the ANC on the relevant issues" (*Global Custodian,* 1994). From a developmental state perspective, the conflicting interests of labour and business seem to have overwhelmed the politics of the RDP. Indeed, contrary to developmental state experiments in East Asia, the politics of the RDP were conspicuous for the absence of the state's political leadership in driving the process in a direction consistent with the redistributionist and developmentalist perspectives. For Nicoli Natrras, the RDP White Paper and the politics that characterized it illustrated the lack of dynamic planning and direction on the part of the new state and political elite. She argued that the lack of leadership would lead to a situation where: "The RDP might simply drown in a mass of sclerotic bureaucracy as activists, parliamentarians and government officials race from one meeting, task team, council, commission, forum or committee to the next" (1994: 39).

Also, she found it incredible that the ANC, which should have a strong background in planning, given its years in exile and flirtations with socialist perspectives, should "end up producing a White Paper that transfers decision-making responsibility to an amorphous and confusing process of consultation" (ibid).

The National Party

The National Party's view of the RDP is crucial not only for its striking resemblance to that of business, but also because the NP was after 1994, a key partner of the ANC in the Government of National Unity. This by implication raises issues of leadership cohesion and the presence or absence of a 'hegemonic project' around which such leadership was organized. The National Party saw the RDP as a forum for negotiating a liberal socio-economic policy outcome for the new South Africa. In this connection, extremist or radical elements on both sides of South Africa's political divide would be marginalized in favour of a 'middle-way' based on the market economy. National Party leader and former apartheid president, F.W. De Klerk, set out his party's vision for the RDP in a parliamentary debate thus:

> We must do everything in our power, irrespective of the political party in which one finds oneself, to control the radical elements in our country. This process has already begun with the launching of the RDP, which provides a worthy rallying point for our national endeavors. Another goal behind which we can all unite is that of our common determination to make South Africa a winning nation in the economic sphere. If we do not succeed in this regard, the RDP will not materialize

And crucially: "We will succeed in the economic sphere only by adhering to universally valid economic approaches and standards" (National Assembly, 18/10.1994, col:3179-3181).

De Klerk's approach to economic transformation in South Africa more generally, was very much in keeping with the advice persistently given to him and his party, as a central condition that should inform the country's socio-economic and political compromise. Margaret Thatcher's views on the matter were typical: "My talks with Mr. De Klerk focused on his plans for the next steps in bringing the ANC to accept a political and economic system which would secure South Africa's future as a liberal, free enterprise country" (1993:532).

As well as arguing for a socio-economic consensus based on the market economy, De Klerk's (1994) speech to the National assembly also reveals a particular interpretation of the RDP. Contrary to the RDP base document and some of the White Paper's pronouncements, De Klerk saw the RDP not as an integrated strategy encompassing reconstruction, development and economic growth in a mutually reinforcing fashion, but as an 'add on'. Economic growth based on what he called 'universally valid approaches and standards', was a separate process that would determine the success of another process – the RDP. In other words, the 'new South Africa' would achieve its developmental goals simply as a by-product of neo-liberal growth strategies.

Secondly, the National Party leader's approach was clearly meant to build support and emphasise the significance of a market-led, as opposed to a state-led economic growth policy trajectory. Indeed, such a liberalized market-led policy approach would be consistent with De Klerk's government liberalization strategies, which began in the 1980s, in response to sluggish economic growth (IMF,2000:25). The National Party also sought continuity (in the economic sphere at least). The fact that the NP did not share the RDP's statist and interventionist foundations, had important implications for the construction of a developmental state in South Africa. Their standpoint illustrated the precarious nature (and lack of cohesion of the political elite that was meant to drive the RDP, and the kind of leadership direction that could emerge from a leadership holding such divergent views on economic policy and ideology.

International Interventions

Although both the IMF and the World Bank had a firm policy of not interfering in the internal policy-making processes of any of their member states, this did not stop either organisation from publishing a series of 'Staff Reports', 'Informal Discussion Papers', and scenarios regarding the best options for South Africa's future economic development path. In the case of South Africa, several such papers were made available to all key stakeholders (World Bank, 1991; Lachman, Desmond and Bercuson, 1992; IMF Staff Report, 1992). Fantu Cherry, Professor at American University in Washington DC, and advisor to the Ethiopian government at the time, argued that these staff reports and related documents were crucial aspects of World Bank and International Monetary Fund strategy in the developing world. Indeed: 'By bringing out various documents, they have been directly influencing the direction of economic policy. They are going to use policy documents and their overwhelming financial assets to shape the development debate in this [South Africa] country" (*Work In Progress*, June, 1992: 32).

What is more, the message from these documents seemed to have close affinities with the views articulated by SACOB and De Klerk above. For instance, the World Bank's 'Informal Discussion Paper on Aspects of the South African Economy' (1993), reached the following conclusions:

> The experience of the successful East Asian countries provides clear evidence of the critical importance of assuring a free trade regime. The East Asian success stories also suggest that establishment of free trade status for export activities can lay initial groundwork for completely liberalizing imports for the domestic market (1993: 62).

Of course, successful developmental state-making elsewhere in the world shows that nothing could be further from the truth. The East Asian experience was in fact a lesson in how to subvert key IMF/WB policy advice in order to achieve sustainable growth and development. Similarly, in their report to the 1992 Interim Consultation with South Africa, the IMF made the following recommendations:

156

the opening up of the external sector to trade would be a necessary condition for moving South Africa to a higher growth path over the medium term (1993:13).

The conclusions in the case of both arguments were not based on any detailed analysis of South Africa's socio-economic and redistribution deficit nor the huge income distribution, inequality and unemployment problems. Neither was it systematically spelt out how, exactly 'free trade regimes' would address the unique set of social and economic challenges confronting South Africa. Instead, the authors relied on a very cavalier, ideological and selective presentation of evidence from the East Asian 'experience'. Both papers neglected to mention the centrality of the role of the state in that experience, and the pervasive involvement of East Asian state actors in formulating, implementing, and monitoring an extremely illiberal trade regime (Wade, 1988; Woo, 1991). Also, consistent with the responses offered by business and De Klerk, the World Bank's Macroeconomic Framework by Kahn, Jenhadjie and Walton (1992), argued for the protection of property rights against state interference. This is despite the well-known historical injustices associated with property ownership in the history of South Africa. More concerning, however, in their objection to nationalization and redistribution, the authors offer no explicit advice on how equity and redress were to be attained. Instead, they argued:

> Whether this takes the form of the possibility of nationalization of strategic industries or attempts to increase equity ownership among the black population. This paper did not survey issues on nationalization, though the international record is not encouraging (1992:20).

It seems to me that references to the East Asian experience should be made more appropriately with respect precisely to this aspect of 'strategic industries' and the role of an interventionist state in using this as catalyst for driving economic development more generally. Nonetheless, World Bank and IMF approaches to South Africa seem to follow the neo-liberal ideological framework and regime of accumulation. Indeed, this was a standard one-size-fits-all package straight off the IMF shelf, recommended to all transitional and developing societies, as IMF Managing Director, Michael Camdessus, made plain in a 1994 seminar for 'economies in transition':

> The transition to a market economy entails inescapable challenges for policy – prices have to be free, the economy has to be opened to the rest of the world, macro-economic stability has to be established, enterprises have to be commercialized and privatized.... As far as the IMF

is concerned, the financial assistance it can provide is necessarily tied to the country's policies (*IMF Survey,* 14th February, 1994).

Such were the general views of key international actors on South Africa's economic policies. Unfortunately, none of these interventions even hinted at the fact that such policy advice had dismally failed to stimulate growth and development in most of the recipient countries for the preceding thirty years.

Summary

This chapter shows that the fight for the heart and soul of the RDP saw the programme being pulled simultaneously in a neo-liberal and statist interventionist directions. On the whole, the pressure of different social interests, all making claims to the programme, made the RDP and its politics incompatible with the politics of developmental state-making. Several other factors militated against the development of the RDP into a developmentalist state instrument. The RDP's popular demands for extensive consultation made it an elastic and incoherent policy instrument, contestable from all quarters. More importantly, the document's focus on laborious consultation processes in some respects undermined its own call for the state to play a leading role. Transferring key decisions on development policy to an open process of consultation could only serve to saturate the economic policy-making process with special interests. Consequently, the RDP became a platform for the expression and contestation of conflicting interests, instead of a state-led developmental programme. This chapter therefore also demonstrates the sheer power of civil society in the South African context, at the same time as it underlines the crying need for leadership.

The need for strong elite or developmental leadership was made all the more important by the fact that the ANC has always been a 'broad church' both ideologically, and in its class orientation. Moreover, COSATU, as an important member of the ANC-led tripartite alliance represented a significant voice in ANC thinking. At the same time, the business perspective was gradually gaining support within the movement (*Financial Times*: 11 June, 1993). For this reason, it would seem that instead of articulating an unambiguous position on the strategic direction of the development process, the leadership elites embarked on a 'balancing act'. The White Paper thus sought to appease all the key social actors. This, together with the absence of what Leftwich (1996;1999) called 'determined developmental elite', severely limited the prospects for the developmentalist and redistributionist elements of the RDP being driven in a developmental state direction.

To resolve the policy impasse, and in response to an acute decline of the currency, the ANC elite sought to take charge of the economic policy process, and to exercise firm leadership over the process. To this end, in March 1996, the Deputy President announced the closure of the RDP Office. The closure was ostensibly a consequence of the programme's success, and therefore, the need to take it into a new level (*Weekly Mail and Guardian*:4th April, 1996). Elsewhere (Marais, 1998; Bond, 2000), it was suggested that the closure of the RDP Office and the announcement in June 1996 of a new programme – Growth, Employment and Redistribution (GEAR)- marked the triumph of the neo-liberal tendency within the ANC alliance. By extension, this period also marked the real defeat of a redistributionist and state-led economic development strategic approach in South Africa.

The Demise of the RDP

According to official statements, RDP functions would be relocated to the Department of Finance and the Deputy President's Office. The RDP remained the official development programme of the government, and the changes were necessitated by the 'positive evolution' of the programme up to that point (*Weekly Mail and Guardian*, 4th April, 1996). It was, however, apparent that the decision to close the office was taken hastily and with no proper consultation even at cabinet level. For instance, when asked to explain the closure of the RDP Office, Trade and Industry Minister, Alec Erwin responded: "The decision to close it was probably taken with not enough reflection as to what would replace it...I still think there is a need to have some oversight at a strong planning level"(*SA Labour Bulletin*, June:1996).

While on the other hand, Gavin Lewis, editor of the RDP newsletter *RDP Monitor* was of the view that most departments had not been transformed into vigorous development bodies. For this reason, institutional and central political coordination was still crucial for the success of the programme (Weekly Mail and Guardian, 4th April, 1996). For Lewis, "if they had thought it through, transitional plans would be in place" (ibid). The absence of such a transitional plan was apparent when Mbeki appointed a 'Task Force' to oversee the reallocation of RDP functions and its staff. As expected, widespread confusion was reported among staff members in the RDP Office, regarding their employment status (*Weekely Mail and Guardian*, 12 April, 1996). Subsequent developments were to disprove government claims that the RDP remained, after the closure of the office, the fundamental policy of the government, for poverty alleviation and economic development. According to an Auditor-General's report to Parliament, on the 31st March 2002, there was R997 million unspent or unallocated, the report also stated that R148 million from the RDP Fund, donated by foreign agencies, was in fact spent to finance the deployment of South African troops to Burundi *(Sunday Times*, 17th November, 2002). Also, the South African National Lottery organisation reported that it had tried and not succeeded in distributing R332 million to the Fund. The difficulty in locating the appropriate authority stemmed from the fact that no one had been tasked to administer the Fund since the RDP Ministry was abolished in 1996 (ibid). There is, thus, merit in the contention that the closure of the RDP Office marked a fundamental shift in policy. Indeed, Thabo Mbeki, pressed by COSATU to explain exactly why the RDP was abandoned, conceded:

> some of the things that we thought doable, might in fact not be doable...We might very well have underestimated the challenges posed by the intricacy of the process of the formation of implementable policies (*The Shopsteward, October/November*, 1996:23).

This also explains the absence of any real alternative institutional mechanism to drive the programme. At the same time, it suggests a conscious and deliberate move by the elites to change policy in a direction deemed to be more 'doable' in the circumstances. This question (as to why the RDP was abandoned) is discussed in greater detail in the next chapter. For now, and for contextual reasons, it is necessary to briefly look at the new economic framework that replaced the RDP.

In June 1996, the government unveiled a new economic growth strategy – GEAR. Deputy President Mbeki spoke of GEAR in the following terms:

> This is the central compass which will guide all other sectoral growth and development programmes of the government aimed at achieving the objectives of the RDP (http://www.anc.org.za/ancdocs/history/mbeki/1996:html).

Addressing the National Assembly of Parliament in Cape Town, Finance Minister, Trevor Manuel emphasized to the chagrin of ANC alliance partners that the Gear was in fact, non-negotiable (Manuel, 1996). The alliance latched on these comments to start a new war on economic policy within the alliance, the ramifications of which can be felt to this day (COSATU, 2014). Not only is it not working, but it will not work, charged ANC National Executive Committee Member, Jeremy Cronin later, but what is more:

> We are unhappy with the closed technocratic process behind GEAR, and we were especially unhappy with the bald declaration that the policy was non-negotiable (*The Citizen*, 11 June, 1997)

This was followed by a string of public outbursts between the leadership elite. Whatever unity the RDP had engendered had been severely tested over the past five years of defining and elaborating especially economic policy strategies. No longer was it possible for the elites to boast of the strength, cohesion and unity of the alliance, for it was open war fare, kitchen sink stuff (*City Press*, 13th October, 2002; *Sunday Times*, 13th October, 2002). Such leadership cohesion, policy coherence and clarity of purpose, are absolutely critical to the success of developmental state-making processes. Quite apart from the issue of consultation, what really seemed to exasperate the ANC's alliance partners was the perception that GEAR was not only undermining the RDP, but placed South Africa unequivocally on a neo-liberal development trajectory (COSATU, 2000: 84-85). A cursory perusal of the GEAR document does indeed, justify their apprehensions with respect to GEAR's departure from the RDP.

GEAR's Overall Policy Assumptions

The GEAR strategy was predicated on the inflow of massive private investment, especially foreign direct investment into the country. The strategy's intellectual point of departure was that the economic policy in South Africa should be grounded in the context of an 'integrated world capitalist system, where markets are the primary actors', and where recalcitrant countries are severely punished by the world market system. In line with this approach, GEAR set out to implement a range of measures (not too dissimilar to the standard neo-liberal package), which included:

- Cutting back government expenditure
- Accelerating the privatization of state assets
- Phasing out exchange rate control regulations
- Lifting trade barriers

Through these measures, the strategy hoped to drive down the budget deficit to 3%, while at the same time, creating 400,000 jobs by the year 2000 (GEAR, 1996:18).

On Investment, Trade and Fiscal Policy

To encourage investment, GEAR would pursue open policies where the market logic could operate unencumbered by the state. State spending had to be curtailed because state-led expansionary fiscal policies:

lead to higher inflation and higher interest rates, exacerbating the burden of interest payments on the fiscus (GEAR, 1996:3).

However, GEAR was silent on where exactly the cuts in state spending would be made, a crucial concern in a country where expectations, especially those of the poor, were so high. Instead of a firm statement, the document could only assert: "The Minister of Finance has initiated a thorough audit of government expenditure, including RDP allocations, to identify those areas in which budgetary cuts can be made" (GEAR, 1996: 8).

This increased suspicion that the strategy was designed to attack the progressive features of the RDP (COSATU, 2000:87-89). Moreover, the strategy neglected to show how trade would be used to ensure economic growth, development and an end to inequality. Instead, it was doing away with measures set out in the RDP, to prevent destabilizing speculative capital flows (RDP, 1994: 76) China has, despite her strict exchange controls, been receiving a very high share of global foreign investment, but so did South Korea and Taiwan in the 1960s and 1970s (*The Economist*, 17th February, 2001). These highly publicized and analysed experiences were not factored into the GEAR modeling and thinking on exchange and tariff controls. Aside from following the well-worn path of the 'Washington Consensus", it is not immediately clear what guided the GEAR document in its proposals for the hasty removal of such controls, which so drastically side-lined state input in these areas and the domestic economy more broadly. The only insight we have is that this reckless removal of controls had to do with some foolish expectation that the world trading system would reward South Africa for hurting its own development prospects (Hirsch, 2005). Also, the important role identified for the state in economic development, in all previous ANC policy and programmatic documents, is done away with in favour of accelerating privatization, cut backs in the public sector, and the state's general absence from the driving-seat of economic development. Instead, the leadership elite, through the GEAR strategy seemed to have defined what Johnson (1982) has referred to as a regulatory role for the post-apartheid South African state. On investment, too, the document declared that gross domestic investment would increase from 20% to nearly 26% by year 2000. This was to be achieved through massive inflows of foreign investment, the equivalent of 41% of GDP coming into the country on the basis of a 'favourable investment climate'. This was despite the fact that all developing and transitional economies (including those from the former Soviet Union), were being encouraged and compelled (as we have seen from the IMFs Mr. Camdessus above), to implement similar policies with unconvincing results (World Trade Organisation, 1995:7; Nattrass, 2001). Chapter six will discuss the impact (success or failure) of these targets on their own terms. Despite official protestations there were quite clearly key differences between the RDP and GEAR, while there were also striking similarities between the 'Washington Consensus' and the policies expounded by the GEAR strategy.

Where the RDP White Paper departed from the original document by attempting to reconcile Keynesian state-led development perspectives with market approaches, thereby creating a confused policy environment, GEAR was unequivocal in its embrace of the neo-liberal framework. The differences between the RDP and GEAR could not have been sharper both in policy and ideological terms. The perspectives of the GEAR document have much more in common with the recommendations of the neo-liberal framework advocated by the IMF and the World Bank (see World Bank, 1993; IMF Survey, 14th February, 1994; Department of Finance – GEAR, 1996). Therefore, whatever the internal and external pressures (we deal with these in the next chapter), the decision to abandon the RDP and embrace GEAR can be interpreted as a consequence of *strategic action.* At the heart of such strategic action was the belief that the GEAR 'stabilisation package' would (as it says on the pack), encourage high productivity in the immediate term, thereby laying the basis for a redistribution of sorts (Nattrass, 2001:13). This is also known as 'trickle-down' by the left and labour movement.

By the year 2000, various observers were jumping on the bandwagon to expose the utter failure of the GEAR programme, both on its own terms and targets, but more significantly, as an instrument for equity-based economic growth, development and reconstruction in South Africa (Marais, 2000; Bond, 2000; Fine, 2002; Sender, 2002). The South African economic debate, especially regarding the role of the state, had thus shifted decisively from a statist to a more orthodox market-centred approach. This led Ben Fine to the conclusion that GEAR in essence, was a sad reflection of a situation wherein: "South Africa became subject to self-imposed stabilization and structural adjustment. Meeting the standards of the World Bank and IMF (Austere economic policies) had taken precedence over meeting people's needs" (Interview, 16th December 2002).

The key question for Fine is not how, but why, did the South African elite shift policy in a neo-liberal direction, especially in such a short space of time (1994-March 1996).

Conclusion

This chapter comprised a comprehensive documentary analysis of the RDP and the pronouncements of key players and agents in defining the ultimate character and content of the post-apartheid policy environment. The analysis has sought to show not only the weakness of the RDP as an instrument for developmental state-making but also that its demise had been foreshadowed in and was a product of, a combination of factors and circumstances. These included the changed geo-political set up, with its emphasis on neo-liberal as opposed to state-led developmental processes. Furthermore, the imposition of the negotiation processes on a largely unprepared liberation movement, led to much organizational and tactical failure, which in turn, meant that economic development was not front and centre in the thinking of the liberation movement. Instead, political development was viewed as the foremost policy area whose resolution would resolve all other policy areas (including economic development). Thus, the Japanese, South Korean and Taiwanese seem to have understood the centrality of the economic structure in shaping the political and social, Johnson (1982) discovered as much in his ground breaking MITI project, as did Marx in an earlier period. As was to be expected, the radical elements of the MERG and to a lesser extent the RDP base documents, were undermined by the structural and subjective constraints permeating the policy environment before, during and in the immediate aftermath of the 1994 political break-through in South Africa. The RDP White Paper provided an important arena for the expression of different socio-economic and political interests. It was an arena not only for the expression and negotiation of such [diverse] interests, but also to resolve these. By observing and analyzing this process, it is easy to determine and demonstrate which interests and ideas triumphed and which came second best.

The above scenario is consistent with the contention of the strategic relational approach that agents bring about change by 'appropriating' the contexts, thereby unleashing political outcomes that impact upon both agents and contexts (Hay, 2002:113). Thus, depending on the strength and power of particular interests (agents) within a selective context (RDP process), the context could be overwhelmed by the 'appropriation', in a way that would affect both agents involved and context itself. Also, sufficient pressure through strategic appropriation by a particular set of interests/agents (for example, local and global business and neo-liberal interests) could have a significant impact on both the participating agents/interests and the selective context in which they operate and are articulated. This, of course, does not detract from the fundamental insight that structural factors will profoundly influence and shape the behavior and conduct of agents (political leaders, power blocs etc),

CHAPTER

but it does not determine the direction and specific choices of such agents. There is thus, always the additional responsibility of subjecting these factors to a forensic analysis to determine why certain and not other policy options were followed. And that is the subject of the next chapter.

Accounting for the Precarious Prospects of Developmental State-making in post-Apartheid South Africa

Introduction

So far the chapters on the RDP have argued that at the very outset, RDP implementation, and by extension, prospects for its evolution into a developmentalist state project were encumbered by important external and internal constraints. On the external front, the constraints consisted of a less than friendly geo-political and intellectual environment. On the internal front, the constraints manifested themselves in the form of a massive role for special interests in the policy arena, absence of ideological and policy cohesion and the absence of a determined developmental leadership to navigate and consistently channel things in a developmentalist direction. However, to anchor this argument, a clearer statement and examination of how such pressures actually exerted themselves on the South African economic policy arena is required. The role of, and rationale behind, elite political action in response to such pressures must be analysed. In other words, there is a need to examine the interaction of structure, agency and power in the collapse of the RDP. On one level, one could easily accept the ANC's account for the policy somersault, which is essentially that early ANC policy views were ill-informed, as Mbeki put it: "because people were not sufficiently aware of the extent of the problem. The effect of being in government with access to statistics and information surely must improve our capacity to resolve the problems and formulate implementable policy" (*The Shop Steward*, October/November, 1996:23)

And Essop Pahad, Minister in the Presidency, would later advance the same explanation thus:

> As the ANC began to look more closely at the kind of economic policies it needed to pursue, you began to see that there was certainty that this was not going to be possible. For example, in terms of nationalization…conditions were not conducive to such a move…. Contact with big South African conglomerates made a number of people in the ANC come to the realization that you could inherit an empty shell…Then when our people got into government for the first time, the enormity of the problems we were facing [was] very very stark (cited in Lyman, 2002:99).

Two critical points arise from both interventions. First, the ANC came into power barefoot and blind, with insufficient information to really understand the implications of implementing the RDP (on investments, trade etc) in other words, it was not ready to govern. Second, once information was obtained, from contact with big conglomerates and government statistics, an influential section of the ANC's leadership elite took a policy (and by extension) an ideological position on economic policy.

However, this explanation is not satisfactory as it fails to encapsulate a range of structural factors at play during the transition. Also, lack of information only partly explain why there was a policy shift, it says even less about the particular direction chosen as a consequence. Adelzadeh (1996) attributed the shift to a "panic response to the recent exchange rate instability and a lame succumbing to the policy dictates of international financial institutions" (1996:5). Indeed, the currency crisis that afflicted the South African economy between 1995 and October 1996 must be added as an important factor in explicating the policy shift in question. According to the South African Reserve Bank (1996), the Rand declined by 14% between late 1995 and the end of June 1996 (*Quarterly Bulletin*, December, 1996:15). Note that the depreciation took place a few months after Reserve Bank Governor Chris

Stals and Finance Minister Trevor Manuel abolished the Financial Rand (a critically important tool for protecting currency from volatile capital account movements). The 'panic response' to the rapid depreciation of the Rand is thus both plausible and constitutes an important explanatory variable in understanding (if only partly) the shift from the RDP to GEAR. To be sure, the timing of the intensification of the crisis, the unceremonious closure of the RDP Office and its replacement with a non-negotiable GEAR strategy, certainly coincided perfectly. The problem however, arises when this part explanation is elevated to *the* ultimate account. Such an account has important analytical limitations. First, it ignores that the neo-liberal compromise was foreshadowed in the early 1990s, when the search for a compromise started. This includes the brief history of the MERG Report, the constant fight for the heart and soul of the RDP and the gradual but determined rightward shift with every version (draft of the RDP itself, culminating in the White Paper). Second, Adelzadeh's depiction of the ANC leadership and policy elites as helpless recipients of neo-liberal policy dictates, over which they had no control or choice is misleading. For it denies agency any independent role as a variable for explaining the process of change. Instead, this approach burdens structural factors (as important as they are) with accounting for the whole process. Crucially, the mutually reinforcing character of the relationship between structure and agency advocated by Jessop and Hay is neglected as a more credible explanatory device.

Tom Lodge (2002) has suggested that it is in the nature of politics for elites to be more pragmatic once confronted by the realities of implementation and for him:

> Presidents and cabinet ministers may take office with particular policy predispositions or narrow social biases, but once in power they will be influenced also by the distinct interests of the state they command (2002:25).

The implication of Lodge's assessment is that the ANC, unlike the developmental elites in East Asia, took office *sans* a Big Idea, if there was a big idea with a determined developmental elite to implement it, it wouldn't melt away so easily and so quickly at the first contact with the 'realities of implementation'. So, both the presence of developmental elites and ideas (the ideational) matter in developmental state-making. Thus, while Lodge's explanation is plausible, it still does not answer a pressing set of political questions. These include why the realities of political office led to the adoption of some and not other policies. And neither does this way of approaching the problem account for why developmental elites in South Korea and Taiwan came to power with developmentalist agenda and went on to single-mindedly implement such plans. Currency crises elsewhere (notably in Malaysia in 1997) have led to a tightening of controls rather than the hastening of liberalization and deregulation and this at the peak of the neo-liberal discourse (see Mahathir Mohamed in *The Hindu*, 5 February, 2001). For their part, Seekings and Nattrass (2002) have based their explanation on the timing of the South African transition. According to this analysis, the South African transition missed out on the post-war economic boom that took place in the "Era of globalization in which capital is more mobile and can exercise more readily the 'exit option' out of a country (or simply not enter in the first place)" (2002:2). The problem with this approach, of course, is that it assumes the global environment is static, unchangeable and not subject to engagement and strategic negotiation. The East Asian developmental elites had to creatively and intelligently navigate a complex set of external factors, and manipulate these in pursuit of set developmentalist objectives. There is also evidence aplenty that in that very post-war globalization era, the rest of the developing world (Latin America, much of the African continent and Asia) did not perform as well, in terms of growth and development. The point is that such single-issue based approaches to the political economy of the South African transition are of limited utility, as I show in the remainder of this chapter. What is needed, instead, is a broader approach creatively encompassing the role of both structure and agency in explaining how and why the opportunity represented by the RDP was lost in South Africa.

In this regard, the key argument I advance in this chapter is as follows. The shift from the RDP to GEAR was a consequence of a particular reading of the global and internal socio-economic and political situation, and the possibilities this held for the South African transition in the 1990s. That reading convinced a key section of the ANC leadership elite that South Africa's survival was contingent on the broad framework of the 'Washington Consensus'. So, the shift was intentional. To summarise, the global context, pressures and expectations and the politics thereof, favoured a neo-liberal outcome, whilst the internal pressures, expectations and ideological posture favoured a more leftist and Keynesian approach. The decisive factor, I shall argue, was the role of a determined section of the leadership elite to drive policy right-wards. Thus, the explanation is sought in the deliberate and conscious actions of political elites in response to their interpretation of the external and internal realities. It is not that there was or is no determined elite in the South African political economic process, the elites at the head of the transition were simply not developmental. Determined but not developmental. I have, in the previous chapters shown how various attempts (MERG, RDP process) with strong state-led developmentalist tints, have been constantly undermined and emptied of their developmental content. Many authors (Marais, 1998; Bond, 2000; Fine, 2002; Lodge, 2002) have also alluded to the unilateral and secretive process that produced the GEAR document, a document that contrasted sharply with the open and consultative processes that produced the Freedom Charter, MERG Report and the RDP. This, in my view, corroborated the argument that the elites took a conscious and determined decision to drive policy in a right-ward direction. The process was secretive because opposition was expected and a sophisticated plan was put in place to win over key potential recalcitrants within COSATU and the SACP. Indeed, in his 'Open Letter', former (now expelled) COSATU general secretary, Zwelinzima Vavi, shows how the first reaction of the SACP to Gear was positive and even welcoming of the policy. The stance was only changed after a stunned COSATU leadership confronted the SACP about the party response to what has come to be dubbed the '1996 class project' (Vavi, 2014).

This chapter is divided into two main sections. The first section explores the various international pressure points confronting the transition, and shows how the leadership and policy elite's response to such international pressures conspired to derail developmentalist state prospects in South Africa. The themes used to explore this argument are the following: world trade issues; the IMF/World Bank; and the role of the United States. The second section shows how the determined and intentional decision to favour neo-liberalism actually frustrated the internal conditions and expectations for state-led Keynesian-inspired approaches. The themes used to explore this argument are the following: civil society; big ideas, leadership cohesion. The chapter concludes by observing that the combination of the above factors has severely circumscribed the prospects for developmental state construction in South Africa. First, the external pressures and the responses they elicited from the leadership elite.

External Pressures

In seeking to explain the role of international processes in the demise of the RDP and its statist policy proposals, one needs to extend the search for clues much further than March 28th 1996, when the RDP Office was formally abolished. A useful point of departure is the role of various international trade agreements, international financial institutions and countries and their influence in defining and determining the nature of the South African transition. It is also important to understand such global interaction within the context of the collapse of the Soviet Union. For the demise of the Soviet Union shattered what had been the ANC's ideological anchorage for a long time. Former Minister of Finance, Trevor Manuel, illustrates the significance of this development for the ANC and its strategic choices: "The collapse of the Soviet Union, the destruction of the Berlin Wall broke the revolutionary romantic illusions of many. The very stark collapse shifted the debate significantly" cited in Habib and Padayachee, 2000: 253).

This development was thus a critically important facilitating factor for understanding South Africa's transition politics, its policy choices and outcomes. In other words, it significantly shaped the international environment and pressures that the ANC elites had to confront. Therefore, how the new South African political elites interacted with and responded to such global economic and political environment holds vital clues. On these grounds, the spotlight falls on three dimensions of the global environment, and these are discussed in turn.

The World Trading System

The South African transition came at a time when (through the General Agreement on Tariffs and Trade (GATT Rounds), the world's socio-economic and political relations were being re-organised and re-ordered in important ways. Although the GATT rounds were generally interpreted as technical and legal arrangements and its documents ostensibly regulating issues of world trade between countries, there is now increasing recognition of the socio-economic and political implications of such agreements (Khor, 1991; UNDP, 1997; Ricupero, 2001). The impact is recognized to be particularly adverse in developing countries (Ricupero, 2001: 5-6). Indeed, a cursory look at the key provisions of the Marrakech Agreement, the final agreement signed in 1994, is instructive. The Uruguay Round document (Marrakech Agreement) is significant also in that its ratification was one of the first orders of international business, of the South African multi-party Transitional Executive Council's (TEC) (Mandela, 1993).

Key Provisions of the Uruguay Round

The final Act of the Uruguay Round signed in 1994, covered a number of trade areas including a General Commandment on Tariffs and Trade. According to this commandment, members should expect:

> Increasing surveillance of their activities through stronger notification and review procedures. [members were required to]... reduce or, as appropriate, eliminate tariffs including the reduction of high tariff concessions among all participants (www.gatt.org/r/english/docs_e/legal-eursum_e.. htm.wtphp).

In other words, the GATT (now World Trade Organisation) would police the world through carefully monitoring the extent of compliance with the organisation's demands for liberalization and openness in its member's trade practices. In another commandment, the General Commandment on Trade and Services stated that each member: "Shall accord immediately and unconditionally to services and service providers of any other party, treatment no less favourable than that it accords to like services and service providers of any other unit…" (ibid).

The implications for members and signatories of these commandments was a substantial reduction of room to maneuver, which the South Koreans and Taiwanese elites afforded themselves in the area of world trade. Concurring fully with the commandments would deny the South African elites any leverage and space of setting the terms of the country's re-insertion or re-entry into the global trading system. Evans (1987) has shown that a critical factor accounting for South Korean and Taiwanese success was the ability of the elites in those countries to set the pace and the terms for their entry into the global trading system (1987: 206). The Uruguay Round's obligation that foreign and domestic firms be treated equally would make it particularly difficult for developing and transitional countries to pursue developmental state-like projects. This was because the objectives of the Round's negotiations aimed, among other things, to:

- Bring about further liberalization and expansion of world trade to the benefit of all countries, including the improvement of access to markets by the reduction and elimination of tariffs, quantitative restrictions and other non-tariff measures and obstacles.

- Strengthen the role of GATT and bring about a wider coverage of world trade under agreed, effective and enforceable multilateral disciplines.

- Increase the responsiveness of the GATT system to the evolving international economic environment, through facilitating the necessary structural adjustment.

- Enhance surveillance in GATT to enable regular monitoring of trade policies and practices of contracting parties (Ministerial Declaration, 1994).

It is clear from the above that the GATT regime would seriously undermine any statist and interventionist policies designed to enhance comparative advantage by strictly monitoring foreign and multi-national and transnational investment and economic activities. If adhered to strictly, the regime would also close off the possibility of favouring local firms, insisting on local content and much more besides. At the same time, however, staying outside the system would effectively side-line South Africa's growth and development drive, and any bi-literal trade relations would invariably have to conform to GATT requirements (as all South Africa's key trading partners and potential partners were also members) (Holland: www.unibas.ch/euro/inhalt). In some instances, WTO arrangements substantially informed the outcome of bilateral trade negotiations (notably the EU/South Africa trade negotiations after 1995) (Teljeur, 1998:3). Given the extent of global pressure and expectations in the trading space, how the South African elites responded to these holds great explanatory force in understanding the policy shifts and turns in this period. Put differently, what was the elite's perception of constraints and opportunities in the world trading system?

The South African Response

The South African response was largely informed by the interaction between the apartheid regime and the GATT Secretariat much earlier than the 1994 democratic breakthrough. Bond (2000) has, however, traced the 'neo-liberalisation' of South African economic policies to the late 1980s, as an attempt by the apartheid regime to stem the downward spiral of the country's economy. It was also after several hints and nudges from various GATT officials and reports that the De Klerk regime took the firm decision to comply with the Uruguay Round's stipulations. Trade and Industry Minister, Derek Keys, said as much in a speech to the National Assembly (Hansard, col.8160: 14th May, 1993). Keys' announcement that his government was reviewing the country's tariff structure and its trade regime broadly followed the public comments by David Hartridge (Policy Advisor at GATT), that South Africa needed to give serious attention to its tariff and trade policies. According to Hartridge, the Uruguay Round was one sure way for the country to normalize its trading activities with the rest of the world (Business Day, 29th April, 1993). This was followed in June 1993 by a GATT Secretariat Report devoted to reviewing South Africa's trade policies. The Report also advised South African politicians to take effective steps to end the policy of protecting certain industries, drastically reduce tariffs and phase-out imports surcharges (Business Day, 3rd June, 1993). As a consequence, South Africa's delegation to GATT was provisionally committed to complying with the GATT Secretariat's proposals, pending a process of consultation with the ANC. Indeed, in July 1993, the South African delegation, armed with a mandate that included the ANC, labour and business, was able to make a firm offer to GATT. The South Africans made the following commitments on the eve of democracy:

- To increase the number of tariffs 'bound' to the WTO from 58% to 98%.

- To replace all quota regimes with tariffs.

- To rationalize its complex tariff structure from 109,000 to 6000 individual tariff lines.

- To reduce the maximum tariff level from 100% to 30 %.

- Terminate its General Incentive Scheme (GEIS) of export subsidies to local firms by 1997.

- To phase-out local content measures in the automobile industry (Hirsh, 1995; Marais, 1998).

As Marais (1998) has shown, in its tariff reductions, the South African government went well beyond its commitments to the GATT. For instance, contrary to South Africa's GATT offer to lower the telecommunications tariff to 20%, the Department of Trade and Industry announced a lowering of tariffs to 0% in the sector (1998: 129). In the auto industry, South Africa's offer meant a reduction of protective tariffs from 110% to 85 % in 1994 (Bond, 2000:67). This prompted an ANC discussion document in the 1997 Policy Conference to proclaim that while "protectionism of the sort applied in previous years, is no longer an option…we must recognize that being more free trade than the norm is unlikely to bring us real benefits" (1997:36). Meanwhile, on realizing the full implications of the implementation of the GATT deal for their industry and jobs, the National Union of Metal Workers of South Africa (NUMSA) threatened strike action in protest. However, the planned action had to be hastily called-off when it came to light that former NUMSA leader (and then deputy Finance Minister) Alec Erwin had in fact, on behalf of his union, consented to the tariff cuts, several months earlier (ibid; *Sunday Times*, 4th September, 1996). The rationale behind South Africa's uncharacteristic haste into liberalization was provided by Department of Trade and Industry economist and former University of Cape Town academic, Alan Hirsh:

> There is nothing in the GATT arrangement to stop a country liberalizing
> more quickly than it is required by the Marrakech Agreement. Indeed, it
> is likely to win admiration. And it may well be appropriate that we follow
> such an accelerated programme for some items (1994: 45)

Thus, the East Asian policy elites at a similar stage of development, were worrying about strategies and tactics to manage, manipulate, navigate and interact with the world trading system. They sought to do this in ways that would advance the putative developmental priorities of their respective countries, the preoccupation and obsession of South Africa's policy elites was 'winning admiration'. In the meantime, the World Bank and the Organisation for Economic Cooperation and Development (OECD) had calculated that complying with GATT requirements would cost South Africa $400million in net annual lost tariff revenues by year 2002 (cited in Bond, 2000:47). The OECD study further suggested that the major beneficiaries of the Uruguay Round would be North America and Europe, while Africa including South Africa, would be net losers (*Third World Economics*, November, 1993: 1- 15).

At the same time, the United Nations Development Programme (UNDP) labeled the WTO an 'unequal partnership', whose formation had accentuated the inequality between north and south, by entrenching and institutionalizing unequal development through the world trading system (UNDP, 1997:86). With respect to agriculture, for example, the Marrakech Agreement gave rise to a situation where the producer subsidy equivalent for European Union products was 50%, while for South Africa it was 15%. Such products were, in terms of the Marrakech Agreement, expected to compete on equal terms both in the European Union market, in third country export markets, and importantly, in the domestic South African market itself (ibid). Interestingly, the study concluded that the Uruguay Round made no provisions for "effective disciplines on export subsidization" (1997:86).

Furthermore, from the perspective of the prospects for developmentalist state construction, the Marrakech Agreement discouraged active state intervention in at least two other ways. First, state action in encouraging export-oriented investment would fall foul of provisions of GATT's Trade Related Investment Measures (TRIMS). In East Asia and elsewhere, such action has included:

- Local content requirements (the foreign company must include a specified minimum ratio of local material in its production).

- Export requirements (obliging a foreign investor to export a fixed percentage of production).

- Manufacturing limitations (reserving certain markets for local firms to protect them from foreign competition).

- Local equity (specifying that a certain percentage of the company's equity be held by local investors) (Khor, 1991:131).

The TRIMS, which insist on equal treatment for all investors and services, thus severely curtail state intervention of the kind indicated here. Secondly, the government is limited in its capacity to use subsidies to encourage exports. In South Africa's case, the General Export Incentive Scheme (GEIS) had to be abolished, as part of the country's commitment to the WTO (Hirsh, 1994: 45). Both forms of intervention were extensively used in the East Asian developmental states, but in terms of WTO arrangements, are not readily available to the South African state (ibid).

Nonetheless, the thinking behind the ANC's acceptance of rules that were surely inimical to a developmental role for the state seemed to be informed, above all, by a firm conviction that, under the circumstances, prudence was the prudent thing to do. That the WTO arrangements would severely circumscribe and undermine the role of the state in driving a developmentalist programme akin to the East Asian projects was not in dispute. To this end, one of the key drivers and authors of South Africa's shift into neo-liberalism, Trade and Industry Minister, Alec Erwin, would concede later: "The generically most problematic issues for a broad spectrum of developing countries in the WTO are agricultural protectionism in industrial countries and the curtailment of the role of the state" (*Global Dialogue*, April, 1999:2). In a lecture to American policy makers at Georgetown University in Washington DC, in May 2000, President Thabo Mbeki articulated his perspective regarding the state of play in the global socio-economic and political arena:

> Many of our countries….do not have and are not likely to have in the foreseeable future, the strength themselves to determine on their own what should happen to their economies. The more they get integrated into the world economy, the further will this capacity be reduced (Mbeki, 2000).

As well as repeating the World Bank mantra that attractiveness to international investors is the only way to stimulate growth in developing countries, Mbeki continued:

> …the world economy disposes of sufficient capital resources whose injection in our countries as long terms investment, would succeed to take us to the 'take-off' stage (ibid).

All the MERG Report/RDP's call for monitoring and directing investment in accordance with the country's developmental needs, were set aside for an unconditional plea for investment in order to trigger the illusive 'take-off' stage. Also, it would seem from this intervention that the ANC elites had satisfied themselves of the adversities of the global balance of forces and thus the limits of state-led developmental policies as called for by the MERG Report and the RDP. Arising from such analyses of the global balance of forces is an ideological and strategic path of what is deemed feasible under contemporary global socio-economic realities. The leadership's perception that there was no alternative to the neo-liberal agenda was put in context in the ANC's 1997 policy conference, partly in response to the ongoing (increasingly heated) economic policy debate within the movement thus:

> No country can maintain protective tariffs and regulatory barriers at the levels they were in the past – unless it is prepared to cut itself off entirely from the global trading system. As protective barriers are lowered, producers oriented towards domestic markets will face increasing competition from potential imports. At the same time, taking advantage of the opportunities available through engaging in export trade has become an objective of many countries (ANC, 1997:35).

The discussion document further argued that, while the East Asian NICs initiated their developmental drive in relatively favourable global circumstances, "South Africa faces the prospect to realize its objectives in this regard at a time when many other countries are trying to do precisely the same" (ibid). This is yet another confirmation of the control persistently exercised by the South African elites over the country's economic policy trajectory. What is more, it is a significant refutation of any approach that neglects the centrality of agency (intentional action) in explaining the role of the world trading system in influencing and shaping policy in South Africa. While an 'impossibility thesis' is clearly evident in the ANC elite's approach, there was also a sense that the developmentalist objectives could be attained (over time) via the neo-liberal route, even if implemented briefly in order to 'stem market volatility'.

In his report to the 49th National Conference of the ANC, Trevor Manuel, emphasized the same sentiment. The report stated that, because of apartheid distortions and requirements of the world trading system, South Africa had to comply fully with the 'rules of the game' in order: " to improve on our ability to produce quality goods and services to meet the basic needs of our people at affordable prices, creating jobs and increasing the local processing and manufacturing of our raw materials" (Manuel, 1994).

Interestingly, the same argument was advanced to justify the government's insistence on honouring the apartheid debt. A large section of anti-apartheid organisations (at home and abroad) under the auspices of the Jubilee 2000 group, including the government's own allies (SACP, SANCO and COSATU), called for the apartheid debt to be written-off. Research from Switzerland and Germany showed that the apartheid foreign debt hovered at around $26 billion (*Mail and Guardian*, 17 September 1999). According to Jubilee 2000, this was an odious debt whose repayment should not be the responsibility of the democratic government. For its part, the South African government has refused to support the campaign, even surreptitiously, pointing to the negative effect such a stance would have on financial markets and more generally, on investor confidence in the new South Africa (ibid). This is despite the massive international good will towards Mandela and the ANC at the time.

Therefore, although the WTO deal came at enormous cost with respect to the state's room for action and intervention, it was the view of the leadership that 'playing by the rules of the game' and in the process (hopefully) extracting massive investment flows, was the only way to go. Nelson Mandela's address to the World Economic Development Congress in September 1993, illustrates the ANC's leadership's approach, even as early drafts of the RDP were on the table for discussion:

> We are therefore ready to address such matters as the security of investments, repatriation of profits and dividends, competitive rates of taxation and stable and predictable public policies. As a token of our commitment to normalize our economic relations with the rest of the world, we are working with the present (apartheid) government of South Africa and other important players to negotiate an agreement on our tariffs in the context of the Uruguay Round.

And crucially:

> we are acutely conscious of the fact that the whole world is competing for limited investment capital. In this regard, we are determined to ensure that the new South Africa is as attractive to the international investor as any other country (Mandela, 1993).

Therefore, the determination of the ANC elite to 'normalise' the economy in the context of the Uruguay Round, coupled with undertakings finally made to the WTO, in part, explicate the matter. The global policy environment being what it is, key sections of the ANC did not only meekly succumb to this reality, there is determination and strategic intent in how trade issues are negotiated. Also, these discussions occurred in the context of heated internal economic policy debate within the alliance (where alternative trajectories were put forth), but our elites were determined to defend and push through the neo-liberal policies. This, more than anything, demonstrate a mutually reinforcing interaction between structure and agency. Next, the focus is on the role of other international players in the South African transition – the World Bank and IMF.

The World Bank and IMF in the South African transition

The World Bank and the IMF played a significant role in actively encouraging the abandonment of statist and interventionist policies in South Africa. These institutions, far from standing on the side-lines, were active participants and must take a large part of the credit for the current 'pragmatic' policy perspectives embraced by the South African government. This section shows that relying only on the 'intellectual and international policy environment' (as an explanatory variable) is inadequate in itself for explaining the policy shift in South Africa. What is required, in addition, is the examination of the agential factors at work in the international environment, and crucially, an analysis of how, who and in what direction such factors actually shaped the intellectual and economic policy context.

The World Bank and the ANC

A brief look at the ANC programmes and documents prior to 1994 shows a huge level of contempt for the IMF and World Bank. And given its history as a national liberation movement and a 'disciplined force of the left', that kind of ideological contempt for Bank and Fund policies, should really come as no surprise. Indeed, as shown in the previous chapter, ANC policies and ideological outlook have historically tended to be diametrically opposed to those advocated by the Bank and the Fund. United States Ambassador to Pretoria between 1992- 1995, Princeton Lyman recalled this hostility in his interactions with ANC leaders in this period. Lyman observed that: "They had even more disdain for the IMF, they felt: this is our policy, we will develop it ourselves. So, they were extremely sensitive about the IMF and World Bank. The leadership from top to bottom were consumed with not falling into a debt trap" (interview: 20 January, 2003).

The same observations were made by the World Bank in a review of the relationship between itself and South Africa, prior to the 1994 democratic elections, in its review, the Bank noted that:

> The Bank then had a very negative image in the country, being perceived by members of the liberation movements, many academics, and other sectors of the country's society as a sponsor of very orthodox and conservative economic policies which, in that perception, had already failed to achieve positive results elsewhere in Africa (World Bank, 1995:2).

This perception of the Bank and the IMF by the ANC leadership thus sets the context within which to appreciate what Bond (2000) has referred to as the elite's ideological shift from developmental statist to market centred policies. It is from this perspective that the extent and success of the Bank's active influencing and coaxing should be viewed. Here, I use the World Bank's "A Successful Approach to participation: The World Bank's Relationship with South Africa", *Working Paper* No.57 July, 1995, as basis for exploration of the Bank's strategy in South Africa.

The Bank's Strategy

Given its inability to interact with the apartheid government in the way it did with other Bank member countries, in the case of South Africa the Bank sought to devise a strategy that would popularize its views among all the key social actors in the country (NGOs, academics, business, labour and political organisations). At the same time, such a strategy would lay the basis for a post-apartheid dispensation, ensuring that whatever the outcome of a democratic election, the new government (or at least important sections within it) would be well disposed towards the Bank and its thinking (World Bank, 1995). The strategy itself had two key discernible elements.

Informal Discussion and Informal Discussion Papers

Such discussions, according to the World Bank review document, were deliberately inclusive and focused on a wide variety of policy topics including macro-economic issues, trade policies, agricultural policies and employment and wage issues (World Bank, 1995: 6- 12). More significantly, from such 'informal discussions' the Bank was able to craft 'informal discussion papers', which it then circulated to relevant structures, most of which had participants in the 'informal' discussions. It would then be the task of these individuals to explain and defend the intricacies of the documents to their colleagues (ibid:12). And so too, would the folly of populist and outmoded policies still held by some in the liberation and trade union movement. In his foreword to two World Bank discussion papers, the Bank's Southern African Department Director, Stephen Denning, underlined the significance of key South African political and economic actors in the compilation of the reports. In the foreword to the Bank's "An Economic Perspective on South Africa" published in 1993, Denning shows that the Bank had been engaged in a protracted and extensive consultation process with a range of South African social, economic and political actors, and that the report represented and was a product of that interaction (World Bank, 1993). Also, with respect to the 'Informal Discussion Paper on Aspects of the Economy of South Africa' published in 1994, Denning emphasized that the Bank's different 'Informal Papers' on South Africa were in fact a product of extensive inputs from a "broadly representative group of South Africans, and involving institutions and researchers" (World Bank, 1994). The informal nature of these forums allowed the Bank to engage with the participants in a relaxed atmosphere, where there was no pressure to articulate or represent strict party political positions. In other words, these were essentially mining research and policy formation exercises. What is more, the technical approaches adopted to tackle the problems and reach solutions made it possible for ideological differences to be rendered largely irrelevant in the workshops. Several documents were crafted in this way and circulated as 'informal discussion documents' including the following:

- 'How can South African Manufacturing Efficiently Create Employment? An analysis of the Impact of Trade and Industrial Policy' (January, 1992).

- South Africa: Macro-economic issues for the Transition' (May, 1992).

- An Analysis of Employment and Wage Behaviour in South Africa' (Ocotber 1992).

- 'South Africa: A Review of Trade Policies' (August 1993).

- 'South Africa: Characteristics of and Constraints facing Black Business in South Africa: Survey Results (November, 1993).

- 'South African Agriculture: Structure, Performance and Policies' (April, 1994).

- Financing South Africa's Metropolitan Areas' (April, 1994).

Patrick Bond (2001) would later conduct an extensive survey of the World Bank's policy advice and its consequences in South Africa. For Bond, as for Cherry (1995), the real impact of the Bank was not through lending, but in policy advice in South Africa. According to Bond, the Agricultural policy discussion document alluded to above:

> ...is a good example of the World Bank's policy advice. The subsequent implementation of that document's recommendations led to the redistribution of less than one per cent of good agricultural land to the landless black people, instead of the 30 per cent advocated by the RDP (Interview:30 September, 2002).

In this context, the fact that the new government announced an Agricultural White Paper "largely based on the conclusions of the joint technical work undertaken in the informal workshops between 1992 -1994" (World Bank,

1995: 13; see also Draft White Paper on Agriculture, RSA, 1994), was no co-incidence. Instead, this was a reflection of the effectiveness of Bank strategy in the South African context (World Bank, 1995: 7). Importantly, the Bank's objective through its informal workshops had always been to cultivate trust with the social actors, and to make sure the product was in the end "owned" by the participants, and by extension, their organisations (ibid).

Capacity Building and Education

The Bank also initiated a six-month internship programme for South Africans. The interns were deployed in various divisions of the Bank and worked with different country teams (ibid:8). The rationale behind this exercise, and certainly the advantage for the Bank, was that the interns were not only exposed to the operations and workings of the Bank, but were also able to appreciate the significance of the Bank in the economic affairs of the rest of the world. The first group of interns commenced their internship in October 1992 and were nominated by the ANC. And crucially: "Since many of these interns have influential positions in South Africa, the programme has made an important contribution towards clarifying the South African perception of Bank objectives, policies and procedures" World Bank, 1995: 8).

An important benefit for Bank strategists was that the impact of their work on South African decision makers did not have to wait for the election of a new government. Since 1990, the economic policy debate had been raging within the ANC, with hegemony shifting constantly between developmental statist and interventionist approaches (MERG Report, RDP), and neo-liberal market centred perspectives (RDP White Paper, closure of the RDP Office, GEAR). This provided the perfect opportunity to start influencing the outcome, especially within what was widely regarded as the *de facto* new government – the ANC. To this end, the World Bank could observe with a good measure of satisfaction that: "During the formulation of ANC economic policy in 1992, the ANC's exposure to the Bank's policy work was evident in the party's policy documentation that emerged" (1995: 13).

Thus, the confusion over the fact that the MERG Report was initiated 'at the highest level' of the ANC leadership, and its rejection a year later at the same level, can be explained as a reflection of the ideological battles within the movement, and no doubt in part, accentuated by the Bank's strategy in that country. Note for instance, that after the MERG document was rejected in September 1993, ostensibly for its statist underpinnings (Marais, 1998; Bond, 2000; Fine, 2002; Sender, 2002), a document advocating similar policy positions emerged from another ally of the ANC – COSATU. The Reconstruction Accord too, advocated state interventionist policies, nationalization of strategic industries and more broadly, socio-economic policies in line with developmentalist state projects. COSATU's insistence on pursuing the 'accord' as platform for engagement with the ANC, in some respects not only re-imposed some of the rejected MERG principles, but also pre-empted the ANC in the launch, at its own initiative, of an economic policy and election manifesto. No doubt COSATU's persistence in holding the ANC government accountable (through a set of economic principles broadly shared by the two organisations) had to some extent to do with COSATU's apprehensions about the economic policy trajectory in the ANC. Also, the acceptance of the broad principles of the accord had in part to do with electoral considerations. Nonetheless, the RDP in its broad sense enjoyed a brief period of hegemony, which was rudely disrupted by the White Paper's interpretation of its broad principles. The social conflict engendered by the fight for the 'soul' of the RDP, provided the state with the opportunity to intervene decisively by articulating an ideologically less ambiguous economic policy strategy – GEAR. It is thus also reasonable to suggest that the zig-zag in the ANC policy positions was in part, inspired by both the internal policy differences on the one had, and the influence the Bank was exerting on key elements of the movement on the other.

At the same time, however, it is also clear that the Bank was not exerting itself on an unwilling and unsuspecting group in the ANC. Princeton Lyman, who was intimately and constantly appraised of the ANC's internal economic policy debates and their interactions with the Bank and Fund, confirms that the elites were not bamboozled into conservative market economics. Instead, the ANC was determined to take any policy decision with its eyes wide open, and with a thorough understanding of the political, social and economic implications of each policy adopted (Interview: 20 January, 2003). Baroness Lynda Chalker, British Overseas Development Secretary and Minister for Africa between 1986- 1997, also confirmed the same impression. Chalker who started to have regular 'formal' contact with the ANC leadership in 1992, noted that:

> ...they were reading and watching what was happening in other parts of the world. So, I think that shift to a more liberal economic policy partly came through realizing what was happening in the rest of the world. I think that's always struck me with some of the younger politicians in South Africa, it was not imposed, it was chosen (interview: 21 January, 2003).

In this context, then, the change from suspicion and hostility towards the Bank and Fund, to active participation in their programmes becomes perfectly plausible. So, too, does the fact that ANC president, Nelson Mandela, met the president of the World Bank in December 1991, "and requested the Bank to gear up for lending to a new government" (World Bank, 1995: 11). The programmes themselves, and the participation of the ANC elite in them, were in part the Bank's response to Mandela's request, which was later endorsed by F.W. De Klerk (ibid).

This section therefore further demonstrates the validity of the argument that the new relationship between the ANC and the Bank was in the ANC's view, not a 'lame capitulation to the dictates' of the Bank. Instead, it was a mutually beneficial relationship entered into consciously and deliberately. Viewed from this angle, it becomes less of a mystery why the ANC leadership was taking the initiative in nominating participants for the Bank's various activities, including the internships. Also, while the notion of the 'international economic and intellectual environment' partly illuminates the reasons for the policy shifts within the ANC, it does not account for the agential factors or the specific ways in which this environment concretely manifested itself in the South African policy arena.

The IMF

ANC relations with the IMF have been particularly hostile for two reasons. First, whereas the Bank cut ties with the apartheid regime, as part of the ANC' sanctions against apartheid drive, the IMF never really ceased its dealings with that regime (Bond, 2001). In the late 1970s and early 1980s, following the Soweto riots and the subsequent price crash, the IMF offered the apartheid regime a $2 billion bailout loan. It was only after the US Congress intervened in 1983 (as a consequence of pressure from the Anti-Apartheid Movement) to prohibit the IMF from further dealings with South Africa, that the IMF reluctantly withdrew the offer (ibid). Secondly, the IMF had a very negative view of South Africa at the time (early 1990s) and the ANC leadership (Layman, 20 January, 2003). However, once the ANC and NP had committed themselves to negotiating a democratic transition, and once president George Bush, after talks with President De Klerk on 24 September 1990, proclaimed that the democratization process in South Africa was irreversible, the IMF changed its attitude (De Klerk, 1999: 189).

The IMF's re-entry into South Africa was facilitated by President Bush's remarks on 24th September, and his subsequent call to Congress to reconsider the relevance of the Comprehensive Anti-Apartheid Act. George Bush had observed of De Klerk's historic 2nd February, 1990 speech: "This is a moment in history which many believed would never be attained. I really firmly believe that this progress is irreversible" (*Congressional Quarterly*,

1991: 4778). And with that, Bush officially lifted sanctions against South Africa on 10th July 1991, amid strong opposition from a significant number of Democrats and the Black Caucus (ibid). These groups, like the ANC felt that it was way too early to lift sanctions against South Africa. It was, however, only after Nelson Mandela's call to the United Nations Special Committee against Apartheid for all sanctions to be lifted, that IMF could really get actively involved in South Africa's economic policy debate (*The Star,* 25 September, 1993). Up to that point, the IMF intervention was mainly in the area of policy advice and influencing the economic policy debate through its 'Working Papers', 'Occasional Papers' and 'Staff Reports'. Key among these were the following:

- 'Apartheid, Growth and Income Distribution in South Africa: Past History and Future Prospects', *Working Paper* No. 91/116 (1991).

- 'Economic Policies for a New South Africa', *Occasional Paper* No. 91 (1992).

The central thrust of both papers was to show the dangers of state intervention in the economy and to argue the case for lean governance, financial liberalization and deregulation. Indeed, since this period, the ANC has, in large measure, stuck almost religiously to IMF inspired policies, prompting the IMF's World Economic Outlook (WEO) to single out South Africa for praise for its persistent pursuit, in recent years, of liberalization of inward and outward capital flows (WEO, 2001; *Finance Week,* 24 November, 2001).

Almost immediately after Mandela's call in the UN, Michel Camdessus, IMF Managing Director, pledged a loan of $850 million to help the transition process, provided a 'letter of intent' signed by both the ANC and NP outlining the country's future economic policy was made available (*Sunday Star,* 26 September, 1993). To this end, the IMF Survey of 10 January 1994, was able to report:

> The IMF has approved a drawing by South Africa equivalent to SDR 614.43 million (about $849 million) under the compensatory and contingency facility (CCF). For the period ahead, the authorities are resolved upon a cautious fiscal and monetary stance that is broadly supported by South Africa's major political groups (*IMF Survey,* 10 January, 1994).

Although the exact contents of the letter of intent remain 'restricted', South Africa's Business Day, did somehow get hold of a copy of the agreement and a summary was printed in the March 24th 1994 edition of the *Business Day*. The letter of intent was ostensibly leaked to reassure those investors and potential investors who were still in doubt regarding the ANC's commitment to 'pragmatic liberal policies' on the eve of the first democratic elections in South Africa. Moreover, the *Business Day* editorial added: "Secrecy over the agreement between government (NP) , the ANC and the IMF on the IMF's special \$850 million loan to this country added to the insecurities of financiers looking to South Africa" (24th March, 1994).

Key aspects of the leaked letter seemed to speak precisely to investor concerns and by extension, were largely in line with general IMF conditionalities. The agreement committed the new government to redressing social backlogs through a macro-economic policy package that would both respect financial constraints and promote investor confidence in the country's economic management (ibid). With respect to fiscal policy, the government would not be pressured by high expectations or the massive socio-economic deficit in the country into spending patterns that would undermine confidence in the new South Africa. The parties however, recognized the significance of addressing people's needs in ways that would sustain social stability. Non-interest recurrent expenditures would be lowered by 22% of GDP in the fiscal year 1994/1995; the figure for fiscal year 1993/1994 was 23% of GDP (ibid). To demonstrate its commitment to fiscal prudence, the government would endeavour to reduce the government deficit to 6% of GDP. More explicitly, the endeavour would be to reduce the budget deficit from 8.5 % of GDP in 1992/93 to a projected 7% in 1993/94. Furthermore, the public service bill would be contained, and this meant that there would be no real increases in wage rates.

The National Party's newly embraced neo-liberal monetary policies would be maintained after the 1994 elections. In addition, there would be significant reductions of tariffs and a general liberalization of trade, deregulation and rapid movement away from anti- GATT protectionist policies *(Business Day*, 24th March, 194). The contents of the letter of intent and the fact of its signing by the ANC continues to be the subject of extreme interest in academic circles and political commentary within South Africa (Marais, 1998; Bond, 2000). The dominant explanation for ANC acquiescence to the demands of the IMF seems to reside mainly in the ANC's alleged capitulation to neo-liberal pressure. Far less attention is paid to the leading role the ANC leadership (notably, Mandela, Mbeki, Erwin etc..) played in actively asking both the Fund and the Bank, for policy advice, training and international connections. A good example of this response is given by former Cape Town Anglican Archbishop, Jongonkulu Ndungane. In his view: "they [ANC] have bought lock, stock and barrel to the policies of the IMF. The challenge I want to throw to Trevor Manuel is to think again about what the International financial institutions are saying" (cited in Ashdon, 2001).

Director of the anti- IMF/World Bank/World Trade Organisation inter-national NGO – '50 Years is Enough' – Njoki Njenu concurred with the Archbishop:

> South Africa for me represented an opportunity to do it right, to do it dif-ferently, it really makes me sad, I think it makes a lot of people sad to see South Africa following the rest of the third world, allowing these institu-tions to dictate their economic policies (ibid).

Both arguments base their claims on the assumption the ANC leadership had somehow been duped by the IMF into the commitments in the letter of in-tent. Moreover, these arguments assume that the ANC leadership and South African state actors were not only overwhelmed by the might of the IMF, but also that they were unwilling or even reluctant objects in a process over which they had no control. For example, after the MERG Report in 1993, heated debate was raging within the liberation movement, reflecting two broad but diametrically divergent views of the policy direction to be pursued by the movement (once in government). These were views generally favour-ing a strong leadership role for the state, nationalization of strategic assets (this view found expression in the MERG Report and earlier versions of the RDP), while on the other hand, a view was represented favouring a leading role for the market, deregulation and the intensification of privatization (this found expression in the RDP White Paper and more un-apologetically, in GEAR). I suggest that until 1996, the leadership was compelled to 'balance' these essentially antagonistic policy perspectives in order to maintain a mea-sure of cohesion within the rank and file. Indeed, the insistence by the leader-ship that the RDP and GEAR were complimentary was in keeping with this effort of 'taking the membership with us'. Thabo Mbeki's comments at the SACP conference in 1998 were typical:

> One of the issues which the right wing parties in our country are very fond of repeating is that our movement has abandoned the RDP. By this means, they hope to turn the masses of our people who voted for us in 1994 against our movement, by seeking to project the notion that we have betrayed the trust that the people placed in the ANC. For some strange reason, when work is then done to translate the perspectives contained in the RDP into actual figures, this is then interpreted as a replacement of the RDP by GEAR (SACP Conference, 1998).

However, *strategic and intentional action* and the ANC's deliberate and conscious orchestration of an intimate working relationship with the Fund is undeniable. An ANC press statement issues in September 1993 illustrates the point:

Over the past two years the ANC has sent delegations to attend the annual meetings of the IMF and World Bank in order to acquaint ourselves with the procedures and functioning of these organisations. This year's annual meeting has coincided with the call by the ANC to lift sanctions. Therefore, our delegation is in Washington to interact with the IMF, World Bank and governments present in preparation for South Africa's re-engagement. ANC President Mandela, who is currently visiting the United States, met the Managing Director of the IMF during which frank and positive discussions were held. We anticipate that the private sector and multi-national institutions, such as the IMF/WB, will begin the process of re-engaging with South Africa. Therefore, any loan from the IMF should be seen within the context of support for the urgent reconstruction and development efforts of our people (www.anc.org.za/ancdocs/pr/1993/pr09h00.html).

From this, the active role of the ANC in driving and strengthening working relations with the IMF is quite apparent. The most plausible explanation for this change in attitude towards the IMF appears to be the ANC's conviction that the IMF way was the best way to achieve the 'urgent reconstruction and development efforts' to which the ANC was committed. Thus, while the international environment was hostile to the implementation of policies akin to East Asian developmental state projects (structure), it is clear that both the IMF and the ANC played a significant role in shifting the economic policy debate in the direction of market liberalization (agency). Structure and agency thus conspired to shift the economic policy paradigm in South Africa, as reflected by various moments in the evolution of economic policy in South Africa.

The Role of the United States

Over and above the efforts of the WB/IMF in shaping and influencing the economic policy debate and its outcome in South Africa in the early 1990s, Princeton Lyman has also shown the significance of the role of the United States government, through its embassy in Pretoria. Indeed, the US government had been aware of the sharp differences within the ANC alliance on the subject of a future economic policy. It was thus important from an American foreign policy and ideological viewpoint to seize the moment and capitalize on these differences. After all, for the longest time, US policy towards South Africa had been informed above all else, by cold war strategic considerations. Herbst (2003) has accessed hitherto classified intelligence reports of the Central Intelligence Agency's (CIA) work on South Africa and the ANC. This is used to reconstruct an interesting picture of the US attitude toward South Africa and the ANC. For instance, a Department of State – 'National

Policy Paper: South Africa' outlined US objectives with respect to South Africa in the early 1970s:

> To align this strategic ally solidly with the Western Powers or at the minimum, to deny it to the Communist Bloc... Difficult as it may be, South Africa's basic value to the free world emphasizes the need to reverse destructive and disruptive influences now present in its situation (cited in Herbst, 2003:95).

However, as the Soviet Union was continuing to experience ever more difficult political and economic problems, and as the anti- apartheid struggle intensified in the mid-1980s, US policy was beginning to reflect these changes too. According to the CIA's intelligence estimate of 1986, Moscow's ability to 'create any insurmountable problem for Pretoria', was regarded as negligible (ibid:102). And for this reason, US National Decision Directorate 187 (written by George Bush senior) was able to outline the new objective of US policy in South Africa as that of "promoting peaceful change away from apartheid, to a system which provides justice and opportunity for all with a government based on the consent of the people" (ibid: 103). This was a significant policy shift, and opened the way for greater American involvement in crafting and defining post-apartheid social, political and especially economic policies. These possibilities were further strengthened by the CIA's work on the ANC. Contrary to the widely held view in the US Administration that the ANC was wholly and inexorably influenced by Moscow and the South African Communist Party, the CIA's intelligence work actually uncovered important differences in the movement's leadership, especially with respect to economic policy (Interview with Lyman, 20 January, 2003). Indeed, as Lyman has contended in his book, this among other things, led to the initiation by George Shultz (US Secretary of State under President Ronald Reagan) of the first ever meeting between a senior US government official and the ANC. Shultz met the late ANC President Oliver Tambo in 1987(Lyman, 2002: 46). In June 1992, the CIA's National Intelligence estimate had this to say on internal leadership differences within the ANC:

> The ANC is not a monolith, nor do we believe it is under the firm control of any one cohesive group. The ANC's alliance with the SACP will survive over the coming year. But differences over future economic policy, ANC attempts to broaden its base of support among relatively conservative voters will ultimately strain the alliance, perhaps to breaking point (cited in Herbst, 2003: 105).

These reports were thus crucial in reshaping American policy towards South

Africa more generally and specifically, towards the ANC. Capitalising on these differences, the US set out to start engaging the ANC leadership and exposing them to the realities of international political economics in the post-cold war era (Interviews with Lyman, 20th January, 2003; Chalker, 21 January, 2003). This approach was designed both to sharpen the differences and thereby hasten the demise of the ANC/SACP alliance, at the same time, it provided the opportunity to directly influence the economic policy debate by arming those among the leadership who were amenable to Washington's economic principles. To this end, Lyman revealed that the US was "actively courting people like Trevor Manuel and Tito Mboweni and saying to them that: look, if you want to have investment in your country, you cannot go down that road" (Lyman, 20 January, 2003). More concretely, the US government was concerned to provide funding for research, conferences and training of key ANC economists. To this end, the US embassy in Pretoria also facilitated a 12-month training programme for leading ANC economist Max Sisulu at the John F. Kennedy School in Harvard. ANC Department of Economic Policy Head, Tito Mboweni was sent to several programmes in the United States, including one on anti-trust legislation (Lyman, 2002: 96-97). Lyman recalled "Mboweni, who had been a long-time supporter of nationalization of key industries, became over time a champion of anti-trust policies instead" (ibid:97). However, for Lyman, two interventions from the US government stood out. One was a series of discussions/workshops run by the Embassy and coordinated by Lyman's Economic Counselor Donald Steinberg (later US Ambassador to Angola). Lyman recalled: "we had a series for two years in Steinberg's home, bringing people together, Tito, Trevor etc. would come along and they would meet once a month- and a lot of ideas got exchanged through that programme (Lyman).

The second area of intervention was through the so-called 'Mont Fleur Scenarios'. This project was funded by a range of private companies and donors including the Swiss Development Agency and the United States. The objective of the project was to put different economic models (and possible development paths) for South Africa, to review the strengths and weaknesses of each model (ibid). Also, the project brought together a diverse group of leading politicians, academics, activists and businessmen to ponder the economic future of South Africa between 1992- 2002 (*Deeper News*, 1999: 1). The four different models (scenarios) that were the object of discussion were referred to as the Mont Fleur Scenarios, after the name of the small suburb near Stellenbosch in the Western Cape, where the meetings were held in 1991. Of the 22 participants in this project, four were leading members of the ANC notably, Mboweni, Manuel, Rob Davies, Saki Macozoma and Gugile

189

Nkwinti (ibid). There were other important political and economic notables who participated in the Mont Fleur process, they included:

Mosebyane Malatsi	Pan Africanist Congress (PAC)
Mahlomola Skosana	National Council Trade Union (NACTU)
Koosan Kaylan	Shell – South Africa
Johan Liebenberg	Chamber of Mines
Christo Wiese	Economic Advisory Council of the President (De Klerk)
Vincent Mapai	Associate professor – UWC

The merits and de-merits of the following scenarios were considered by the group, all named after different birds:

The Ostrich Scenario

This scenario concerned the possibility of the National party government, buoyed by its success in the whites-only referendum (in support of a nego-tiated settlement) in 1992 and thus deciding to harden its negotiation posi-tions. This in turn, would lead to the escalation of socio-political conflict and the 'Lebanonisation' of South Africa, where the country's infrastructure is virtually destroyed by the conflict. Like an Ostrich facing trouble, the group felt that such a scenario would be tantamount to government burying its head in the sand. It was agreed that this was not desirable and, it was in the interest of all parties to ensure the success of a negotiated settlement.

Lame Duck Scenario

This scenario represented a drawn out and protracted negotiations processes which eventually lead to a weak government (an enforced coalition), which incapacitated the new government. Such a government, the group, agreed, would lack decisiveness to play any significant role in leading the transi-tion process. International investors would remain uncertain, and this would thereby lead to limited, if any, investment, growth and development in the country. Also, the economic 'take-off' would thus never materialize (*Deeper News*, 1999: 13).

The Icarus Scenario

The scenario given here was one of a popular government spurred on by a popular mandate and massive redistributive demands to implement popular but unsustainable policies. Such policies would include huge deficit spending, inducing a brief spurt of high economic growth inspired by price controls, strict foreign exchange controls and heavy government involvement in the economy. The scenario showed and the group agreed that, in due course, such an approach would lead to an economic slump, worse than that inherited from the apartheid regime. The assault on Icarus was, of course, also an assault on many aspects of the Freedom Charter and the MERG Report. It also helped the [neo-liberal] cause that the policy options in this scenario were vulgarized and the possible negative outcomes exaggerated and crude.

The Flight of the Flamingos

The new government in this scenario adopts sound economic policies and observes macro-economic constraints. The government also observes international monetary, trade, and economic conventions as exercised through such organisations as the IMF, WB and the WTO. In so doing, the government's approach created credibility for the transition in the eyes of the international community. This attracts much needed investment into the country and above all, there is social and macroeconomic stability. The economic 'take-off' therefore, not unlike a family of flamingos, is slow, but steady and in time, is effective and impacts the whole country. Hence the flight of the flamingos. Thus Lyman argued: "The scenario that came out best was the Flamingo...was the policy that basically you now see in South Africa, which says that you start off at a sort of modest rate and then steady and steady growth takes place. And that had a lot to do with Mont Fleur Scenarios" (Interview, 2003).

According to Patrick Bond (2000) however, the Mont Fleur process was rigged from the start, and its fundamental mission was to discredit the ANC alliance's 'growth through redistribution' strategy, the maiming of poor Icarus' (2000:71). Nonetheless, the bulk of the political and business elites were keen on the 'flight of the flamingos' model, including F.W. De Klerk (ibid). Within the ANC too, this scenario found resonance and received good reviews. Rob Davies, SACP Central Committee member had this to say on the feasibility of the different scenarios: "The Flamingo scenario sketches the bare bones of a successful national democratic project of the kind that is feasible under prevailing conditions in South Africa" (Deeper News, 1999: 18).

However, like the World Bank strategy discussed earlier in this chapter, the Mont Fleur process according to Adam Kahane – facilitator of the process – was not a strict and formal political forum. Instead:

> The process was an informal, open conversation. The Mont Fleur team gave vivid, concise names to important phenomena that were widely known, and previously could be neither discussed nor addressed. The aim of such non-negotiating processes is…to find and enlarge common ground (www. futurenet.org/7peacebuilding/innovations.htm.).

These, therefore, were the key processes that contributed to the re-shaping of ANC economic policy in the early 1990s. From all possible points of influence discussed thus far, there is no evidence to suggest that the ANC was either duped or unwillingly compelled to adopt market centred policies. Instead, the available evidence seems to confirm the active role of the ANC leadership in the evolution of economic policy in South Africa. Moreover, the voluntary and intentional role of the ANC is clearly evident, and so too, are the reasons for this policy shift. Nowhere are these as clearly stated as in the ANC National Executive Committee's response to its allies, during the ongoing internal leadership conflict over economic policy. In its 'Briefing Notes' released in October 2001, the NEC argued: "we are made to believe that GEAR is the problem, however, we go into detail logically to explain why GEAR was necessary at that stage to stabilize our economy and prevent a meltdown; to acknowledge that within GEAR were compromises – bitter medicine – without which we could not have cured the ills left by the apartheid regime; to demonstrate that as a result of GEAR we have now achieved macro-economic stability which made it possible for us to introduce programmes of state intervention in promoting growth" (ANC, 2001: 7).

And Further: "There is no national democratic revolution that is more radical than the ANC is implementing under current conditions" (ibid:9).

Arising from the above is therefore a very clear sense of intention in the ANC's policy shift, a shift inspired by the belief that market centred policies would lead to macro-economic stability and eventually, create conditions for state intervention. A similar body of evidence can be reconstructed with respect to the role of the British government in influencing and shaping the ANC's economic policy perspectives. However, here too, what is apparent is intention and willingness to play the free market game, on the part of the leadership. To this end, Lord Renwick (British Ambassador to Pretoria between 1987 – 1990), observed:

> We therefore did believe that we had some influence on the evolution of ANC economic policy and that a negotiated transition was likely to be followed by the adoption of cautious and moderate economic policies (Interview, 7th April, 2003).

However, like Lyman, Lord Renwick refuses to take all the credit for the economic policy somersault in the ANC, he believes that leaders like Mandela and Mbeki had a very good idea of the limits of statist policies and sought to steer clear of these (ibid).

Summary

This section has sought to draw attention to the mutual interdependence of structure and agency in real political life. Specifically, it underlines the combined effect of structural and agential factors in limiting developmental state prospects in the South African transition. It also follows from the above assessment that the politics of the South African transition were significantly different from the politics of East Asian developmental states. Moreover, the above assessment also shows that the two experiments were confronted by a qualitatively different set of global realities with respect to geo-politics, trade and finance. At the same time, the elite response to such global realities was different. In each context, the elites, guided by their examination of the global context, and the extent to which it lent itself to the implementation of its strategic objectives, took a course of action deemed most appropriate under the circumstances. This, in turn, has important implications for the developmental state debate. Above all, it suggests that the extent to which policies associated with developmental state-making are replicable is a function of politics and political action (and inaction). The next section seeks to review the key internal political factors and processes that explain the progressive erosion of developmental state prospects in the South African transition.

Internal Factors

In this section the focus is on the internal political factors that explain the collapse of a state-led developmentalist drive through the RDP. While the developmental state debate has thrown-up several features and components to explain East Asian developmental state-making, it is important to re-iterate here that those conditions and the resultant policy positions could not be replicated in South Africa with exactly the same effect. Indeed, it is not the object of this section to explore that kind of replication. Instead, the objective here is to provide an overview of the key internal political and strategic factors responsible for the collapse of a state-led developmentalist project in South Africa. In this regard, three themes are explored to explain the diminished prospects of developmental state politics in the South African transition and the RDP, these are then contrasted with the successful East Asian projects. These themes are: strength of civil society, the RDP document and the role of cohesive leadership elites. The section concludes by underlining the absence in the South African transition of the political conditions (in sufficient force) associated with developmental state construction. But first, in order to anchor this overview within the strategic relational approach, I offer a succinct discussion of the internal structural context that inspired agential processes (choices) that led to the collapse of the developmentalist project in transitional South Africa.

Internal Political Pressures and Influences

A combination of internal structural factors and circumstances account for the rapid abandonment of the developmentalist policies contained in the RDP, in favour of the neo-liberal approach advocated by GEAR and beyond. As in the previous section, the key argument here is that to understand this policy shift, one needs to look not only at the broad structural factors, for on their own, they are of limited analytical and explanatory utility. But neither should the search for explanations (for the demise of the RDP) be confined to agential factors (role of individual leaders and the processes they embarked upon). Such an approach is also restricted in terms of the explanatory light it can shed. The strategic relational approach, helpfully, departs from the premise that structure and agency are inextricably interlinked, it holds that they constantly influence and reinforce one another. Thus, in the South African context, the negotiated compromise, the balance of military power, and the intellectual environment crucially influenced the shape and content of the transition. But, there is little doubt that at the same time, the different social class forces, political organisations and individual decision-makers (eg. De Klerk and Mandela), had as crucial a role in influencing the outcome of the transition. It is in the mutually reinforcing relationship of structure, agency and power that the complex internal political reasons for the collapse of the RDP (and with it, the developmental state prospects) are to be found.

The South African Context

The broad internal structural and institutional factors that conditioned the shape of the South African transition, and hence the country's approach to economic development can be summarized as follows: First, as a consequence of the stale-mate between the apartheid regime and the anti-apartheid liberation movement, the need for a negotiated settlement became an increasingly unavoidable reality. Pressure for negotiations was brought to bear on the major players not only by the Western Countries, as shown in the last section, the Soviet Union (key supporter of the ANC) was equally insistent on a negotiated settlement. ANC/SACP leaders recalled:

194

> When I was in Lusaka (exile) between 1987 and 1990, somewhere in the
> middle of that, I remember comrades from the SACP being called into the
> Soviet Embassy and told that we could no longer expect the same levels
> of support. We needed to move rapidly towards some kind of negotiations.
> This was what the Soviet Embassy was telling the ANC/SACP in the late
> 1980s and clearly, they were just desperate to remove the burden of solidar-
> ity and support (www.comms.Dcu.ie/sheehanh/za.cronin02.htm).

After all, for over forty years, and despite its military and repressive capa-
bilities, the apartheid regime had failed miserably to effectively suppress the
anti-apartheid movement. At the same time, however, many years of international and internal protests, including sanctions and armed struggle, had put
the anti-apartheid movement no nearer to the attainment of its goals. Second,
the downward spiral in the South African economy, especially in the mid-
1980s, continued unabated and with no real prospect of resolution. There
were both political and economic reasons for this. The political reasons
concerned sanctions and the international isolation of the apartheid regime,
while the intensification of political opposition (internally) to the system did
little for stability in the country. This, too, predisposed the apartheid regime
and its allies to a negotiated settlement with its principal adversaries. The
economic reasons concerned the failure of the apartheid capitalist regime of
accumulation to replicate itself in the new global conditions. Thus, apartheid
leadership elites had come to the conclusion that there was a need to pursue
an IMF/WB sponsored neo-liberal policy path, but that the strategy of accumulation needed to be altered in such a way that key sections of the black
majority were also accommodated. For both these reasons, the stage was set
for a reformist resolution of the racial capitalist system. Crucially, since there
was no insurrectionary seizure of power, the complexion of the post-apartheid order was set to reflect not the hegemony of the victors, but rather the
plurality of the Government of National Unity (GNU).

Therefore, the apartheid regime released political prisoners and reversed
the ban on the ANC and other political formations. For its part, the ANC
abandoned the armed struggle and accepted the 'give and take' of a negotiated settlement and the associated compromises. These were early indications
of how these 'pacted arrangements' would shape the political economy of
the new South Africa. By its very nature, a negotiated settlement implied
compromise and deviations from previously held maximalist policy positions. Thus, the ANC was sucked into a situation where it had to be content
with both qualitative and quantitative compromises (Slovo, 1992:38). The
specific compromises (agreements and decisions) relevant to the abandonment of the RDP developmentalist state prospects include the following:

> An Interim Constitution, which entrenched power-sharing in the form of the GNU. This meant that the NP, ANC and IFP sat in cabinet and ran the country together, despite the hugely divergent strategic and ideological orientations of the three parties. This arrangement, as is to be expected with pacted governments, made for weak policies, strategies and weak states

The Interim Constitution allocated (in keeping with the spirit of the GNU) greater powers to the provinces, thereby further weakening central state co-ordination, planning, reach and leadership at a national level. This arrangement also scattered decision-making on policy issues to provincial Premiers and cabinets, particularly emasculating and polarizing for the ANC elite was the lack of real access to provinces not under ANC control (notably, KwaZulu/Natal and the Western Cape provinces).

The Interim Constitution, in the give and take of deal-making also provided for the appeasement of the apartheid bureaucracy. For a period of five years, the apartheid incumbents in the bureaucracy had to be guaranteed job security. This would make transforming the bureaucracy into a developmentalist instrument an almost impossible task. At the same time, it posed the danger of policy sabotage by those members of the bureaucracy who did not share the new government's policies.

Section 28 of the Interim Constitution that dealt with property rights made redistribution a virtually unattainable objective. This section effectively entrenched the apartheid property rights, making it very difficult for the new elite to effect redistribution. It also prevented nationalization programmes in support of a state-led developmental process.

In broad terms, these were some of the key strategic limitations imposed by the internal structural realities of the South African transition on developmental state-making prospects. South Africa was thus poised to evolve not a developmental state type project, but a 'pacted democratisation' process with important neo-liberal foundations (Webster and Adler, 1999: 348). But in what concrete ways did these play themselves out in the policy arena, and what did this mean for South Africa's developmentalist state prospects?

The Strength of Civil Society

The last chapter has demonstrated in detail the power of the key social actors in South Africa's economic policy processes. The collapse of the RDP and thus the prospects for developmental state construction has been shown here to be associated with the varied strength and importance of civil society in South Africa, as compared to East Asia. Both in South Korea and Taiwan, when the state elites embarked on their economic development programmes, the industrial working class was virtually non-existent, and the bourgeoisie was too weak and largely dependent on the state for inputs and general economic survival (Vertiairianen, 1999:224). However, when labour militancy did rear its head, the state response was generally swift and brutal (Deyo, 1987; Moon and Kim, 1996). Similarly, those members of the business classes who resisted the state's interventionist programmes in the economic life of the country, were threatened with confiscation of their assets and prosecution (Weiss and Hobson, 1997). Alternatively, through institutional linkages set up by the state, and enticement with promises of investments, recalcitrant business groupings were co-opted, infiltrated and compelled to cooperate (Chu, 1989; Cheng, 1998).

Two important conclusions can be drawn from state-society relations in Taiwan and South Korea. First, the economic policy arena was in large measure the exclusive domain of the state. The extent and manner of involvement by social groups was likewise largely determined by the state, and crucially by the extent to which such involvement would advance the elite's development programmes. The politics of state and civil society relations were thus very much in line with developmental state construction in both the Taiwanese and South Korean contexts. By contrast, South Africa in the 1990s had a powerful and extremely vocal civil society, one that insisted on active involvement in shaping and defining the country's post-apartheid economic policy. As shown earlier, such involvement by both labour and capital was in the first and last instance motivated by the interests of the social group concerned. In other words, during the RDP debate, the overriding instincts of labour and capital were maximization of their sectional interests in the economic policy process. This contrasts markedly with the East Asian experiences, where the state pursued and led an economic development programme in the putative interest of society at large. Nonetheless, the management of disparate class and social interests proved to be an important burden on the new South African leadership elite's ability to dictate a radical state-led economic development programme.

Labour

Contrary to East Asia where the *modus operandi* was typically repression, infiltration and co-option, the South African labour movement was an intrinsic part of the ANC/COSATU/SACP alliance, and in partnership with the new ruling elite. Furthermore, post-apartheid labour law reflected the rapprochement between the state and labour, in stark contrast to say, South Korea and Taiwan. For example, the Labour Relations Act No. 66 of 1995 stated "every employee has the right to participate in forming a trade union or federation of trade unions and to participate in its lawful activities including strike action…protest action to promote and defend socio-economic interests of workers" (Act No.66, 1995). These rights were further entrenched in sections 15, 16 and 17 of the country's 1994 Interim Constitution. The Constitution of South Africa, being the supreme law of the land, also had provisions that would significantly affect labour law and thus state-labour relations in South Africa including:

> the right to equality and freedom from discrimination; freedom of assembly, demonstration and petition; freedom of association and freedom of economic activity (www.oefre.unibe.ch/law.icl.sf10 000-html).

Such wide ranging rights not only gave workers enormous power in the work place, but also actively invited workers to take part in the policy process in support of their constitutional rights. The autonomy of the state in economic policy implementation would, in such circumstances, be very difficult to sustain and similarly, shedding the economic policy process off special interests could not be realistically attained. Developmental state construction is greatly enhanced by the relatively free reign the state enjoyed in the area of policy formulation and implementation. The historical strength and warm relations between the new political elites and labour in South Africa, made the East Asian route (repression of labour) an untenable option. Furthermore, the South African labour movement was not only strong numerically and politically, but it was also very strong ideologically. This made the state's ability to bully the labour movement into accepting anti-worker ideological positions that much harder. Thus, one important condition for East Asian developmental state construction was absent in 1990s South Africa- a weak and subordinated civil society.

Capital

Like labour, the business sector had significant space to extend its interests in the policy process, and thereby limited the state's autonomy to pursue a developmental programme designed to advance not only sectional, but also broader social interests. Act No. 66 of 1995 allowed employers to establish organisations and federations as they pleased. Also, the Act stated: "no person may do or threaten to do the following: require an employer not to be a member of an employer's organisation; to give up membership of an employer's organisation; prejudice an employer because of the past, present or anticipated –participation in the lawful activities of an employer's organisation or federation of employers' organisations (Act No.66, 1995).

First, the provisions of this Act taken together with those of the Constitution, virtually took away any leverage the state could have over the activities and operations of the business sector. By contrast, General Park in South Korea was able to create sufficient room for the state to extract from, and cajole strategic sections of business into cooperation with the state's developmental programme. Secondly, unlike the South Korean scenario, the South African business sector was, by 1994, well developed, and could count on its extensive international connections for loans and investments. Above all, the South African business community was, in large measure, a firm believer in the neo-liberal project and its rejection of the role of the state. The RDP, for its part, failed to define a developmentally consistent relationship between state and capital. Instead, this relationship, so critical to the success of developmental states in East Asia (Weiss, 2000: 23), was captured thus in the RDP:

> Multipartite policy forums representing the major role players in different sectors should be established and existing forums restructured to promote efficient and effective participation of civil society in decision-making. Such forums must exist at national, provincial and local levels (ANC, 1994: 132).

Developmental state literature shows that state and society relations were determined by the leadership elite on the basis of national developmental objectives set by those elites. Therefore, the multipartite forums envisaged by the RDP significantly departed from the developmental state norm, since they implied the undermining of the leadership role of the state in policy formulation. Furthermore, this role was being delegated to an amorphous forum with no clearly defined strategic objectives, certainly none that would be in the putative interest of society more broadly. But the RDP approach also provided no scope for a developmentally driven state-capital relationship led by the state. What is more, the RDP assigned this role to special interests. Therefore, with respect to capital too, South African political conditions were very much at odds with the East Asian experience. Thus, the pluralist nature of the policy-making process in South Africa foreclosed a predominant role for the state. Indeed, some analysts have advanced the view that "the power of capital relative to both labour and the state is greater than ever before" and that the very politics of the transition were dominated and shaped by capital and the interests of capital (Seekings and Nattrass, 2002: 2). This state of affairs would most certainly constitute a major deviation from the developmental state-making experiences in East Asia. For this reason, the internal political conditions and prerequisites for developmental state construction were not present in 1990s South Africa. The above were not the only deviations from the developmentalist perspective – more were to be found in the RDP document itself.

The RDP Document

Several aspects of the RDP document, which was meant to be the new elite's unambiguous programme towards a state-led interventionist project, proved in fact to be vague and in some respects, contrary to the developmental state perspective. The ideological and strategic vagueness of the RDP document was a reflection of the competing interests within the ANC alliance for the 'heart and soul' of the RDP. At the same time, it also reflected the varied interests and economic policy positions held by the different partners in the GNU. Thus, the document sought to maintain a precarious balance, which took on board contradictory policy positions. As a consequence, a number of its aspects in fact undermined developmental state prospects in transitional South Africa. In this sub-section some of the most salient (and counter-developmental state) aspects are explored.

A People-driven Process

In the RDP document, the explicit commitment to be a leading role of the state in economic development is underplayed by another (contradictory) commitment to a 'people-driven' process. This approach to implementation runs directly against the developmental state emphasis on 'state-driven' developmental processes. Careful consideration of the RDP document shows that a disproportionately large part of the document was devoted to the relegation of key decision-making responsibilities to an amorphous mix of consultative processes, negotiations 'with stake holders', and people's forums. Under normal circumstances such an approach would, of course, be commendable. For one thing, it would deepen democracy and consolidate popular participation and encourage active citizenry. There are, however, questions about whether more energy and focus should not have been expended in driving a rapid state-led developmental agenda. One directed at expeditiously curbing poverty, inequality and unemployment. The social sciences have yet to come to grips with the relationship between democracy and development. Far too often this relationship is presented as mutually re-enforcing and uncontroversial. Historical evidence, especially from the developing world (including post-apartheid South Africa), would seem to suggest that much research and analytical work is called for in understanding this dynamic. At any rate, the RDP had a preference for decentralized decision-making and implementation. There were several examples:

> In taking this approach we are building on the many forums, peace structures and negotiations that our people are involved in throughout the land ANC, 1994: 5).

Also:

> In the course of 1994, trade unions sectoral social movements and community based organisations (CBOs), notably civics, must be encouraged to develop programmes of action and campaigns within their own sectors and communities...Trade unions and other mass organisations must be actively involved in democratic public policy-making. This should include involvement in negotiations ranging from the composition of the constitutional court to international trade and loan agreements (ibid:131).

There may well be very legitimate and convincing historic-political reasons unique to South Africa for this apparent over-generosity of the RDP, regarding powers to drive economic strategy. However, from a developmental state view point, at least two aspects make these provisions inimical to developmental state-making. First, these provisions violate the relatively autonomous role of the state in setting and implementing economic development policy. By actively advocating that social groups should have such far-reaching roles in policy development and implementation, the RDP was in fact inadvertently flooding the economic development policy process with special interests. Given the high developmental stakes and high levels of inequality and unemployment, such an approach was bound to undermine developmental state-making. For instance, it is extremely difficult to contemplate capital and labour in the manufacturing and export sectors formulating mutually acceptable international trade policies. It is even more unlikely that such a policy, assuming it eventually materialized, would reflect the broad socio-economic and developmental interests of the country as a whole. The previous chapters have shown that only a developmental state would have incentive to pursue such a project. And would be facilitated by the relative distance of the state from such sectional interests.

Secondly, the leadership role of the state and its ability to deliver on its chosen developmental path would be seriously compromised by the requirements for wide and endless consultation (Nattrass, 1994; Wolpe, 1995). Thus, the relegation of decision making to amorphous structures and forums was in fact a critical constraint on the leadership role of the state, which was the hallmark of successful developmental state-making elsewhere.

Bureaucratic Transformation

Were the East Asian development projects were led by meritocratic and well trained bureaucrats, South Africa faced much more complex challenges in this regard. To start with, the GNU compromise entrenched in the Interim constitution (1994) insisted that the jobs and perks of the old apartheid civil service be protected (1994: section 236). In terms of this section of the Constitution:

> (1) A public service, department of state (including a police force), adminis-
> tration... or other institution which immediately before the commencement
> of this constitution performed government functions....shall continue to
> function as such in accordance with the laws applicable to it...(2) A person
> who immediately before the commencement of this constitution was em-
> ployed by an institution referred to in sub-section (1) shall continue in such
> employment subject to and in accordance with this constitution and other
> applicable laws regulating such employment (RSA, 1994: section 236).

Thus, through the constitutional compromise, the new elites found that they had denied themselves the possibility of initiating an economic development programme implemented by a meritocratic but relatively loyal bureaucracy. Instead, in South Africa, 95 % of senior bureaucrats were white and the vast majority were Afrikaner males, with little sympathy for the new state elites and what they represented (*Business Day*, 2nd May 1994).

Indeed, the period before the 1994 elections saw a number of strike actions designed to 'cripple the new government', which were led by the white conservative Public Service Association (Davies, 1994: 4). The central grievance behind the industrial unrest that spread throughout the country was objection to the creation of 11,000 affirmative action posts within the bu-reaucracy, in order to promote representativeness and equity (Moroke, 1994; Hadland, 1994). Government efforts to transform the civil service within the limited confines set by the Interim Constitution in turn, attracted stinging criticism from political commentators. Such lack of genuine bureaucratic transformation was said to be a major obstacle to development. Anton Har-bor, a veteran journalist, suggested that the bureaucracy was:

> too big, too old, too costly and too much apartheid duplication. In fact, the
> problem has been the inability of the Commission for Public Administra-
> tion headed by Minister Zola Skweyiya, to rise to the challenge of trans-
> forming the civil service (Harbor, 1995: 22).

Yet others accused the new leadership of the country of having:

> ...treated the civil service gingerly, hoping respect will be re-paid with loyalty and worrying that confrontation will generate resistance (Keller, 1994: 1).

What was clear, however, was that the bureaucracy, a critically important pillar of developmental state-making, was struggling to conform to the East Asian meritocratic and developmentally driven bureaucratic state types. ANC member of Parliament and President of the civic movement, SANCO, Letchesa Tsinoli observed: "In the GNU there are some people who do not believe in the RDP...and we have to fight for its implementation" (*Natal Witness*, 24th May, 1994).

In the meantime, Jeff Radebe, Minister of Public Works, was reported as attacking (predominantly white) senior management in government for inefficiency, adherence to old apartheid priorities, and for acting to protect the interests of the old order (*Sunday Time*, 9 April 1995). Moreover, for the *Sunday Times:* "The unprecedented public row captured the tensions between the old guard in the civil service and the ANC over attempts to transform the country" (ibid).

Unlike the South Korean and Taiwanese experiences, there was no positive bureaucratic inheritance. Instead, a white bureaucracy with allegiance to the National Party, which had carefully cultivated a patronage relationship with the civil service for decades, was at the cutting edge of post-apartheid policy implementation. The possible and perceived loss of such patronage also largely explained the hostility and disdain of the civil service for the new ANC dominated GNU. Once the RDP structures were put in place, the task of translating the base document into an implementable legislative framework, was removed from the principal architects of the document. This task was instead taken up by senior management associated with the National Party's neo-liberal Normative Economic Policy (NEP). The elaboration of the RDP thus fell on: "a new generation of bureaucrats, not necessarily involved with the conception of the RDP, [who] were in the forefront of translating the base document into concrete legislation"(Interview with Phadu, 22 August, 2002).

Furthermore, the Interim Constitution did not allow the new elite to effect any real changes to the bureaucratic set up for at least five years, especially changes that concerned sacking the apartheid era bureaucrats. Aside from the constitutional arrangements, the new elites themselves were loath to rock the boat of reconciliation, lest this led to conflict and instability. Above all, for a significant section of the ANC leaders, nothing could be contemplated that had the potential to undermine business confidence in the transition. For all these reasons and much besides, the internal political factors (bureaucratic transformation in this instance) were not amenable to developmental state construction. And more significantly, the RDP document itself was limited.

Institutional Arrangements

I have shown that, in some respects, the RDP's institutional arrangements conformed to those that coordinated and led the East Asian economic development projects. However, there were also important differences and limitations inherent in the RDP structures, especially from a developmental state viewpoint.

First, the constitutional deal-making and compromise meant that the RDP would largely exist side by side with, and in some instances, rely on old apartheid agencies for its success. Such agencies included the DBSA, CEAS, CSS and NPI, all operating according to and guided by a completely different social agenda and ethos. Secondly, there was extreme confusion and lack of clarity both among government Ministers and the public more broadly regarding the exact role of the RDP Office. Was it meant to be a 'Super Ministry' auditing the activities of line departments, a developmental planning agency initiating new transformation projects, or a monitoring agency (Munslow and FitzGerald, 1995; Blumenfeld, 1997)? The RDP document itself and different government spokespersons laid claim to all these possible roles. For instance, ANC National Executive Committee Member and senior bureaucrat, Phillip Dexter noted:

> It seems to me that when we went to government, the first mistake we made was to create a ministry of the RDP. By creating a ministry, you are making the RDP an 'add-on' instead of a government-wide programme. Moreover, you are setting the Minister of the RDP against his peers in government (Interview: 21 August, 2002).

These remarks underscore a crucial deviation from the developmental state approach. For in the East Asian contexts, the economic development structures had real power and authority. In turn, these structures stemmed from the convergence of ideological and strategic views among the elite, which was unencumbered by the type of constitutional and political constraints confronting the South African elites. The development of institutional arrangements appropriate to the task of state-led economic development was given priority, hence the status and location of such institutions in the Presidency. For this reason, the Minister in the Presidency was given real power and presidential support, thereby making it easy for the incumbent to exercise his/her role unconstrained by territorial and power struggles. In the final analysis, the key was the presence of a clearly defined and firmly supported development programme, and its single-minded implementation by the entire leadership elite. The RDP fell short of these qualities when its detailed proposals were scrutinized and examined closely. These caused internal strife and divisions rather than cohesion among the elite. For these reasons, RDP institutional arrangements did not measure up to the carefully constituted Council on International Economic Cooperation and Development (CIECD) in Taiwan, or the Economic Cooperation Board (ECB) in South Korea. Whereas economic policy was coherent and emanated largely from the Presidency in the East Asian context, in South Africa:

> There were three key centres of economic policy formulation and implementation in government, and these did not always work in sync. The RDP Ministry, Finance Ministry; and the Presidency (Phadu, 2002).

This was another legacy of the post-apartheid settlement and the ANC's apprehensions about inspiring business confidence and attracting foreign investment. In the Finance Ministry, Derek Keys, and in the Reserve Bank-Christian Stals (Bank Governor), were retained by the new government. According to an Africa *Confidential* report, the retention of these two had everything to do with appeasing business sentiment and the need for individuals who could " categorically reject budgetary demands from spending Ministries" (20th May, 1994). Unsurprisingly, a key target of the Finance Minister's austerity measures would be the RDP 'spending Ministry'. Note that after all the massive reconstruction and development that the RDP Ministry set for itself, the fraction allocated to this programme in the fiscal year 1994/95 was the equivalent of only 3% of current general government consumption expenditure (*Financial Mail*, 18th July, 1994). The Finance Minister had apparently only agreed to stay on provided President Mandela and his deputy, Mbeki undertook to give his handling of the country's finances their full backing (*Africa Confidential*, 20th May, 1994). This is also consistent with Lyman's experience of the ANC leadership's apprehensions about a potential debt trap (interview, 2003). This lack of power and authority in the RDP Office, and the concomitant absence of a single policy centre constitute another crucial deviation from the developmental state approach.

Yet another important deviation concerns the size and significance of the RDP Office. Indeed, it is extremely difficult to reconcile the stated objectives of the RDP and its role in the transformation process on the one hand, with the size, capacity and resources allocated to the RDP and RPP Office on the other. First, the RDP had a very small staff compliment and the highest-rank-ing official occupied the position of Deputy Director-General (Blumenfeld, 1997:75). The Ministry also had no administrative department devoted to actual implementation of adopted RDP policies. The rest of the government's line departments were headed by Directors- General, a ministry and fully fledged departments (ibid). Blumenfeld's work has further shown that the powers and authority of the RDP Ministry were, on closer inspection, quite limited. For example, although the RDP Minister had a veto over all projects, in practice, projects had to be submitted and approved not by the RDP Minister but an inter-ministerial cabinet committee, chaired by the RDP Minister. In other words, it was not his decision per se, but had to be taken jointly with other line Ministers, whose departments (through the top-slicing of part of their departmental budgets), had a stake in and represented special interests. Significantly, the actual disbursement of funds for such projects was the responsibility not of the RDP Minister but the Finance Minister, who administered all government funds. Therefore, while theoretically, the RDP Minister had a lot of power and authority, at the operational level, this quickly dwindled into insignificant ceremonial powers. In this respect, too, political conditions in South Africa were not amenable to developmental state construction. The above speak to poor coordination, in part, I would argue, a consequence of poor cohesion at the leadership top.

The East Asian developmental state-making experiences have shown that a critical condition for success was the presence of a cohesive leadership elite (Leftwich, 1996: 285). Furthermore, the fundamental basis of such cohesion had been shown to reside in the single-minded commitment of the elites to a common strategic objective – state-led economic development (Johnson,1982: 306). The significance attached by the elites to successful economic development was inspired by a number of factors at the core of which was defence against possible military and ideological invasion. This sub-section explores the presence of this crucial component or developmental state features in South Africa's transitional politics.

Developmental Elites

In both South Korea and Taiwan, the developmental elites were the driving force behind the success of these country's projects. Moreover, such elites stood out for their developmental determination and single-minded commitment to growth and transformation in their respective countries. Another critical basis for developmental elite formation, and more broadly, developmental state-making, has been the role of war-making. In 19th century Europe, Japan and more recently South Korea and Taiwan, war and the threat of war have been crucial in shaping developmental states and developmental elites (Tilly, 1985; Weiss and Hobson, 1995). Also, more often than not, such elites were associated with founding fathers of independence, liberation and the struggles that preceded liberation (notably, Park in South Korea and Lee in Singapore) (ibid). Above all, however, the significance of developmental elites symbolized the centrality of politics, political leadership, and political commitment and determination in driving and achieving institutional changes comparable to the East Asian 'miracle'. It is only with the direction of such a cohesive leadership guided by a clear 'hegemonic project' that consistency and policy coherence can be maintained (Pempel, 1999: 160). Consistency and determination are particularly critical attributes given the complexity and the many pit-falls on the way to developmental state-making, and these are in turn, made possible by the presence and pursuit of a 'hegemonic project' or 'big idea' for change. In the case of the Korean and Taiwanese elites, the hegemonic projects were crafted around three key elements:

- Enhancement of national economic development interests – for national defence.

- A rejection of the Western concept of the 'market', opting instead, for active market manipulation.

- A rejection of communism (although many Marxist-Leninist institutional features continued to define the KMT party apparatus) in Taiwan (ibid).

Therefore, a crucial rallying-point for the formation and substance of the East Asia elites was the notion that the respective countries were under threat and the conviction among the elites that economic development was the *sin qua non* of regime survival (Evans, 1998). To what extent was the RDP and the politics of transition in South Africa consistent with the above developmental state feature?

Founding Figures

The ANC and its allies have always been seen as the foremost South African liberation movement, and indeed, its leadership (Tambo, Mandela, Slovo) indisputably fitted the 'founding fathers' label. With respect to the ANC/COSATU/SACP alliance, a policy of overlapping membership strengthened cohesion, and led to mutual influence on a range of issues including economic policy. The reverence with which the alliance leadership were held in society was not diminished by the failure of the insurrectionary strategy to materialize either, the land slide victory of the ANC in the 1994 elections illustrates the point. However, unlike the Taiwanese and South Korean experiences, where the elites more or less imposed themselves through power, the ANC elite had to forge its hegemony through struggle over time. Thus, an immediate contrast between the two experiences was the authoritarian basis of the East Asians and the open democratic (pluralist) basis of the position of the ANC founding figures. Another important contrast relates to the absence in the South African context of a military threat either facing the country itself or the region. Certainly, South Africa did not have the equivalent of the North Korea threat that faced South Korea, or the People's Republic of China in the case of Taiwan. Consequently, the absence of this factor saw the development of radically different roles for the founding figures in the two situations.

Hegemonic Project

The broad basis of the ANC elite's project has always been non-racialism, non-sexism, democracy, redistribution and equality for all, as a counter-veiling force to the apartheid nationalist project. However, once the economic policy propositions were unpacked (through the RDP White Paper), these noble ideas proved strategically and ideologically pliable and open to a range of interpretations. There were reasons for this. Unlike the East Asian elites, there was no strong position on the role of the market or communism among the elites. Instead, the authors of post-apartheid economic policy sought to pursue an ideologically vague 'non-capitalist' development path. The reasons for this are not hard to find, the ANC is a broad ideological church and thus, ideology and economic strategy are precarious and very sensitive matters. Accordingly, indelicate handling of these is likely to unsettle the organisation (Lodge, 2002; Barrell, 2002). Moreover, economic policy has always been recognized as a potentially polarizing factor in the ANC alliance (*Africa Confidential*, May, 1994; CIA, 2003). Therefore, the ANC/CO-SATU/SACP alliance, while a useful leadership elite to preside over a broad non-racial and non-sexist national democratic project during the struggle, compared poorly with the East Asian 'developmental elites'. In particular, the alliance has proved unable to sustain itself in government and incapable of translating the RDP into a coherent 'strategic, hegemonic project' or an effective 'counter-veiling project' to apartheid capitalist hegemony. Instead, different ideological tendencies represented within the alliance and the ANC have seen the RDP crumble and replaced by GEAR as a strategy representing the hegemonic neo-liberal section within the alliance. Therefore, the RDP's ability to constitute a hegemonic project comparable to those led by East Asian elites was easily undermined.

Leadership Cohesion

The ideological differences noted above eventually exploded the cohesion of the alliance so carefully sustained over the past forty years. The trigger for (what could have been) the beginning of the alliance's collapse is generally associated with the abandonment of the RDP and the introduction of GEAR as the central macro-economic platform for the South African transition. Various leaders have conceded:

> That the introduction of GEAR has bedevilled the alliance ever since. That was combined with the fact that, people in government were saying 'we are in government, we are going to govern, we rule', which is problematic if you are in an alliance. You can't really govern and expect your allies to support you when they don't understand what you're doing (Dexter: interview, 2002).

Similarly, Jeremy Cronin has observed:

> the ANC itself or significant parts of the ANC got seduced. Whether from panic or deep concern, laden with the responsibilities of governing, they were seduced or persuaded of certain aspects (not necessarily the whole package) but core aspects of the neo-liberal paradigm became very influential in government circles and leading parts of the ANC (www.comms.dcu. ie/sheehanh/za/cronin02.htm).

These views were, in turn, in line with the SACP Central Committee resolution, which stated:

> The SACP is more and more convinced that a thoroughgoing review of macro-economic policy is essential. Too much emphasis has been placed [by GEAR] on creating an 'investor friendly climate' and then hoping that the market will do the rest. It is not working, and it will not work (SACP, 1997).

The two million strong labour ally, COSATU also had serious misgivings about the GEAR strategy. In particular, the labour federation saw the strategy as compromising the RDPs redistributionist thrust. Thus, the Central Committee of COSATU insisted in a press briefing held on the 14th September 1996:

> The Federation remains opposed to the basic thrust of the government's macro-economic framework (GEAR) which was released in June this year. We are concerned at the impact that drastic cuts in the fiscus can do to

209

programmes such as health, education, social benefits, housing, and delivery by the state. This does not in any way suggest opposition to debt management, but to the government's chosen route (www. Cosatu. Org.za/press/1996/pro0914.01).

For his part, ANC President, Thabo Mbeki, accused critics of the government's GEAR programme of having "an all-consuming desire to present themselves as the sole and authentic representatives of the progressive movement and ready to use the hostile message of the right and thus join forces with defenders of reaction to sustain an offensive against our movement" Mbeki, 1998: 6).

While State President Mandela told an SACP conference more starkly:

> GEAR is the fundamental policy of the ANC. We will not change it because of your pressure. If you feel you cannot get your way, then go out and shout like the opposition parties. Prepare to face the full consequences of that line (*Financial Mail*, 3 July, 1998).

Of course, the SACP was not and has not been prepared to face the consequences of that line since. There has, instead been increasing rapprochement between this socialist party and the conservative policies pursued by the ANC government especially after 2007. The most cynical observers have linked this acquiescence of the SACP with an ideological framework and a set of policies that are fundamentally at odds with what any communist party should stand for with the clever deployment of leading lights of that party into key government positions.

Therefore, not only was there no leadership cohesion at the top, but the alliance leadership was openly and publicly trading insults. Above all, there was no agreement on economic policy and no 'hegemonic project', around which leadership cohesion could be forged. Cohesion was further undermined by the nature of the Government of National Unity.

The Government of National Unity

It was not only within the ANC alliance that cohesion was shaky, but it was even more precarious in the ANC/NP/IFP governing coalition, which was an 'elite-pacting arrangement based on bargaining, trade-offs and compromise' (O'Meara, 1996: 405). Moreover, as Przeworski has shown, in such circumstances, the key participants in the coalition invariably struggle on two fronts. First, they attempt to fulfil the objectives of the coalition, but at the same time, they "seek to create conditions that would be most conducive to the realization of its own interests in future conflicts against current allies"

(1993:63). In this sense, F.W. De Klerk's assessment of the agreement that brought the GNU into being, is remarkable:

> For our part [National Party], we would get continuity, on the Interim Constitution with a justiciable Bill of Rights, fairly strong regional government, a multi-party GNU and the assurance that the final constitution would have to comply with pre-arranged constitutional principles (2000:254).

Not quite a model or a basis of developmental state-making, although the South African transition politics seem to have more in common with the developmentally limited capacity and conservative nature of multi-party democratic arrangements. In these cases, both the decision-making processes and policy output are generally conservative in that they normally involve inter-elite accommodation, compromise, consensus and incrementalism.

Room for Manoeuvre

Developmental elite determination to succeed was reflected not only locally, but also in the policies advocated to engage in the international arena. These policies included restricting entry and carefully monitoring imports, 'both qualitatively and by means of tariffs' (Wade, 1990: 57). Operational space to implement national developmental policies was also created through a "deliberate approach to international integration through a measured and properly sequenced set of policies towards trade, capital flows and FDI" (Akyuz, Chang and Kozul-Wright, 1998: 29). For instance, on commencement of their developmentalist projects, South Korea and Taiwan opened different sectors of their economies to foreign competition, all in line with their national policy objectives and what were considered 'strategic industries' at a given time (ibid). Can a similar strategic approach to international trade be deciphered in the RDP and the policies of the ANC during the South African transition? WTO arrangements were not only regarded as sacrosanct, but policy makers considered it prudent to 'liberalise more quickly than required...to win admiration' (Hirsh, 1994: 45). The RDP itself offered no broad strategic objectives to guide South Africa's trade policies other than the call for a minimization of disruption when tariffs were revised (ANC, 1994: 90). Indeed, the RDP saw the GATT agreement as cast in iron, rather than as a terrain of policy engagement and implementation. On this subject, the RDP stated: "The recent GATT agreement has necessitated painful adjustment in certain quarters, and policy should aim to reduce and share out the impact of that adjustment while at the same time promoting efficiency" (ibid:88).

Thus, no thought was given to the strategic approach of subordinating adherence to WTO arrangements to the country's national development priorities. Furthermore, the direction for South Africa's interaction with WTO requirements was the task not so much of the country's political elite, guided by clearly defined economic and developmental imperatives, but the task of an amorphous multi-party and multi-sectoral National Economic Forum (NEF). The absence of strategic bottom-lines and the constant search for room to manoeuvre, during the trade talks constituted yet another important deviation from the East Asian experience. There, the elites armed with clearly defined policy alternatives and developmental project, constantly sought room to manoeuvre and to manipulate the world trading system in ways that advanced their set objectives. In this regard, Akyuz *et al* remind us that the East Asian elites had to "exercise a considerable amount of policy ingenuity and administrative and diplomatic skills to maintain some of their policies" (1998: 30). Furthermore, "While the WTO multilateral agreements have reduced the scope of policy options, measures comparable to those applied by the East Asian countries can still be applied" (UNCTAD, 1996: 39).

All that is required is a determined developmentally focused and astute leadership elite, that can constantly seek and find intelligent ways to meet its country's developmental objectives, within an ever hostile world trading and economic environment. In the South African context, it would appear that there was no intention to engage with the world trading system, as this possibility was closed off well before 1994, when the TEC made far-reaching and poorly conceived commitments. The idea that a country like South Africa, that so desperately needed as much room to manoeuvre as it could possibly win, would opt to forgo this option in favour of winning admiration, remains inexplicable. So too, is the naiveté that led to the belief that the world trading system is a family picnic, where kindness is rewarded. At any rate, in politics there is always room to manoeuvre, for those state and political actors that are determined to achieve their objectives. South Africa's case, it would seem from the above analysis, is a function of an elite in peace with and in some instances, confident in the ability of the inherited ideological framework to meet South Africa's growth and developmental needs. Jacob Zuma's recent response to a parliamentary question is instructive: "trade issues are determined by WTO and other international organisations, that determine how trade should go between countries….How trade moves in the world is determined by market forces…" (Hansard, August 06 2015).

Summary

The transition was impaired in its ability to advance into a state-led developmentalist project from the start. The internal politics of the transition were largely stacked against such a project. It may well be that some elements within the elite were desirous of the developmentalist growth path discussed above, but the key decision-makers had taken a conscious political decision not to rock the boat of negotiations and deal-making. But above all, even in the deal-making process, there was determination not to upset the core elements of the neo-liberal growth path. In practice, this has meant very limited deviation from the inherited accumulation strategy that was under-pinned, first and foremost, by a racially defined inequality. So, the source of this fundamental contradiction of South African society (the South African question), has yet to be tackled head-on, via the introduction of a hegemonic project that overhauls and fundamentally alters power and economic relations in South Africa.

Conclusion

Structural and agential factors combined to frustrate developmental state prospects both with respect to the external and internal realities. This chapter has sought to underline the absence (in sufficient force) of politics associat-ed with developmental state construction in the RDP and the South African transition. Instead, I show that South Africa followed a growth path largely accommodative of, and in line with the hegemonic neo-liberal approach, which is, in many respects anti-thetical to developmental state-making. Cru-cially, however, I reject the dominant explanation for the policy choices, which hold that either the new state elites were overwhelmed by the realities of office or that they got 'cold feet'. I show, instead, that the policy choic-es and the maintenance of the current ideological framework were all very much *intentional* and well thought through (see Turok, 2014: 53- 57). In sum, internal and external pressures, politics, ideology and policy choices conspired against the emergence of a developmental state path in South Af-rica.

At the same time, the deliberate and conscious political decisions taken by the new elite largely fell in line (rather than challenged) the strategic di-rection dictated by the prevailing and predominant structural set up. And this was largely *animus* to developmental state-making.

CHAPTER

'No Developmental State, No Development'

Introduction

The principal preoccupation of this book has been the exploration of the political economy of developmental state-making in post-apartheid South Africa. The analysis underlines the primacy of politics and ideology in comprehending and explicating the flows and ebbs of post-apartheid policies, politics and state-making processes. To be sure, ideology, politics and human agency (intentional action or choices) largely explain the particular direction taken by post-apartheid South Africa, as against what was on the script for much of the ANC's existence. These variables also explain post-apartheid South Africa's current internal and external developmental positioning. It is essentially a story of missed opportunities, unfulfilled promises, unmet expectations and socio-economic growth and developmental possibilities insufficiently explored. Both the East Asian developmental states of South Korea and Taiwan on the one hand, and the state-making processes associated with Afrikaner nationalism, have much to bequeath current endeavours in South Africa's state-making processes. True, the analysis in the preceding chapters shows that developmental state-making processes in post-apartheid South Africa have encountered powerful

215

head winds. However, unlike much analytical conclusion on this subject, I reject the notion that such internal and external structural realities were visited upon an unsuspecting and helpless leadership elite. I argue, instead, that far too often, the role of the subjective factor (leadership choices and actions) is underplayed at the expense of the 'material conditions'. Such analyses generally have limited explanatory utility, as they deny post-apartheid elites agency. Thus, while such structural factors do indeed, shape and condition leadership behaviour, it is not the case that structure determines such behaviour, choices and decisions. Leaders consciously and deliberately interpret the internal and external circumstances under which they operate, they identify strengths, flaws and room to manoeuvre. In the post-apartheid South African case, I show that a variety of policy options were on the table, as demonstrated by the intense internal jostling (within the ANC alliance) for the adoption of various policy positions (and not others). By the same token, this is by no means an afro-pessimistic view of developmental state-making prospects in South Africa, far from it, both the internal and external socio-economic conditions present a lot of strategic gaps, opportunities and room to manoeuvre. What has been missing is a developmental leadership that will both identify and appreciate such opportunities and one that has the strategic wherewithal to navigate the difficult (but not insurmountable) hurdles towards developmental state-making. The past twenty-two years have not been 'anti-developmental' but they have been 'non-developmental'. This distinction is important as it recognizes hard work and quantitative efforts at transforming South African society. At the same time, however, there is also recognition that such efforts were largely thwarted by bad politics and a bad ideological framework. The next few pages underline and summarise the developmental performance, obstacles and prospects in post-apartheid South Africa. This chapter also provides some pointers regarding how the transition in post-apartheid South Africa could somehow be re-imagined in pursuit of different ideological, political, policy and developmental outcomes. In this regard, the following themes are discussed, each in turn: Ideology and developmental state-making, the primacy of politics and a brief statement on developmental state prospects in South Africa, moving forward.

Developmental State-making and ideology

The ideological framework and accumulation strategy currently operating in post-apartheid South Africa has its roots in the late 1800s, with the discovery of minerals. True, there has been periodic tinkering with aspects of policy and strategy, but in the main, the fundamental ideas guiding South African growth and development paradigm have not fundamentally altered in the past hundred years or so. I have shown in chapter three that in the early 1950s, following the National Party victory and the ascendance to power of a new nationalist elite, important changes were effected to the operations and workings of the system. The idea was to overhaul the structure of accumulation in such a way that a new social agenda (Afrikaner nationalism is served and advantaged). What was novel and innovative about the apartheid state however, had to do with the post-war socio-economic environment and the new ideas this spawned. The need for post-war reconstruction, job creation and poverty alleviation, put states and state-centred developmental approaches (Keynesianism, social democracy, socialism etc), at the centre of much development thinking in the 1950s and 1960s. The Apartheid state was thus not immune to these influences, and this partly explains the developmentalist state attributes discussed in chapter two. The dominant (statist) ideas of this period seem to have chimed and coincided with the Afrikaner elite's desire to effectively drive a race-based developmental agenda, that fundamentally transformed the human development and economic status of Afrikaners in particular and whites in general. I have also suggested that the East Asian developmental elites benefited and made effective use of the post-war surge in statist theories. However, this period and the ideas associated with it started disintegrating in the early and mid- 1970s. The first trigger point was the collapse of the gold standard, which opened the way for a new regime of flouting currencies and money derivatives. Secondly, the oil price crash occasioned by the Arab oil embargo and a seventy per cent oil hike (between 1973 and 1980, oil prices increased ten-fold), and later the Iranian revolution. The gradual and later very rapid and stark unravelling of the Soviet Union would set the scene for a new era of global economic and social organisation. These developments, of course, paved the way for the reversal of state-led developmental experiments and the intellectual discourse this had spawned. In response to and to counter-act what was seen by liberal and neo-classical theorists as massive state failure, high deficits, rent-seeking, a suffocation of the market mechanism, and in general, 'macro-economic populism', a new set of policy ideas were aggressively and enthusiastically introduced. The alternatives were ostensibly simple and straight-forward. Lower tariff barriers, elimination of restrictions on imports, stabilize, liberalise and privatise. Consequently, demand-management policies, income distribution, equality, employment creation and shared prosperity were all kicked sideways in favour of the new orthodoxy. More than thirty years down the line, very few proponents of this policy suit care to interrogate and indeed, to explain why it is that implementation of these policies have not eventuated in

217

radically improved economic and developmental performance. The performance has been particularly dismal in the developing world. Instead, most countries that benefited from these policies were economically and socially ruined. Despite this poor record and a deeply tarnished image, neo-liberalism continue to shape and drive policy (as in Greece). In response to the generalized socio-economic crisis engulfing South Africa, the South African Institute on Race Relations (SAIRR), recently called for a return to GEAR (SAIRR, 2015). Clearly, it will take time, commitment and a great deal of effort for these flawed and discredited ideas to be finally put to bed. After all, a whole generation of economists have staked their careers and reputations on them. That partly explains the resilience. Remarkably, socio-economic improvements were experienced in those countries that went out of their way to avoid or actively resist neo-liberal policies (Korea, Taiwan, China, Vietnam etc). Post-apartheid South Africa, as I show, unfortunately and with all the benefit of what transpired in those countries that embraced the neo-liberal package, nonetheless, chose to follow the same policy and ideological path. This has largely been to the detriment of developmental state-making, growth, genuine efforts at attending to the structural underpinnings of unemployment and inequality. Twenty-two years down the line, we have yet to see the deployment of a set of policies designed to unravel the racially defined wage structure; racially biased and deeply segmented labour market and an economic structure designed to serve a tiny minority of the population. This is notwithstanding the introduction of various growth and development strategies the fundamental institutional and structural basis of which remain steeped in neoliberal orthodoxy. However, as I show in chapters five and six, the policies adopted and vigorously pursued in post-apartheid South Africa, do not, as many have sought to suggest, represent a neo-liberal capitulation. Instead, the current policy trajectory represents and is a reflection of the views of winners in the internal economic policy battles within the ANC-led alliance.

A dominant ideological and intellectual environment in and of itself does not guarantee developmental success. A critical element in turning things around one way or the other, resides in the role of the subjective factor. This refers to the role of philosophers, economists, economic historians, social scientists, academics, policy-makers and other opinion-makers and leaders, in shaping and driving public opinion and in the process, reinforce and spread the reach of the dominant ideas. And, as part of this neo-liberal 'counter-revolution', it has become learned convention that drivers of economic policy in most International Financial Institutions (IFI) and National Treasuries have to be conservative economists, engineers and other technocrats. This is due to the belief in such institutions that developmental and economic policy is not a deeply ideological and political process, but a technical and administrative one. In this regard, what is required are professionals armed with various econometric models and templates, in order to solve what are essentially straight-forward growth and developmental problems in the world, especially the developing world. Indeed, for decades, World Bank economists and other technocrats failed miserably to accurately explicate the phenomenal developmental success of East Asian countries. For, the fundamentally political and heterodox ideological explanations did not conform to ready-made models and templates. Instead, what these experiences called for was something foreign and completely out of the reach of the technocrats charged with policy - political analysis and a solid grasp of the global regime of accumulation that shaped and reproduced flawed policies and poor economic performance. It also took the spectacular failure of structural adjustment programmes and later, 'good governance' interventions for sanity to prevail. Though the numbers are far from adequate, there is, at least, increasing recognition of the importance of social and political scientists, economic historians and other non-technocratic professionals in the international development policy field. Indeed, the difference is discernible in the quality of papers, reports, research and other works of organisations such as the UNDP, World Bank, World Economic Forum etc. It could very well be, that IMF director, Jonathan Ostry, with an academic background in philosophy and politics represent a long overdue rapture in the quality of the Fund's research and recommendations. Ostry (2016) and colleagues is the author of a stinging critique of the policy and developmental impact of neo-liberal policies in both the global north but especially in the south. The paper warns that neo-liberal policies have stunted growth and has increased inequality. This is a tiny and inadequate step in the right direction but one that nonetheless requires recognition, for it does go some way in tempering with one-sided, one size-fits all technocratic and ideologically inspired models in the global and national development policy discourse. Whereas at the level of International financial institutions (IFI) and international development agencies, there is a gradual recognition of the need for ideological plurality and heterodox policy approaches, states in the developing world have generally been slow in following suit. From Treasury, the Reserve Bank, economic development and trade departments, there is still an engrained belief that senior employees (if not technical advisors from IFI), must at least be traditional (neo-classically trained) economists. As a consequence, these state departments remain bastions of economic conservatism, prudence and poor developmental performance. They generally receive good feedback from rating agencies and

IFIs for their prudence and excellent management of the fiscus. However, while there is much blame gaming about poor governance, corruption etc., rarely do these IFIs pause to interrogate the fault-lines inherent in the dominant framework. Therefore, part of the big ideological challenge is that of deliberately and consciously imposing non-economists in key global development policy organisations and internally – in departments traditionally reserved for technocrats. The significance of this reside in the fact that it will open doors for continued interdisciplinary intellectual engagement, in the search for solutions to the growth and developmental problems confronting humanity in the twenty first century. Ultimately, in order to overhaul the current flawed transformation template in South Africa, determined policy, ideological and intellectual action needs to be taken in order to attend to its ideological (institutional and structural) foundations. Doing so will require the eschewal of orthodoxy in all its forms, and a move towards more heterodox approaches to state-making, policy-making and developmental change more broadly. There is a preponderance of voices crying out for more heterodox approaches to economics and economic policy formulation (Chang, 2014). The critical point is that the economics taught in most of our universities, neo-classical economics is not the only way of doing economics. Instead, Chang argues, there are nine different schools of economics, none of which, on their own, have been helpful in apprehending the complex socio-economic and developmental phenomena of our times. There is much to be learnt from each school, and in the process to produce qualitatively new knowledge, in aid of growth and development in the developing world. For, the few developmental success stories that have made waves in recent times, have achieved their success through creative, dynamic and crucially, unorthodox policy means. However, as I argue throughout the book, the state (its role differently conceived) will have to be at the heart of such exploration and re-imagination of developmental change. So, it matters who runs the state and what suit of policy skills they bring both individually or as teams. The role and place of ideology is not always sufficiently appreciated and factored into developmental theories, I show throughout that this omission has been to the detriment of such theories. Not only is much development theory the poorer for this neglect, but it has also left it analytically blunt and ineffectual, in apprehending and comprehending the structural, institutional and ideological framework within which such developmental process take place. Unsurprisingly, the income and inequality gap between rich and poor countries has widened in the past thirty years or so. And, so too, has the gap, as Piketty (2014) so eloquently demonstrate, between rich and poor within countries widened.

History is littered with real life and very tragic consequences of this neglect of ideology and the structural underpinnings of underdevelopment and sluggish growth. The Duvalier dynasty ruled Haiti for twenty-nine years from the 1960s. Their reign is remembered less for its economic performance – growth and development and more for its repression, poverty and *'le misere'* (misery). The critical point I am bringing to the fore, however, is that it has been more than thirty years since the fall of the Duvaliers in Haiti, and there have been very determined efforts by local and external policy players to rebuild that country. Still, *le misère,* poverty, underdevelopment, unemployment, and hopelessness continue to be the defining feature and hallmark of Haitian society. I suggest that this developmental failure is largely a function of both ideology and politics. On the ideological front, the ideological and structural underpinnings of Duvaliarism have yet to be confronted and effectively dealt with by the various developmental plans designed by international developmental agencies. And, these international development agencies stubbornly refuse to move away from discredited neo-liberal policy templates, that do very little to confront the structural underpinnings of underdevelopment and sluggish growth. I show with respect to both East Asia and post-apartheid South Africa that no matter how well intentioned and how determined the efforts of individuals and groups of individuals, if such efforts do not take cognizance of and give due attention to ideology and structural issues, these efforts will invariably founder. But for the ideological issues to be effectively tackled, a particular type of politics and leadership are called for – developmental politics driven by a developmental leadership.

In Mobutu Seseko's Zaire too (now the Democratic Republic of Congo), close to thirty years after the demise of Mobutu's predatory regime, the DRC has yet to recover from that legacy. True, the country has experienced intermittent war and instability, but as I show constantly, post-war reconstruction has been known to pave the way for growth and development. However, to be able to take advantage of the post-war reconstruction possibilities provided by a war situation, a particular type of politics and political processes are called for. Developmental states driven by developmental leadership do more than just drive a growth and developmental processes – they do so in ways that affect and fundamentally shake the institutional, ideological and structural foundations of the old order. As the recent history of both DRC and Haiti abundantly demonstrate, developmental failure invariably lead to greater reliance on repression and naked force – as the citizenry demonstrates its discontent. Of course, post-apartheid South Africa is not here yet, but parallels are hard to ignore, especially if the down-ward spiral (structural unemployment, inequality and sluggish growth), is not arrested soon. Indeed, the

Marikana massacre and the recent # Fees must fall student movement, and the response of the state security services all point to the desperate and urgent need for a re-imagination of the South African transition. I thus conclude as I argue throughout the book that the key fault-lines in South Africa's 1994 transition prospectus reside in a fundamentally flawed ideological framework and a politics (including leadership) that is non-developmental. What is bewildering about post-apartheid South Africa's insistence on traversing the well-worn path of neo-liberal growth and development strategies is that there is statistical evidence aplenty to demonstrate that growth, development and relative equity in the past twenty five years have been experienced in countries that have embraced heterodox strategies. Indeed, a cursory look at the World Bank's 2015 statistical information is instructive in so many different respects. However, this information does confirm the main thesis of this book, this is not only that ideology matters but also that those countries (whether through conscious state leadership or the exigencies of war and post-war reconstruction), seem to have done consistently well in terms of GDP (over a twenty-five-year horizon). On the other hand, the rest of the developing world (including post-apartheid South Africa), that elected to stick with neo-liberal prescripts have generally experienced economic decline and deceleration in the same period. It is worth reprinting this table for emphasis.

Gross Domestic Product – average annual % growth

Country	1989 - 2000	2000 – 2009	2009 – 2013
Cambodia	7.0	9.2	7.0
China	10.6	10.9	8.7
Indonesia	6.0	7.6	6.9
Iraq	10.3	3.8	8.1
Lao PDR	6.4	7.0	8.2
Qatar	11.1	13.5	10.2
Singapore	7.2	6.0	6.3
South Africa	2.1	4.0	2.7
Vietnam	7.9	6.8	5.8

Source: World Development Indicators (2015)

No doubt, there are caveats, faults and loopholes aplenty to throw at these countries. Nonetheless, in this day and age, any country or group of countries that can sustain such spectacular levels of growth over such a prolonged period, surely deserve looking into. I suggest that much of the explanation has to do with the implementation of policies that deviate from the neo-liberal norm. The policy mix is generally heterodox, home-brewed and above all, informed by the concrete socio-economic challenges confronting the countries concerned. It has also not hurt these country's growth and development prospects that they have inserted themselves into the global trading system largely on their own terms.

So, for these and many other reasons besides, ideology matters in developmental theory in general and developmental state-making processes in particular.

The Centrality of Politics in Developmental state-making

Like ideology, politics and political processes play an extremely important role in shaping the character and content of any developmental change process. This is because, in large measure, the developmental objectives of these state types have been politically driven, and the politics developmentally driven. This dialectical relationship between developmental theory and political processes and practices is not always sufficiently captured in developmental state-making processes. Throughout the book, I underline and emphasise the role and place of politics and political processes, and I do this for two reasons. First, emphasizing politics and political processes enriches and enhances the explanatory force of developmental theories in general and developmental state-making processes in particular. Secondly, and crucially, politics and political processes are at the very heart of all developmental and social processes and as such 'taking politics out' of development studies and developmental economics is to obscure the inner kernel of this sub-field. And, if politics is to be understood as the dynamic and contingent relationship around which conflicts over the use, production, distribution and deployment of resources inside and outside the state, at local, provincial and national level, then it should be clear why it matters so much in developmental state-making. After all, however such conflicts are resolved, they invariably alter power dynamics in the societies affected. Simply put, politics and political processes create winners and losers, annihilates or weakens old vested interests and create new ones, it shapes and affects the proximity of certain groups and individuals to power (negatively and positively, as the case may be). Key political variables associated with developmental state-making have included leadership cohesion, institution-building, state-society relations, attitude and approach to graft, bureaucratic power - all of which have important implications for South Africa's post-apartheid state-making attempts. An important political variable is the ability of the leadership elite to accurately define and understand the socio-economic, ideological and political factors confronting the country. Once such diagnosis has been made, political leadership must be prepared to set in motion political strategies and plans designed to destroy the power and politics that sustain such socio-economic problems. Typically, in the South African context, such problems will include poverty, unemployment, and inequality. Developmental state politics mean that the leadership does much more than just tinker with these social problems but goes much further and attend to the institutions, power, power relations, politics and structural arrangements that sustain and reproduce these social ills. I show throughout the foregoing chapters that post-apartheid South African politics distinctly lacked the developmental sting associated with East Asian developmental state politics. In large measure, the underwhelming developmental performance of the post-apartheid state has its roots in the deployment and pervasiveness of a politics that can be termed 'non-developmental'. However, there are several political factors and circumstances that simply do not chime with successful developmental state-making politics.

Developmental Leadership

This is a critically important developmental state attribute that is to be found in all successful developmental states. I have shown that in both South Korea, Taiwan and latterly, China, successful state-led growth and development experiments were determined by the ideological coherence and common values of the leadership elites. The politics in these societies reinforced such coherence and in turn, drove the momentum for developmental change. Thanks to the real or perceived dangers of foreign or communist domination, like in Stalin's Russia or in Park's South Korea, the elites in these countries saw economic development and modernization of their back-ward countries as the only solution to the perceived threats. In practical terms, this cohesion was reflected in the careful monitoring and restriction of the economic role and trading activities of foreign firms in these countries. Clarity of purpose and leadership cohesion was also demonstrated in the insistence on challenging (rather than an uncritical acceptance) and skilfully manipulating complex global and geo-political pressures, in the developmental interest of society as a whole. Consistent with the developmental leadership's commitment of economic growth and development, the states were turned into decisive instruments for driving these objectives and in the process, radically redefined the social structures and organisation of these societies.

True, rent-seeking and corruption are an integral part of any state-making process, this is more prevalent in instances where the role of the state is pervasive. None of the successful developmental states have been spared the scourge of corruption and rents, but there are reasons why these phenomena have not eclipsed human and economic development success stories. The first reason has to do with the fact that at the summit of their developmental state-making processes, the overriding and most pervasive activities in society had to do with constructive state-led developmental processes. So focused were the state actors on their *raison' detre* – economic development, that corruption and other anti-social and unethical activities (while very much prevalent), took a back seat relative to the good work of driving economic growth and development. The second reason has to do with leadership cohesion driven by a common political and ideological outlook. This has meant that even senior party officials who negate the developmental agenda set by the developmental elite face the full might of the law. A recent *New York Times* report has suggested that Malaysian Prime Minister, Najib Razak, who has allegations of corruption hanging over his head, faces significant opposition and appears isolated in his own party (07, October 2015). At the same time, reports from the People's Republic of China would seem to suggest that President Xi Jinpin has intensified the party's anti-corruption drive, leading to the life imprisonment of a senior politburo member Zhou Yongkang and many others. Not only does such swift action against (especially) senior government and party personalities, build public confidence in the state, but it also helps to sustain the country's growth and developmental momentum. It focuses the attention and energies of all on socio-economic and developmental challenges. In the absence of such swift and decisive action, however, developing countries can and do easily get swept into a developmental imbroglio, that eats away at the developmental gains (not unlike the Philippines under Marcos, or Mobutu's Zaire). In the context of post-apartheid South Africa, the critical political factor is that developmentally driven politics give rise to a developmental state culture and developmental leadership, which will have the foresight and political wherewithal to deal mercilessly with anti-social and anti-developmental tendencies. Especially when such tendencies affect senior leadership personalities, as in the Malay Prime Minister. Post-apartheid South Africa has yet to produce this kind of politics and the associated developmental leadership.

Indeed, reports by Corruption Watch and Transparency International seem to suggest that corruption is trumping growth and economic development, in the public discourse. According to the 2014/15 Corruption Watch Annual Report, corruption and impropriety, especially within the state, has increased unabated in South Africa, with the country jumping five places to 67 in rank. This means that South Africa scored 44th in the Corruption

Perception Index (CPI). Transparency International regards any country that scores below 50 as having a significant corruption problem. Poor leadership over this and other counter-developmental tendencies has had knock-on developmental effects. The country and the leadership get sucked into defending corrupt colleagues and party members and in the process get completely de-focused. This is a surefire way of how not to do a developmental state. The biggest leadership problem in post-apartheid South Africa has been its non-developmental character and its 'softness' and lack of capacity and capability in relation to the complex and difficult tasks confronting developmental states.

Role of the State

The analysis of developmental state politics in East Asia and elsewhere in the world, shows the role of the state to be a critically important political variable for explaining developmental success or failure. Specifically, the state's role in steering and overhauling the economic policy trajectory in a developmental direction, stands out as a game-changer in state-making processes. Furthermore, developmental state theory brings to the fore the need for political and bureaucratic leadership with the credentials and capacity to resist capture by vested interests. Such tactical and strategic capacity, as a rule, will include the ability of the political and bureaucratic leadership to make effective use of all available policy tools to drive a growth and development agenda. Typically, some of these instruments will fall outside the neo-liberal policy templates, but will be part of a broader, very diverse and heterodox policy mix. Developmental state theory suggests that an essential condition for effective state economic intervention is the ability of state actors to steer clear of special/social pressures and interests. Quite often, these special interests are not individual local corporates. The main driver for the reproduction of flawed policies is the debilitating fear or firm belief that the deployment of a policy mix that falls outside the template will lead to loss of investment. This despite tons of empirical evidence (China, Vietnam, DRC, Tunisia, South Sudan etc), disproving this misconception of what essentially drives foreign direct investment. Although I have shown that there are historically specific conditions that gave rise to and facilitate what Marx referred to as 'Bonapartist states' in East Asia, It does appear that the political and developmental experience of post-apartheid South Africa has spawned a politics and state-type that was readily malleable to corporate and ideological capture. In other words, the leadership elite attached the state and defined its role in accordance with the prevailing and dominant ideological discourse. Thus, the efficacy and developmental impact of the state is contingent on two important aspects, as the post-apartheid state-making process shows: the relative distance of the state elite to vested interests (especially, class, finance and conglomerates) and crucially, the politics, capacity and ideological orientation of those who exercise power over the state. Such relative distance does not imply hostility. Instead, it has meant that the state has been able to act unencumbered by sectional interests or has generally been able to avoid state capture and consistently acted in the interest of growth and development.

My examination of the South African transition shows that, contrary to the East Asian experiences, the new leadership and state elites were not able to position the state and a developmental trajectory away and above vested class, corporate and social interests. Instead, the policy making process (especially the economic policy making process) was intensely contested, with both labour and capital seeking to influence the shape and content of the new economic order. Moreover, I also demonstrate that the strategic posture of the leadership elite, during the constitutional negotiations did much to undermine developmentalist prospects. The entrenchment of property rights in the Interim Constitution did much to undermine the kind of redistributive role of the state that the South Korean, Taiwanese and indeed, Maoist states were able to push through in East Asia. As I have shown, in those countries, early redistribution, land and agrarian reforms did much to impose equity, redress and social stability. Above all, however, such agrarian reform did not only dynamise and stimulate rural economic growth but this set the foundation for high level industrial growth and development. It is germane too, that it took most East Asian elites no more than two years to resolve (redistribute) the land and agrarian problems in those countries. Thus, the strength of social classes and vested interests in the South African transition, and the politics, political processes and prospectus that undergirded that transition precluded relative state autonomy and the decisive leadership role that the East Asian developmental states are renowned for.

State-society Relations

Whereas the Japanese, Koreans and Taiwanese state elites designed extensive and comprehensive strategies to penetrate all sectors of society, no such plan is discernible in the South African transition (apart for a very brief moment when there was a drive to make the RDP people-centred and people driven). Another missing variable in the South African context are the growth and developmental coalitions created by East Asian states, designed to impose a growth and development agenda on the one hand, and to impose mutually beneficial state-business partnerships on the other. In the main, these were comprehensive coalitions that stretched to all sectors of the economy (especially those deemed as strategic to the state's developmental agenda). It was through these partnerships that the trade regime and trade relations of the state were defined – in the putative interests of the country's growth and development objectives. If there is one political variable that really accounts for the rare developmental success of East Asian developmental states, it must be their institutional arrangements. There is general consensus in the literature that the institutional arrangements designed and located at the apex of the decision-making, implementation and monitoring pipe-line, were a critical developmental success factor. If developmental objectives are to be achieved, then the structures and institutions of the state must be organized around and be poised to achieve that which defines the state and its principal priority – economic development. In the case of Japan, it was MITI, The Economic Planning Board in Korea, The Economic Development Board in Singapore and in all cases, the president is a key member of such institutions. This gave them power, prestige and incredible levels of autonomy and space to act decisively unencumbered by normal bureaucratic red tape. Such was the case in the successful attempts at developmental state-making. I show that in post-apartheid South Africa, undergirded by a different type of politics, there was only the briefest flirtation with institutional arrangements designed for developmental success. This was the RDP Office, which was hastily abandoned, as it struggled to sustain competing policy, political, ideological and developmental priorities and personal tensions between ministers. Unlike Korea or Taiwan were labour and the left were relatively weak at the onset of the industrial process, South Africa and post-apartheid South Africa presented a different reality. A strong and vocal labour and left movement was an important inheritance of the post-apartheid elite. This was always going to be a curse or blessing depending on the ideological, political and policy trajectory that emerged after an intense internal policy conflict within the alliance. Vested interests, expectations, opportunism and political intrigue was also going to be key in the positioning of the labour and left movement within the alliance. As it happened, the first few years of democracy saw a very uneasy and often acrimonious relationship between labour and the left on the one hand and the new state elites and capital on the other. Officially, the cause of conflict was economic policy and specifically, what came to be dubbed the '1996 class project' (the abandonment of the RDP in favour of a thoroughly neo-liberal GEAR programme). The change of political guard at the ANCs Polokwane conference in 2007, has not given rise to any new ideological and policy trajectory. Instead, the neo-liberal structural and institutional foundations of the regime of accumulation have been consolidated and adapted to the post-2008 recession realities (of austerity, increased inequality, unemployment and a predominance of state-less and borderless finance capital). Despite the intensity of the squeeze on the working classes and the poor in the post- 2008 period, it would seem a significant section of the labour and left movement (at least within the alliance), has found strategic convergence and a rapprochement of sorts within the broad neo-liberal regime of accumulation. The most cynical analysts have attributed this acquiescence of labour and the left with the essential elements of the '1996 class project' to the clever deployment of leading left personalities to government positions. Indeed, not only are these voices muffled, at government level, leading left and labour elements are at the forefront of implementing much the same policies that they had so vociferously objected to, not too long ago. At any rate, as I show throughout, this kind of ideological convergence and or co-option does not a developmental state make, what is required instead, is a leadership cohesion built around the imperatives of growth, development, equity and redistribution.

Meritocratic bureaucracy

Often, the meritocracy, capacity, technical competence and relative insulation of the East Asian bureaucratic administrators are counter-posed to so-called cadre deployment. The comparisons are not all that neat and straight-forward. But some inferences are certainly possible. First, it makes a world of difference when the country is overseen by a strong developmentally and ideologically cohesive leadership. When bureaucrats know the line of march, there is less likely to be confusion in implementation and strategy. Second, and this is a world phenomenon, all political elites prefer and do deploy individuals who are sympathetic to their cause to senior government positions. However, what does discredit cadre deployment is the flooding of the bureaucracy with poorly qualified, incompetent and technically challenged party sycophants. Also, it is soul-destroying when the few party members and sympathisers who are competent professionals are subjected to destructive political interference and pressure. Often for nefarious reasons that have absolutely nothing to do with fixing the country's many ills. The Koreans and Taiwanese certainly spent a lot of money on training, not only were the bureaucrats recruited from the most prestigious national schools and universities, but large numbers were also sent to the best institutions in the US, UK and elsewhere in Europe, to further their studies.

It was precisely because of the confidence and trust the politicians had in the loyalty and competence of the senior bureaucrats that these are credited with driving developmental policy, often contradicting one myopic and self-interested political agenda or the other. Of course, the insulated policy development and implementation institutions and institutional arrangements facilitated this. Also, their relative insulation helped to keep rent-seeking and corruption in check, somewhat. Third, so committed were these states to their developmental objectives that they were readily and often did actively compete with the private sector in terms of remuneration. This was especially the case in respect of the finance bureaucracy (mostly economists, lawyers, senior army types etc), who also ran and expanded the developmental role of state owned enterprises (SOE). In the final analysis, the relative success of developmental states and the failure of some aspirant developmental state elites reside in the mutually reinforcing relationship between institutions, competence and a supportive political and ideological system.

Prospects for developmental state-making in post-Apartheid South Africa

Between 1988 -2002, real GDP growth in South Africa was 1.4 % annually. GEAR predicted 6 % to 7% by the year 2000 (TIPS, 2002). According to Statistics South Africa, official unemployment increased from 19.3 % in 1996 to 29 % in 2001, and the expanded rate increased from 33 % to 37 % over the same period (SSA, 2001). Meanwhile, the South African branch of Norway's Institute for Applied Social Science, reported that the poorest 50 % of the population received about 10 % of national income, while the richest 10 % took 50% of total income (www.news24.com26/02/2003). This survey also found that household income inequality had actually increased since 1994 (ibid). The new government's stated objectives of poverty alleviation and denting the apartheid inheritance remain hampered by bureaucratic incapacity and the inability of the new state elites to exert their authority over the process of change. This state of affairs would appear to give credence to the overall argument and conclusion of this book, and this is that without an activist state orchestrating and directing economic development, growth in South Africa will remain slow and inadequate. At any rate, the rates of inequality and deprivation are so high and the development prospectus so flawed that no amount of growth is likely to address poverty, inequality and unemployment. For these social problems are not transient, nor momentary encumbrances on an otherwise excellent regime of accumulation and distribution (the 'fundamentals' are not only not in place, but what fundamentals are in place are completely at odds with redistributionist and developmental challenges confronting the country). Furthermore, these 'contradictions' are deeply structural and institutional and owe their existence and endurance to the chosen development trajectory. The experiences of Bolivia (where a similar development trajectory was followed in 1989) are instructive. That country rapidly disintegrated into instability and violence, as the poorest sections of the community felt the disempowering impact of such policies. At the same time, the Bolivian state responded with increasing violence and authoritarianism to these legitimate protests. It was only after the democratic election of Evo Morales in 2006, following a sustained and successful campaign against neo-liberalism, by a broad section of the community, that Bolivia's developmental prospects improved. My comparative examination of the politics and ideas that underpinned South Korea, Taiwan and South Africa, seem to suggest that South Africa's continuing socio-economic strife can only be prevented through a growth and development strategy akin to those driven by developmental states. In other words, a new kind of politics and a new set of ideas are called for, radical, developmentalist and redistributionist. Ironically, despite their anti-democratic and authoritarian stigma, a significant section of left and ANC allied thinkers, have increasingly been sifting through the developmental state literature in search of working alternative development models. There is now broad convergence among left thinkers on the need for:

> a feasible menu of developmentalist-state interventions along East Asian lines. Such strategic policy positions should include the imposition of a watertight exchange controls; strategic state spending and the redirection of finance to social uses; increasing nationalization of strategic sites of the economy....and a more general commitment to get the prices wrong (Patrick Bond: Interview).

The RDP was highly important, and presented the new elite with immense opportunities for crafting a growth and development path akin to the East Asian developmental states. However, as the foregoing chapters and pages clearly demonstrate, the ideas and politics of post-apartheid South Africa just did not lend itself to the construction of such a state type. The internal and external political and ideological factors and circumstances, interests and expectations seem to have overwhelmed the thin reeds on which the transition rested. Instead, new political challenges have emerged, placing evermore pressure on the prospects for developmental state-making in South Africa. These include the prominence of corruption, the desperate need for economic and political leadership, in order to re-imagine the transformation prospectus. For this to happen, a new set of ideas, policies, politics, institutional and structural instruments are called for. The recent poor showing of the ANC in Local Government Elections 2016, may not be unrelated to the gradual erosion of confidence and legitimacy of the former liberation movement in the eyes of an ever growing number of South Africans. Yet, following a four day 'soul-searching' exercise, the National Executive Committee (NEC) of the ruling party, came out insisting on staying the neo-liberal course. In a detailed press statement, the ANC believe firmly that at the heart of its poor electoral showing and eroding support from its traditional base are subjective issue: corruption, organisational weaknesses, lack of leadership capacity at various levels of the organisation and poor performance by some state entities, notably, South African Airways, South African Broadcasting Corporation and the electricity entity – ESKOM. Not only did the soul-searching exercise fail to identify a lack of developmental leadership and intelligent state activism as a contributory factor for dwindling support for the ANC. There was also no reference to the urgent and pressing need for a review of the structural arrangements underpinning the country's development strategy. There is consensus that the current intellectual discourse is unlikely to change in the near future.

In the final analysis, the poor economic and developmental performance in post-apartheid South Africa is closely bound up with the absence and failure to construct a capable developmental state.

Conclusion:
'No developmental state no development'

The critical aphorism 'no developmental state no development' rings very true for post-apartheid state-making, for all the reasons set out in the foregoing pages. This raises the question of whether South Africa's moment for developmental state-making has been squandered never to return? True, much international good will, developmental momentum and expectation could and should have been managed better. In those early days, the delicate balance between democracy and development could also have been managed differently. Post-apartheid South Africa's insertion (and the sequencing of that insertion) into the global trading system and the global economic system should have been managed with better care for the developmental challenges and inequalities confronting the country. However, as I indicate in the beginning, this is by no means an afro-pessimistic take on South Africa's developmental prospects. Furthermore, I stand firm in my belief that in politics, there is always room to manoeuvre, policy choices and intentional action. So, NO, prospects for developmental state-making may have been severely circumscribed in the intervening twenty-two years, but scope and room for re-imagination of the post-apartheid transition (ideology and politics) remain.

Apart from the re-imagination of the ideological prospectus, its politics and policy mix, the past few years have sharply brought to the fore several other variables and determinants for a change in direction. These include: the need for a developmental leadership, an understanding of unemployment, poverty and inequality as structural and not transient, a focus on foot-loose levels of corruption, effective developmental institutional arrangements, smart economic management (growth coalitions at local, provincial and national levels), and of course, cohesion and renewal of key agents for change. These are critically important variables that require attention, but the point of departure, as I show throughout, is to get the ideology and politics right.

References

Abedian, I. and Standish, B. (1984) 'An Analysis of the Sources of Growth in State Expenditure in South Africa 1920 – 1982' *South African Journal of Economics*, Vol. 4, No 52

Abedian, I. and Standish, B. (1985) 'Poor Whites and the Role of the State', *South African Journal of Economics*, Vol. 53 No. 2

Aberbach, J. D. , Dollar, D. and Sokoloff, L. K. (eds) (1994) *The Role of the State in Taiwan's Development* (New York, M.E. Sharpe, Inc.)

Adelman, I. G. and Robinson, S (1978) Income Distribution Policy in Developing Countries: a case study South Korea (Stanford, Stanford University Press)

Adelzadeh, A. and Padayachee, V. (1994) 'The RDP White Paper: Reconstruction of a Development Vision', *Transformation*, No 25, 1994

Adler, T. (ed) (1977) *Perspectives on South Africa: A Collection of Working Papers*. African Studies Institute (Johannesburg, University of Witswatersrand).

Africa Confidential (1993) Vol. 34 No. 20 (London, Miramoor Publications Ltd)

Africa Confidential (1993) Vol. 34, No 24 (London, Miramoor Publications Ltd)

Africa Confidential (1994) Vol. 35, No. 10 (London, Miramoor Publications Ltd)

Ahluwalia, M. S. (1974) 'The Scope for Policy Intervention' in H.B. Chenery (ed.) *Redistribution with Growth* (London, Oxford University Press)

Akyuz, Y.; Chang, H. and Kozu-Wright, R. (1998) 'New Perspectives on East Asian Development' in *Journal of Development Studies,* Vol. 34, No. 6

Alexander, N. 91992) 'National Liberation and Socialist Revolution' in Callinicos, A. `*Between Apartheid and Capitalism'* (London, Bookmarks)

Allen, T. and Thomas, A. (1992) Poverty and Development in the 1990s (Oxford, Oxford University Press)

Alson, L. S.; Eggertsson, and North, D.C. (1996) *Empirical Studies in Institutional Change: Political Economy of Institutions and Decisions* (Cambridge, Cambridge University Press)

Amin, S. (1996) 'The New Capitalist Globalisation- Problems and Perspectives' *Links,* No. 7 July-October 1994 (Australia, New Course Publications)

Amuwo, A. (2008) 'Constructing The Democratic Developmental State in Africa' – A Case Study of Nigeria, 1960 – 2007, Institute for Global Dialogue, Occasional Paper No. 59

Amsden, A. (1998) Asia's Next Giant: South Korea and Late Industrialisation (New York, Cambridge University Press)

ANC (African National Congress) (1996) Morogoro Conference Documents. (www.anc.org.za/ancdocs/history/morogoro.html)

ANC (African National Congress) (1985) Kabwe Conference Documents. (www.anc.org.za/ancdocs/history/kabwe.html)

ANC (African National Congress) (1990) DEP Discussion Document: Economic Policy, (Johannesburg, ANC)

ANC (African National Congress) (1994*) Reconstruction and Development Programme, (*Johannesburg, Umanyano Publications)

ANC (African National Congress) (1994) The Reconstruction and Development Programme: A Policy Framework (Johannesburg: ANC)

ANC (African National Congress) (1996) 'The State and Social Transformation' ANC Discussion Document (Johannesburg: ANC)

ANC (African National Congress) (1997) 'ANC National Policy Conference- 1997' (Johannesburg, ANC NEC)

ANC (African National Congress) (2001) 'Briefing Notes on the Alliance' ANC Discussion Document, (Johannesburg, ANC Head Office)

ANC (African National Congress) (2002) 'Draft Discussion Document on allegations of Neo-Liberalism' (Johannesburg, ANC NEC)

Ardington, E. and Nattrass, N. (eds) (1990) *The Political Economy of South Africa* (Cape Town, Oxford University Press)

Arendt, H. W. (1988) 'Market Failure and Underdevelopment' in *World Development* Vol. 2, No.16

Astro, A. (1983) Zimbabwe: A Revolution that lost its way? (London. Zed Press)

Assies, W. (2003) 'David versus Goliath in Cochamba: Water Rights, Neo-liberalism and the Revival of Social Protests in Bolivia' *Latin American Perspectives*, Issue 130, Vol. 30 No. 3

Aoki, M. et l (eds.) (1997) The Role of Government in East Asian Economic Development: Comparative Institutional Analysis (Oxford, Clarendon Publishers)

Bagchi, A.K. (1987) Public Intervention and Industrial Restructuring in China, India and the Republic of Korea (New Delhi, ILO)

Baker, P.; Borain, A. and Krafchik, W. (eds.) (1992) *South Africa and the World Economy in the 1990s* (Washington DC, Brookings Institute)

Barber, J. (1999) South Africa in the Twentieth Century: A Political History – In Search of a Nation State (Oxford, Blackwell Publishers)

Bauer, P.T. (1976) *Dissent on Development* (London, Cox and Wyman Ltd)

Belli, P.; Finger, M. and Ballivian, A. (1993) 'South Africa: A Review of Trade Policies' Discussion Paper 4 (Washington DC, The World Bank Southern Africa)

Berry, I. and Cline W.R. (1979) The Agrarian Structure and Productivity in Developing Countries (Baltimore, John Hopkins University Press)

Bhagirath, Lal Das (1999) The World Trade Organisation – A Guide to the Framework for International Trade (London, Zed Books Ltd)

Bhorat, H and Leibbracht, M. (1999) Correlates of Vulnerability in the South African Labour Market, DPRU Working Paper (Cape Town, University of Cape Town)

Bhorat, H. (2000) 'How to Reduce South Africa's Wage Gap' *Essays on the South African Labour Market* (Development Policy Research Unit – University of Cape Town)

Bhorat, H., Tseng, H., and Stawix, B. (2014) 'Pro-poor Growth and Social Protection in South Africa: Exploring the Interactions', *Development Southern Africa*, 31 (2)

Bird, A. (1991) 'Developing a "Technology-sensitive" Human Resource Strategy for South Africa' Paper presented at Technology and Reconstruction Colloquium, 4th May (University of Cape Town)

Black, A. and Stanwix, J. (1987) 'Manufacturing Development and the Economic Crisis: Restructuring in the Eighties', *Social Dynamics*, 13 (1)

Black, A. (1991) 'Manufacturing Development and the Economic Crisis: Reversion to primary production? in Gelb, S. (Ed) *South Africa's Economic Crisis,* (Cape Town, David Philip Publishers)

Black, A. (1994) 'The Role of the State in Promoting Industrialisation: Selective Intervention, Trade Orientation and Concessionary Industrial Finance' in Lipton, M. and Simkins, C. *State and Market in Post-Apartheid South Africa* (Johannesburg, Witswatersrand University Press)

Black, and Gerwel, (2014) 'Shifting the Growth Path to Achieve Employment Intensive Growth in South Africa' *Development Southern Africa*, 31 (2)

Blackbourn, D. (1997) Fontana History of Germany: 1780 – 1918, The Long Nineteenth Century (London, Fontana Press)

Blumenfeld, J. (1997) 'From Icon to Scapegoat: The Experience of South Africa's Reconstruction and Development Programme' in *Development Policy Review*, Vol. 15

Brand, S. (1976) 'Alternative Patterns of Industrial Development in South Africa' in Truu, M. (ed) *Public Policy and the South African Economy* (Oxford, Oxford University Press)

Brotz, H. (1977) The Politics of South Africa: Democracy and Racial Diversity (Oxford, Oxford University Press)

Browne, G. W. G. (1983) 'Fifty Years of Public Finance' *South African Journal of Economics*, Vol. 1, No. 51

Braun, G. (1989) 'The Afrikaner Empire Strikes Back: South Africa's Regional Policy' in Brewer, J.D. (ed.) *Can South Africa Survive? Five Minutes to Midnight* (London, Macmillan Press)

Brown, G. (2010) Beyond the Crash: Overcoming the first crisis of Globalisation, (Free Press, London)

BTI (Board of Trade and Industries) (1945) *Manufacturing Industries in the Union of South Africa*, Report No.282 'Investigation into manufacturing Industries in the Union of South Africa, First Interim Report (Pretoria, U.G)

Bond, P. (1990) Commanding Heights and Community Control: Economics for a New South Africa (Johannesburg, Ravan Press)

Bond, P. (1991) South African Socialists in Crisis: The State and the Economy (Johannesburg, Phambili Books)

Bond, P. (2000) Elite Transformation from Apartheid to Neo-liberalism in South Africa (London, Pluto Press)

Bond, P. (2001) *Against Global Apartheid: South Africa Meets the World Bank, IMF and International Finance* (Cape Town, University of Cape Town Press)

Bozzoli, B. (1997) 'A Comment on Capital and the State in South Africa' presented at the African Studies Seminar (Johannesburg, University of Witswatersrand)

Botha, P.W. (1979) *P.W. Botha: A Political Backgrounder* (The South African Embassy, London)

Bundy, C. (1979) *The Rise and Fall of the South African Peasantry* (London, Heinemann Educational Books)

Burroway, M. (1982) 'State and Social Revolution in South Africa' in *Kapitalistate*, Vol. 9

Burkett, P. and Hart-Landsberg, M. (2000) *Development, Crisis and Class Struggle: Learning from Japan and East Asia* (London, Macmillan Press ltd)

Business Day 04 November 1992

Business Day 08 December 1992

Business Day 29 April 1993

Business Day 03 June 1993

Business Day 04 November 1993

Business Day 24 January 1994

Business Day 24 March 1994

Cameron, R. and Tapscott, C. (2000) 'The Challenges of State Transformation in South Africa' in Public Administration and Development, *The*

Journal of International Management Research and Practice, Vol. 20, No. (2)

Callinicos, A. (1986) 'Working Class Politics in South Africa' reprinted from *International Socialism,* No. 31, (London, Socialist Worker's Party)

Callinicos, A. (1988) *South Africa: Between Reform and Revolution* (London, Bookmarks)

Callinicos, A. (2000) Equality (Cambridge, Polity Press)

Cammack, P. (1990) 'Statism, new Institutionalism and Marxism' in The Socialist Register (London, Merlin Press)

Castells, M. (1992) 'Four Asian Tigers with a Dragon Head: A Comparative Analysis of the State, Economy and Society in the Asian Rim' in Appelbaum, R. and Henderson, J. (eds.) *State and Development* (London, Sage Publications)

Cape Times 19 November   1995

CPS (Centre for Policy Studies) (1996) 'Making the Means Justify the Ends? The Theory Practices of the RDP' *Research Report* No. 45, Social Policy Series (Johannesburg)

Chang, H.; Akyuz, Y. and Kozul-Wright, R. 91998) 'New Perspectives on East Asian Development' Journal of Development Studies, Vol. 34 (6)

Chang, Hajoon (1999) 'The Economic Theory of the Developmental State' in Meredith Woo-Cumings (ed.) *The Developmental State* (Ithaca, Cornell University Press)

Chazan, N. et al (1992) *Politics and Society in Contemporary Africa*, 2nd edition (Boulder- Colorado, Lyn Rienne)

Chazan, N.; Lewis, P.; Martimer, A. R; Rotchield, D. and Stedman, J.S. (1999) *Politics and Society in Contemporary Africa*, 3rd edition (Boulder-Colorado, Lynne Rienne

Cheng, J.; Haggard, S. and Kang, D. (1998) 'Institutions and Growth in Korea and Taiwan: The Bureaucracy' *Journal of Developmental Studies* Vol. 34 (6)

Cherry, F. (1992) 'Debt, Development and Democracy – The IMF/World Bank in Africa' *Work in Progress*, No. 82, June

Chibber, V. (1999) Building a Developmental State: The Korean State Reconsidered' *Politics and Society*, Vol. 27, No. 3, (Sage periodicals Press)

CIIR (Catholic Institute for International Relations) (1986) South Africa in 1980s State of Emergency (London, CIIR)

Clapham, C. (1996) 'The Developmental State: Governance, Comparison and Culture in the Third World' in Imbeau, L.M. and Mickinlay (eds.) *Comparing Government Activity* (London, Macmillan Press)

Clark, S. (1978) 'Capital, Fractions of Capital and the State: Neo-Marxist Analysis of the South African State' in *Capital and Class*, 5

Clark, G. and Dearlove, M. (1984) *State Apparatus: Structures and Language of Legitimacy* (Hemel Hempstead, Allen and Unwin)

Clarck, N.L. (1994) Manufacturing Apartheid: State Corporations in South Africa (London, Yale University Press)

Crankshaw, M. (1990) 'Apartheid and Economic Growth: Craft Unions, Capital and the State in the South African Building Industry, 1945-1975' *Journal of Southern African Studies*, Vol. 16 (93)

Cronin, J. (1993) 'Is Nelson Mandela for Real? *Work in Progress*, No. 87, February

Cronin, J. (2002) 'Interviews' [www.comms,dcu,ie/sheehanh/za.cronin02. htm]

Crush, J.; Jeeves, A. and Yudelman, D. (1991) *South Africa's Labour Empire: A History of Black Migrancy to the Gold Mines* (Cape Town, West View Press)

Collier, D. (ed.) (1987) 'Overview of the Bureaucratic Authoritarian Model' in *The New Authoritarianism in Latin America* (Princeton- NJ, Princeton University Press)

Colclough, C. and Manor, S. (eds.) (1991) *States or Markets? Neo-liberalism and the Development Policy Debate* (Oxford, Clarendon Press)

Commonwealth Secretariat (1991) *Beyond Apartheid: Human Resources for a new South Africa*, (London, Commonwealth Secretariat)

COSATU (Congress of South African Trade Unions) (1994) 'Submission on the RDP White Paper to the Parliamentary Standing Committee on the RDP', 28/10/94, (Cape Town, COSATU NEC)

COSATU (Congress of South African Trade Unions) (1996) 'Decisions of the Central Executive Committee, 14/09/96: www.cosatu.org.za/ press/1996.pr0914.01

COSATU (Congress of South African Trade Unions) (1996) COSATU Discussion Paper: ' A Draft Programme for the Alliance' (Johannesburg, COSATU H/Q)

COSATU (Congress of South African Trade Unions) (1996) 'A Summary of COSATU's Submission on Tariff Policy to the Trade and Industry Portfolio Committee, *Shopsteward*, Vol. 5.5, October/November

COSATU and SACP (1999) Building Socialism Now: Preparing for the New Millennium (Johannesburg, COSATU & SACP)

COSATU (Congress of South African Trade Unions) (2000) 'Accelerating Transformation: First Term Report of the COSATU Parliamentary Office' (Cape Town)

Cornevin, M. (1980) Apartheid Power and Historical Falsification (Paris, UNESCO)

Cox, A.; Furlong, P. and Page, E. (1986) *Power in Capitalist Societies: Theory, Explanations and Cases* (Brighton, Wheatsheaf Books)

Cumings, B. (1987) 'The Origins of the Northeast Asian Political Economy: Industrial Sectors, Product Cycles and Political Consequences' in Deyo, F.C. (ed.) The Political Economy of the New Asian Industrialism (Ithaca, Cornell University Press)

Cumings, B. (1999) 'Web with spiders, Spiders with no Webs: The Genealogy of the Developmental State' in Meredith Woo-Cumings, (ed.) The Developmental State (Ithaca, Cornell University Press)

Dahl, R. (ed.) (1970) *Foundations of Modern Political Science Series* (London, Prentice-Hall International Inc.)

Datta-Chaudhuri, M.K. (1981) 'Industrialisation and Foreign Trade: Development Experience of South Korea and the Philippines' in Lee, E. (ed.) *Export-led Industrialisation and Development* (Geneva, International Labour Organisation)

Davies, R.H. ((1979) Capital, State and White Labour in South Africa, 1900 – 1960 (Brighton, Harvest Press)

Davies, R.; O'Meara, D. and Dlamini, S. (1985) The Struggle for South Africa (London, Zed Books)

Davenport, T.R.H. (1991) South Africa: *A Modern History*, Fourth Edition (Houndmill-Basingstoke, Macmillan Press Ltd)

DBSA (Development Bank of Southern Africa) (1994) South Africa's Nine Provinces: A Human Development Profile

De Crespigny, A. and Schirer, R. (eds.) (1978) The Government and Politics of South Africa (Cape Town, Juta and CompanyLtd)

Deegan, H. (1999) South Africa reborn: Building a new Democracy (London, UCL Press Ltd)

Deeper News (1999) The Mont Fleur Scenarios- What South Africa be Like in the year 2002 (California, Global Business Network)

Denoon, D. and Nyeko, B. (1972) Southern Africa Since 1800 (London, Longman Group Ltd)

De Klerk, M. (1991) 'The Accumulation Crisis in Agriculture' in Gelb, S. (ed.) South Africa's Economic Crisis (Cape Town, David Phillip Publishers)

De Klerk, F.W. (2001) The Autobiography (London, Pan Books)

Deutcher, I. (1961) Stalin: A Political Biography (London, Oxford University Press)

Deyo, F.C. (ed.) (1987) The Political Economy of the New Asian Industrialism (New York, Cornell University Press)

Deyo,F.C. (1989) Beneath the Miracle: Labour Subordination in the Asian Industrialism (Berkeley and Los Angeles, University of California Press)

Drew, A. (ed.) (1996) South Africa's Radical Tradition, a Documentary History, Vol. 1, 1907 – 1950 (Cape Town, University of Cape Town Press)

Drew, A. (ed.) (1997) South Africa's Radical Tradition, a Documentary History, Vol. 2, 1943 – 1964 (Cape Town, Univeristy of Cape Town Press)

Dubow, S. (1995) 'The Elaboration of Segregationist Ideology' in Beinart, W. and Dubow, S. (eds.) *Segregation and Apartheid in Twentieth-Century South Africa*, (London, Routledge)

Du Toit, A. (1998) 'The Fruits of Modernity: Law, Power and Paternalism in the Rural Western Cape' in Howarth, D.R. and Normal A. (eds.) S*outh Africa in Transition: New Theoretical Perspectives* (New York, London and St. Martins Press)

Ellis, A. and Kumark, K. (eds.) (1993) Dilemmas of Liberal Democracy – Studies in Fred Hirsh's 'Social Limits to Growth' (London, Tavistock Publications)

Evans, P.B. (1979) Dependent Development – The Alliance of Multinational, State and local Capital in Brazil (New Jersey, Princeton University Press)

Evans, P.B.; Rueschemeyer, D and Skopal, T. (1985) 'On the Road toward a more Adequate Understanding of the State' in Evans,P. and Rueschemeyer, D. (eds.) *Bringing the State back In* (New York, Cambridge University Press)

Evans, P.B. (1987) 'Class, State and Dependency in East Asia: Lessons for Latin Americanists' in Deyo, F.C. (ed.) The Political Economy of the New Asian Industrialism (Ithaca, Cornell University Press)

Evans, P.B. (1995) *Embedded Autonomy: States and Industrial Transformation* (Princeton, Princeton University Press)

Evans, P.B. (1997) 'State Structures, Governance-Business Relations and Economic Transformation' in Maxfield, S. and Sneider, B.R. (eds.) *Business and State in Developing Countries'* (New York, Cornell University Press)

Evans, P.B. (1998) 'Transferable Lessons: Re-examining the Institutional Prerequisites of East Asian Economic Policies', *Journal of Development Studies*, Vol. 34, No.6

Evans, P. (2010) 'Constructing the 21st Century Developmental State' in

Evans, I. (1997) Bureaucracy and Race. Native Administration in South Africa (London, University of California Press)

Fage, J.D. (1995) *A History of Africa*, Third Edition (London, Routledge)

Falkena, H.B. (1980) *The South African State and its Entrepreneurs* (Johannesburg, A.D. Donker ltd)

Farlam Commission of Inquiry:

Fisher, J. (1969) *The Afrikaners* (London, Cassel and Company Ltd)

Finance Times 11 June 1993

Financial Mail 03 July 1998

Finance Week 23 July 2001

Fine, B. (1994) 'Politics and Economics in an ANC Economic Policy': An Alternative Assessment in *Transformation* No. 25 (Durban, University of Natal Press)

Fine, B. and Stoneman, C. (1996) 'State and Development' *Journal of Southern African Studies*, Vol. 22(1)

Fine, B. and Rustomjee, Z. (1996) *The Political Economy of South Africa* (Boulder-Colorado, Westview Press)

Fine, B. (2010) 'Can South Africa be a Developmental State'? in

Frankel, P.; Pine, N. and Swilling, M. (eds.) (1988) *State, Resistance and Change in South Africa* (USA, Croon Helm)

Frankel Max Vinderine INC, SANLAM, Ernst and Young and HSRC (1993) A Labour-Intensive Development Strategy for South Africa, *South Africa International*, Vol. 23, No. 4 (South African Foundation)

Friedman, M. (1962) *Capitalism and Freedom* (Chicago, Univeristy of Chicago Press)

Fry, M.J. (1985) 'Financial Structure, Monetary policy and Economic Growth in Hong Kong, Singapore and South Korea, 1960 – 1983' in Corbor, V. Krueger, A. and Ossa, F. (eds.) *Export Oriented Development Strategies* (Boulder- Colorado, Westview Press)

Fourie, F. (1997) How to Think and Reason in Macroeconomics (Cape Town, Juta)

Fukuyama, F. (1992) *The End of History and the Last Man* (London, Penguin Group)

Fujita, N. and James, E.W. (1990) 'Export Oriented Growth of Output and Employment in Taiwan and Korea' *Weltwirtschaftliches Archives,* Vol. 126, No. 4

Gamble, A. (1988) *The Free Economy and the Strong State* (London, Macmillan)

Gann, L.H. and Duignan, P.(1981) Why South Africa will Survive(London, Croom Helm)

Gauteng Government (1995) 'Proposed Role and Structures of the RDP' (Johannesburg, Gauteng Government)

Gawith, P. (1992) *Southern African Business Intelligence*, 1: 1-3

Geddes, B. (1994) *Politician's Dilemma: Building State Capacity in Latin America* (California, University of California Press)

Gelb, S. (ed.) (1991) *South Africa's Economic Crisis* (Cape Town, David Philip)

Gelb, S. (1996) 'The Post-Apartheid Political Economy' in Swatuk, L. and Black, D. (eds.) *Bridging the Rift: The New South Africa in Africa* (Boulder- Colorado, Westview Press)

Gerschenkron, A. (1962) Economic Backwardness in Historical perspective – A Book of essays (Cambridge, Harvard University Press)

Giliomee, H. and Schlemer, L. (1989) *From Apartheid to Nation-building: Contemporary South African Debates* (Cape Town, Oxford University Press)

Glaser, D. (2001) Politics and Society in South Africa (London, Sage)

Global Custodian (1994) 'Ogilvie Thompson's Take on the New South Africa' Summer, 1994

Global Dialogue (1999) 'Interview with Alec Erwin' (www. Igd. org.za/publications/globaldialogue/interview/Erwin.html)

Graaf, J. (1990) 'Towards an Understanding of Bantustan Politics' in Nattrass, N. and Ardington, E. (eds.) *The Political Economy of South Africa* (Cape Town, Oxford University Press)

Greensberg, S.B. (1980) Race and State in Capitalist Development: Comparative Perspectives (New Haven, Yale University Press)

Greenberg, S.B. (1987) Legitimating the Illegitimate: State, Markets and Resistance in South Africa (Berkeley, University of California Press)

Grootte Schuur Minute (1990) (www.anc.org.za/ancdocs/history/transition/minutes/html)

Gouws, R. P. (1989) The Rise of the Public Sector and use of Privatisation Proceeds in South Africa (Johannesburg, Rand Merchant Bank)

Habib, A. and Padayachee, V. (2000) 'Economic Policy and Power Relations in South Africa's Transition to Democracy', *World Development*, Vo. 28, No.2

Hadland, A. (1994) 'Public Servants get a Hearing at TEC', *Business Day*, 18th April 1994

Hagopian, F. (1992) 'The Compromised Consolidation: The Political Class in the Brazilian Transition' in Mainwaring, S.; O'Donnell G. and Valenzuela, J.M. C. (eds.) *Issues in Democratic Transition* (Indiana, University of Notre Dame Press)

Hall, P. (1986) Governing the Economy – Politics of State Intervention in Britain and France (Cambridge, Polity Press)

Hamilton, N. (1992) The Limits of State Autonomy: Post-Revolutionary Mexico (Princeton, Princeton University Press)

HA (Hansard- National Assembly) (1952) Speech by Brooke MP: col. 1289, 01/02/52

HA (Hansard- National Assembly) (1953) Speech by Schoeman MP: col. 1899, 19/08/53

HA (Hansard- National Assembly) (1982) Speech by Koornhof MP: cols 308-10

HA (Hansard-National Assembly) (1993) Speech by KeysMP: col. 8160, 14/05/93

HA (Hansard- National Assembly) (1995) Speech by Sisulu MP: col. 3358

HA (Hansard- National Assembly) (1995) Speech by Carrim MP: cols. 3362-63

HA (Hansard – National Assembly) (2015) Speech by JG Zuma: cols.

Harbor, A. (1995) *Weekly Mail and Guardian* 17th January 1995

Hausner, J.; Jessop, B. and Nielson, K. (1993) (eds.) *Institutional Frameworks of Market Economies: Scandinavian and European Perspectives* (Aldershot, Ashgate Publishing Company)

Hay, C. (2002) Political Analysis – A Critical Introduction (New York, Pelgrave)

Heinz, J. (1998) The South African Labour Market, Discussion Paper (Johannesburg, NALEDI)

Henderson, W.O. (ed.) (1983) Friedrich List: The Natural System of Political Economy- 1837 (Cornwall, TJ Press Ltd)

Herbst, J. (2003) 'Analysing Apartheid: How Accurate were US Intelligence estimates of South Africa, 1984 – 1994' *African Affairs*, Vol. 102, No. 406, January

Hindson, D.C. (ed.) (1983) *Working Papers in Southern African Studies,* Vol. 3 (Johannesburg, Ravan Press)

Hindson, C. (1987) Pass Controls and the Urban African Proletariat (Johannesburg, Ravan Press)

Hirsch, A. (1993) *Trading Up: Towards a Trade Policy for Industrial Growth in South Africa.* Industrial Strategy Project Draft Final Report. Cape Town (Cape Town, Development Policy Research Unit)

Hirsch, A. (1994) 'GATT: The Way Forward', Indicator South Africa, Vol.12, No. 1

Hirsch, A. (2005) Season of Hope: Economic Reform Under Mandela and Mbeki (Pietermaritzburg, University of KwaZulu-Natal Press)

Hirsch, A., Bhorat, H., Kanbur, R. and Ncube,M. (2014) Economic Policy in South Africa: Past, Present and Future, DPRU Working Paper, 201401 (DPRU, University of Cape Town)

Hirschman, A.O. (1987) 'The Political Economy of Latin American Development: Seven Exercises in Retrospection', *Latin American Research Review* 22(3)

HSRC (Human Sciences Research Council) (1995*) A Profile of Poverty, Inequality and Human Development in South Africa* (Pretoria, HSRC)

Hobsbawm, E. (1994) Age of Extremes: The Short Twentieth Century, 1914 – 1991 (London, Abacus)

Hobart, D. and Dagut, J. (1973) *Source Material on the South African Economy: 1860 – 1970*, Vol. 3 (London, Oxford University Press)

Holden, B. (1993) *Understanding Liberal Democracy* (Hertfordshire, Harvester Wheatsheaf Press)

Holloway, J. and Picciotto, S. (1977) 'Capital, Crisis and the State' *Capital and Class*, No. 1

Holland, M. (1994) 'The European Union's Foreign and Security Policy – The Joint Action on South Africa' (www. Unibas.ch/euro/inhalt)

Horwitz, R. (1967) *The Political Economy of South Africa* (Weidenfeld and Nicolson)

Hua wu Yin (1983) Class and Communalism in Malaysia (London, Zed Books)

Huff, W.G. ((1997) 'Turning the Corner in Singapore's Developmental State'? (University of Glasgow, Unpublished *mimeo*)

Huff, W.G. and Dewit, G. (1998) 'Credibility and Reputation Building in the Developmental State: A Model with East Asian Applications' (University of Glasgow, Unpublished *mimeo*)

Hutt, H.W. (1964) *The Economics of the Colour Bar* (London, Merrit and Hatcher Ltd)

Hugo, P. (1992) Redistribution and Affirmative Action: Working on South Africa's Political Economy (Johannesburg, Southern Book Publishers)

Islam,I. and Chowdhury, A. (1997) *Asia Pacific: A Survey* (London, Routledge)

ILO (International Labour Organisation (1985) *World Labour Report*, 2 (Geneva, International Labour Office)

ILO (International Labour Organisation (1993) *Year Book of Labour Statistics*, 52nd Issue (Geneva, International Labour Office)

ILO (International Labour Organisation) (1996) *Year Book of Labour Statistics* (Geneva, International Labour Office)

IMF (International Monetary Fund) (1994) *IMF Survey*, May 2 1994

IMF (International Monetary Fund) (2000) 'Exchange Rate Regimes in an Increasingly Integrated World Economy' *Occasional Paper,* 193 (Washington DC, IMF)

IMF (International Monetary Fund) (2000) 'Trade and Trade Policies in Eastern and Southern Africa' *Occasional Paper* 196 (Washington DC, IMF)

IMF (International Monetary Fund) (2015)'South Africa: Concluding Statement of an IMF Staff Visit' (Communications Department, IMF)

Jenkins, R. (1992) 'Theoretical Perspectives' in Hewitt, T., Johnson, H. and Wield, D. (eds.) *Industrialisation and Development* (Oxford, Oxford University Press)

Joffe, A., Kaplan, D., Kaplinsky, R and Lewis, D. (1994a) 'Meeting the Global Challenge: A Framework for Industrial Revival in South Africa' in Baker et al (eds.) *South Africa and the World Economy in the 1990s* (Cape Town, David Phillip)

Johnson, C. (1082) *MITI and the Japanese Miracle* (Stanford, Stanford University Press)

Johnson, C. (1987) 'Political Institutions and Economic Performance: The Government – Business Relations in Japan, South Korea and Taiwan' in Deyo, F.C. (ed.) *The Political Economy of the New Asian Industrialism* (Ithaca, Cornell University Press)

Johnson, C. (1995) Japan: Who Governs? (New York, W.W. Norton and Company)

Johnstone, F. (1976) *Race, Class and Gold* (London, Routledge and Kegan Paul)

Jones, S. and Muller, A. (1992) *The South Africa Economy*, 1910 – 1990 (Macmillan Academic and Professional Ltd)

Jones, S. (1992) Financial Enterprise in South Africa since 1950 (London, Macmillan)

Ka, Chi-Ming (1995) Japanese Colonialism in Taiwan (Boulder, West View Press)

Kahn, B. (2000) 'Debates over IMF Reform in South Africa' www.fes.org.za/english/debate.ifa6-00-imf.pdf

Kantor, B.S. and Kenny, H.F. (1977) 'The Poverty of neo-Marxism: The Case of South Africa' *Journal of Southern African Studies*

Kaplan, D. (1974) 'Capitalist Development in South Africa: Class conflict and the State' IDS Discussion Paper (Brighton)

Kaplan, D. (1976b)' An Analysis of the South African State in the 'Fusion' Period, 1932 – 1939' Discussion Paper (London, Institute of Commonwealth Studies)

Kaplan, D. (2010) 'Science and Technology and Economic Growth in South Africa: Performance and Prospects' in Xiaolan Fu and Luc Soete (eds.) The Rise of Technological Power in South Africa (Pelgrave, Macmillan)

Kaplan, D. E. (2015) 'The Structure and Performance of Manufacturing in South Africa' in Naude, W., Szrmei, A. and Haraguchi, N. (eds.) Structural Change and Industrial Development in the BRICS (Oxford University Press)

Kapstein, E. (1996) 'Workers and the World Economy' *Foreign Affairs* 75, 3 (May – June 1996)

Keller, B. (1994) 'Same old Bureaucracy Serves the new South Africa' *New York Times* (04 June 1994)

Kentridge, M. (1993) *Turning the Tanker: The Economic Debate in South Africa* (Johannesburg, Centre for Policy Studies)

Khor, M. (1991) 'Third World Economic Sovereignty at Stake: The Uruguay Round' in Turok, B. (ed.) *The African Response: Adjustment or Transformation* (London Institute for African Alternatives)

Kim, Y.H. and Choo, L. J. (eds.) (1994) *Korea's Political Economy: An Institutional Perspective* (USA, Westview Press)

Kraak, A. (1991) Beyond the Market: Comprehensive Institutional Restructuring of South African Labour Markets, Education, Training and Work (Johannesburg: Education Policy Unit, University of Witswatersrand)

Krasin, Y. (1981) The Contemporary Revolutionary Process: Theoretical Essays (Moscow, Progress Publishers)

Kohli, A. (1999) 'Where Do High-Growth Political Economies Come From? The Japanese Lineage of Korea's "Developmental State"' in Woo-Cumings, M. (ed.) The Developmental State (Ithaca, Cornell University Press)

Koo, H. (1987) 'The Interplay of State, Social Class, and the World System in East Asian development: The cases of South Korea and Taiwan' in

Deyo, F.C. (ed.) *The Political Economy of the New East Asian Industrialism* (Ithaca, Cornell University Press)

Korner, P., Maas, G., Siebold, T. and Tetzald, R. (1986) *The IMF and the Debt Crisis. A Guide to the Third World's Crisis* (Avon, Zed Books Ltd)

Kotze, P. (1987) 'Aspects in Devising an Industrial Strategy' in Van der Walt and Van Pletzen (eds.) *Modern Trends in Industrialisation with Reference to South Africa* (Cape Town, Haum)

Kuznets, S. (1955) 'Economic Growth and Income Inequality' *American Economic Review,* Vol. 45

Lavigne, M. (1995) The Economics of Transition: From Socialist Economy to Market Economy (Macmillan)

Lazar, J. (1987) Conformity and Conflict: Afrikaner Nationalist Politics in South Africa, 1948 – 1961, DPhil Thesis (Oxford University)

Lecky, W. E. H. (1896) *Democracy and Liberty* (London, Longman, Green and Co.)

Leftwich, A. (1993) 'Governance, Democracy and Development in the *Third World' Third World Quarterly* 14 (3)

Leftwich, A. (1994) 'The Developmental State' (Working Paper No. 6) Department of Politics, University of York

Leftwich, A. (1996) (ed.) Democracy and Development, Theory and Practice (Cambridge, Polity Press)

Le Roux, P. (1986) 'The State as Economic Actor: A Review of Divergent Perceptions of Economic Issues', paper delivered at the South Africa Beyond Apartheid Conference (York University)

Legassick, M. (1974) 'South Africa: Capital Accumulation and Violence', *Economy and Society*, 3. 3

Legassick, M. (1974a) 'Legislation, Ideology and Economy in Post-1948 South Africa', *Journal of Southern African Studies*, 1

Legassick, M. (1975) 'South Africa: Forced Labour, Industrialisation and Racial Differentiation' in Harris, R. (ed.) The Political Economy of Africa (John Wiley and Son)

Leibbrabdt, M., Woolard, I., Finn, A. and Argent, J. (2010) Trends in South African Income Distribution and Poverty since the Fall of Apartheid, OECD Social, Employment and Migration Working Papers, No. 101, OECD Publishing <http://dx.doi.org/10.1787/5Kmmsot7p1ms-en>

251

Levin, D. and Crisp, B.F. (1999) 'Venezuela: The Character, Crisis and Possible Future Democracy', in Diamond, L., hartlyn, J., Linz, J.J. and Lipset, S. M. (eds.) *Democracy in Developing Countries – Latin America* (London, Lynne Rienner Publishers)

Lewis, S. (1990) 'The Economics of Apartheid' (New York, Council on Foreign Relations)

Lemon, A. (1976) *Apartheid: A Geography of Separation* (England, Saxon House)

Lenin, V.I. (1992) *The State and Revolution* (London, Penguin Books)

Lester, A., Nell, E. and Bins, T. (2000) South Africa: past, Present and Future, Gold at the End of the Rainbow? (London, Pearson Education)

List, F. (1857/1983) The Natural System of Political Economy (London, Frank Cass)

List, F. (1885/1996) The National System of Political Economy (New York, A. M. Kelly)

Lipton, M. (1974) 'Towards a Theory of Land Reform' in Lehmann, D. (ed.) *Peasants, Landlords and Government* (New York, Holmes and Meier)

Lipton, M. (1985) *Capitalism and Apartheid – South Africa, 1910 – 1986* (England, Wildwood House)

Liang, K.S. and Lee, T.H. (1975) 'Taiwan', in Ichimura, S. (ed.) *Economic Development of East and South East Asia* (Honolulu, University Press of Hawaii)

Lim, Youngil (1981) *Government Policy and Private Enterprise: Korean Experience in Industrialisation*, Korean Research Monograph No.6 (Berkeley Institute of East Asian Studies, University of California)

Little, I. (1979) 'An Economic Reconnaissance', in Galenson, W. (ed.) *Economic Growth and Structural Change in Taiwan* (Ithaca, Cornell University Press)

Lodge, T. (1999) *South African Politics Since 1994* (Cape Town, David Phillip Publishers)

Lodge, T. (2002) Politics in South Africa – From Mandela to Mbeki (Cape Town, David Phillip Publishers)

Lombard, J. (ed.) (1974) Economic Policy in South Africa, Selected Essays (Cape Town, Haum)

Lombard, J. and Du Pisanie, J. (1985) A Memorandum for Assacom, Removal of Discrimination against Blacks in the Political Economy of

South Africa (Bureaux for Economic Policy and Analysis, University of Pretoria)

Lubeck, P. (1992) 'Malaysian Industrialisation, Ethnic Divisions and the NIC model', in Applebawm, R.P. and Henderson, J. (eds.) *State and Development in the Asian Pacific Rim Countries*) (London, Sage Publishing)

Luedde-Neurath, R. (1988) 'State and Export Oriented Development in South Korea' in White, G (ed.) *Developmental States in East Asia* (London, Macmillan Press)

Lyman, P. N. (2002) Partner to History – The Role of the US in South Africa's Transition to Democracy (Washington DC, United States Institute of Peace Press)

Maasdorp, G (ed.) (1990) 'The Role of the State in the Economy' in Critical Choices for South Africa. An Agenda for the 1990s (Oxford University Press)

Mabin, A. (ed.) (1989)' Organisation and Economic Change' Southern African Studies Vol. 5 (Johannesburg, Ravan Press)

Mail and Guardian 17 September 1999

Mail and Guardian 11 April 2003

Mandela, N. (1956) 'Freedom in Our Lifetime' in *Liberation* (June 1956)

Mandela, N. (1990) 'Message to USA Big Business, 19 June 1990' *<www.anc.org.za/ancdocs/history/mandela/1990/sp900619.html>*

Mandela, N. (1993) 'ANC Statement at the World Economic Development Congress, Washington DC, 24 September 1993'

Manuel, T. (1994) 'ANC 49th National Conference' Ministerial Reports, (Johannesburg, ANC)

Manuel, T. (1996) ANC Press Statement, 14 January, 1996 <www.anc.org.za/press/html>

Mann, M. (1984) 'The Autonomous Power of the State: Its Origins, Mechanisms and Results' *Archives Europe' ennese de Sociologie* (25)

Manpower Survey (1995) www.statssa.gov.za/default3.asp

Makgetla, N. (1997) Issues on Labour Market Policy in South Africa, Discussion Paper, (COSATU, Johannesburg)

Marais, H. (1998) South Africa – Limits to Change: The Political Economy of Transformation (Cape Town, University of Cape Town Press)

Marsh, D. and Stoker, G. (eds.) (1995) *Theory and Methods in Political Science* (Hampshire, Macmillan Press Ltd)

Martin, M.T. (1999) *Third World Quarterly,* Vol. 20, No. 4

Marx, K. (1971) *Capita*l (Moscow, Progress Publishers)

Marx, K. (1852) 'The Eighteenth Brumaire of Louis Bonaparte' in Fernbach, D. (ed.) (1973) *Karl Marx: Surveys* from Exile (Hamondsworth, Penguin)

Maxfield, S. and Schneider, B.R. (eds.) (1997) *Business and the State in Developing Countries* (New York, Cornell University Press)

Maundeni, Z. (2000) Development and the Developmental State: A Comparative Analysis of Botswana and Zimbabwe (DPhil Thesis, University of York)

Mayall, J. (1988) 'The South African Crisis: The Major External Actors', in Johnson, S. (ed.) *South Africa: No Turning Back* (London, Macmillan Press)

Mbeki. T.M. (1996) 'Challenges Facing the ANC in Government', *The Shopsteward*, Vol. 5.5 (October/November 1996)

Mbeki, T.M. (2000) 'Lecture in Georgetown University' (Washington DC, 23 May 2000)

Mcgrew, A. G. et al (1992) *Global Politics* (Polity Press)

Michael, T. M. (1999) *Third World Quarterly*, Vol. 20, No. 4

Mckinley, D. T. (1994) 'South Africa: Class, Democracy and Socialism' *Links*, No. 3 (Australia, New Course Publications)

Mckinley, D. T. (1997) The ANC and the Liberation Struggle: A Critical Political Biography (London, Pluto Press)

MERG (Macro-Economic Research Group) (1993) *Making Democracy Work – A Framework for Macroeconomic Policy in South Africa* (Cape Town, Centre for Development Studies)

Ministry in the Office of the President (1995) The RDP: The First Year Reviewed, (Pretoria, Ministry in the Office of the President)

Mitchel, M. and Russel, D. (1989) 'Political Impasse in South Africa: State Capacities and Crisis Management' in Brewer, J. D. (ed.) *Can South Africa Survive: Five Minutes to Midnight* (London, Macmillan Press)

Mitchie, J. and Padayachee, V. (1997) The Political Economy of South Africa's Transition: Policy Perspectives in the late 1990s (London, Dryden Press)

Mkandawire, T. (1996) ' Thinking about Developmental States', United Nations University website_www.unu.edu/nq.academic.pg-area4/makandawire.html

Mohr, P. and Rogers, C. (1996) *Macroeconomics* (Johannesburg, Lexicon Publishers)

Moll, G. P. (1991) *The Radical's Guide to the South African Economy* (Johannesburg, Skotaville Publishers)

Morales, j. A. (1996) 'Economic Policy After the Transition to Democracy: A Synthesis' in Morales, J. A. and McMahon, G. (eds.) *Economic Policy and the Transition to Democracy – The Latin American Experience* (Ottawa, International Development Research Centre)

Morris, M. and Kaplan, P. (1976) 'Labour Policy in the State Corporation: A Case Study of the South African Iron and Steel Corporation' *South African Labour Bulletin*, Vol. 2, No. 6, Jan. (part 1). Vol. 2, No.8, April (part 2)

Morris, M. (1993) 'Who's In, Who's Out? Trying to side-step a 50% Solution' *Work in Progress*, 87

Moroke, M. (1994) 'Transvaal Hospital Crisis Deepens', *The Star*, 26 January, 1994

Moon, C. I. and Kim, Y. C. (1996) 'A Circle of Paradox: Development, Politics and Democracy in South Korea', in Leftwich, A. (ed.) *Democracy and Development* (Cambridge, Polity Press)

Mpumalanga Government (1994) The Provincial RDP: Some Thoughts Regarding the Process of Implementation (Nelspruit)

Murphy, C. and Tooze, R. (eds.) (1991) The New International Political Economy (Bourlder, Lynne Rienner Publishers)

Munslow, B. and Fitzgerald, P. (1997) 'The Reconstruction and Development Programme', in Fitzgerald, P., Mclennan, A. and Munslow, B. (eds.) *Managing Sustainable Development in South Africa* (Cape Town, Oxford University Press)

Munck, G. (1994) 'Democratic Transitions in Comparative Perspective' *Comparative Politics,* 26 (3)

255

Murray, R., White, G. and White, C. (eds.) (1983) Revolutionary Socialist Development in the Third World (Brighton, The Harvester Press Publishing Group)

Murray, M. (1994) The Revolution Deferred: The Painful Birth of post-apartheid South Africa (London, Verso)

Myers,R. (1986) ' The Economic Development of the Republic of China on Taiwan, 1965 – 1981', in Lau, L.J. (ed.) *Models of Development* (San Francisco, ICS Press)

Myrdal, G. (1968) Asian Drama: An Inquiry into the Poverty of Nations, 3 Vols. (New York, Pantheon)

Myrdal, G. (1970) 'The Soft State in Underdeveloped Countries', in Streeten, P. (ed.) Unfashionable Economics. Essays in Honur of Lord Balogh (London, Weidenfeld and Nicholson)

Mzala, C. (1985) 'Cooking the Rice Inside the Pot' *Sechaba*, January, 1985

Naidoo, J. (1995) 'Taking the RDP Forward' Report by Minister Jay Naidoo, 31 October (RSA, Pretoria)

National Training Board/ Human Sciences Research Council (1991a) *Investigation into National Training Strategy for the Republic of South Africa* (Pretoria, HSRC)

Nattrass, J. (1981) *The South African Economy: Its Growth and Change* (Cape Town, Oxford University Press)

Nattrass, N. (1990) 'Economic Power and Profit in post-war Manufacturing', in Nattrass, N. and Ardington, E. (eds.) *The Political Economy of South Africa* (Cape Town, Oxford University Press)

Nattrass, N. (1994) 'Politics and Economics in ANC Economic Policy', *African Affairs* 93

Nattrass, N. (1994) 'The RDP White Paper – A Cocktail of Confusion', *Indicator* SA Vol. 12, No. 1, Summer 1994

Nattrass, N. (2001) 'High Productivity Now: A Critical Review of South Africa's Growth Strategy', in *Transformation* 45

Ndungane, N. (2001) 'Two Trevors go to Washington' in a *Video* by Cashdon (Johannesburg, Seipone Productions)

NIEP (National Institute for Economic Policy) (1993) *Macro Economic Research Group: Structure, Regulations and Programme* (Johannesburg, NIEP)

256

NIEP (National Institute for Economic Policy (1994) 'An Appraisal of the White Paper Discussion Document on the RDP', NIEP Occasional Paper Series No.1, October 1994 (Johannesburg, NIEP)

NIEP (National Institute for Economic Policy (1996) 'Form RDP to GEAR: The gradual embrace of Neo-Liberalism in Economic Policy', Occasional Paper Series No.3 August 1996 (Johannesburg, NIEP)

Njeku, N. (2001) 'Two Trevors go to Washington' in *Video* by Cashdon (Johannesburg, Seipone Productions)

NEECC (1991) *Annual National Conference Report* (Johannesburg, National Education Coordinating Committee)

Nolan, P. (1990) 'Assessing Economic Growth in the Asian NICs', Journal of Contemporary Asia Vol. 20, No1

Nolan, B. (1995) 'Poverty, Inequality and Reconstruction in South Africa', *Development Policy Review* 13 (2)

Nordlinger, E. (1981) *On the Autonomy of the Democratic State* (Harvard University Press)

Norman, H. (1940) Japan's Emergence as a Modern State – Political and Economic Problems of the Meiji Period (Connecticut, Greenwood Press Publishers)

North, C.D. (1981) *Structure and Change in Economic History* (New York, Norton and Company)

O'Donnell, G. and Schmitter, P. (1986) Transitions from Authoritarian Rule: tentative conclusions about uncertain democracies, vol. 4 (Baltimore, John Hopkins University Press)

O'Dowd, M. C. (1978) 'The Stages of Economic Growth and the Future of South Africa', in Schlemer, L. and Webster, E. (eds.) *Change, Reform and Economic Growth in South Africa* (Ravan Press)

O'Meara, D. (1975) 'White Trade Unions, Political Power and Afrikaner Nationalism', (*SALB*, Vol. 1, No. 10)

O'Meara, D. (1983) Volkskapitalisme: Class, Capital and Ideology in the Development of Afrikaner Nationalism, 1934 – 1948 (Cambridge, Cambridge University Press)

O'Meara, D. (1996) Forty Lost Years: The apartheid state and the politics of the National Party, 1948 – 1994) (Athens, Ohio University Press)

O'Meara, (1996a) Politics in the Apartheid State: Analysing the Materiality of the Political, Social Dynamics, Vol. 22 (2)

Olsen, M. (1982) The Rise and Decline of Nations – Economic Growth, Stagflation and Social Rigidities (New Haven and London, Yale University Press)

Onis, Z. (1991) 'The Logic of the Developmental State', *Comparative Politics* 24 (1)

Ozay, M. (1986) Development in Malaysia: Poverty, Wealth and Trusteeship (London, Croom Helm)

Padayachee, V. (1995b) 'Foreign Capital and Economic Development in South Africa: Recent trends and post-apartheid Prospects', *World Development* 23 (2)

Palais, J. (1973) 'Democracy in South Korea, 1948 – 1972' in Baldwin, F. (ed.) *Without Parallel: The American – South Korea Relationship since 1945* (New York, Panteon Press)

Pempel, T. J. (1999) 'The Developmental Regime in a Changing World Economy ', in Woo-Cumings, M.(ed.) *The Developmental State* (Ithaca, Cornell University Press)

Penman, J.S. (1923) *The Irresistible Movement of Democracy* (London, Macmillan and Co. Limited)

Pettman, R. (1979) State and Class – Sociology of International Affairs (Redwood Burn Ltd)

Pheko, M. (1999) <http://www.paca.org.za>

Picard, L.A. and Garrity, M. (1997) 'Development Management in Africa', in Fitzgerald, P., Mclennan, A. and Munslow, B. (eds.) *Managing Sustainable Development in South Africa* (Cape Town, Oxford University Press)

Pillay, V. (1993) ' Oliver Tambo Memorial Lecture, November 5 1993' www. anc.org.za/ancdocs/speeches/1993/sp931105.html

Pretorius, L. (1994) 'The Head of Government and Organised Business' in Shrire (ed.) *Malan to De Klerk: Leadership in the Apartheid State* (London, Hurst and Company)

Pretoria News 12 August 2015

Price, R. (1991) The Apartheid State in Crisis: Political Transformation in South Africa, 1975 – 1990 (New York, Oxford University Press)

Posel, D. (1991) The Making of Apartheid South Africa, 1948 – 1961: Conflict and Compromise (Oxford, Oxford University Press)

Posel, D. (1999) 'Whiteness and Power in the South African Civil Service: Paradoxes of the Apartheid State' *Journal of Southern African Studies*, Vol. 25 (2)

Poulantzas, N. (1973) 'Marxism and Social Classes', *New Left Review, No.* 78

Qureshi, A.H. (1996) The World Trade Organisation – Implementing International Trade Norms (Manchester, Manchester University Press)

Raghavan, C. (1991) 'The Uruguay Round: The Political dimension', in Turok, M. (ed.) *The African Response: Adjustment or Transformation* (London, Institute for African Alternatives)

Ramutsindila, M.F. (2001) 'Down the Post- Colonial Road: Reconstructing the post- colonial state in South Africa' *Political Geography* Vol. 20

Randall, P. (ed.) (1970) Anatomy of Apartheid: Occasional Publication No. 1 (Johannesburg, SPRO-CAS)

Randall, P. (ed.) (1971) Some Implications for Inequality: Occasional Publication No. 4 (Johannesburg, SPRO-CAS)

Randall, P. (ed.) (1971) Towards Social Change: Occasional Paper No.6 (Johannesburg, SPRO-CAS)

Rantele, J. (1998) The ANC and the Negotiated Settlement in South Africa (Johannesburg, J.L. Van Schaick Publishers)

Rao, D. (1978) 'Economic Growth and Equity in the Republic of Korea', *World Development*, Vol. 6, No. 3

RDP Monitor (1994) Volume 1, No. 1, June/July/August (Pinegowrie, Stock Press)

RDP News (1995) April, No. 4 (Pretoria, South African Communication Services)

RDP News (1995) October, No.10 (Pretoria, South African Communication Services)

Republic of South Africa (RSA) (1978) Report of the Commission of Enquiry into the Monetary System and Monetary policy in South Africa (De Kock Commission) (Pretoria, Government Printers)

Republic of South Africa (RSA) (1979) Report of the Commission of Enquiry into Legislation Affecting the utilization of Manpower (Riekert Report – RP/32) (Pretoria, Government printers)

Republic of South Africa (RSA) (1985) Department of Manpower <u>Annual Reports</u> – 1985 – 1990 (Pretoria, Government Printers)

Republic of South Africa (RSA) (1986) Central Statistical Services: South African Statistics (Pretoria, Government Printers)

Republic of South Africa (RSA) (1996) *Growth, Employment and Redistribution: A Macro-Economic Strategy* (Johannesburg, Ministry of Finance, Unpublished)

Reekie, D.W. (1993) 'Should South African parastatals be privatized?in Lipton, M. and Simkins,C. (eds.) *State and Markets in post-Apartheid South Africa* (Boulder, Westview Press)

Rogers, H. (1949) *Native Administration in the Union of South Africa* (Pretoria, Government Printers)

Rostow, W. W. (1960) *The Process of Economic Growth* (London, Oxford University Press)

Rothchild, D. and Chazan, N. (eds.) (1988) *The Precarious Balance: State and Society in Africa (*Boulder, Westview Press)

Rowthorn, R. and Chang, H. (1995) 'The Role of the State in Economic Change: Entrepreneur*ship and Conflict Management', in Rowthorn, R. and Chang, H. (eds.) The Role of the State in Economic Change* (Oxford, Oxford Clarendon)

Rueschemeyer, D., Stephens, E. and Stephens, J. D. (1992) *Capitalist Development and Democracy* (Cambridge, Polity Press)

Sabatier, P.A. (1993) Policy Change and Learning: An Advocacy Approach (Boulder, Westview Press)

SACOB (1994) *Reconstruction and Development Programme – A Business Perspective* (Cape Town, South African Chamber of Business submission to the Parliamentary Portfolio Committee on the RDP)

SACOB (1997) Implementation of the GEAR Strategy (<u>Discussion Document</u>, South African Chamber of Business)

Samson, M. (2000) 'The Macroeconomics of Job-creating Growth' (Cape Town, Economic Policy Research Institute)

Sagarra, E. (1980) *An Introduction to Nineteenth Century Germany* (Hong Kong, Sheck Wah Tong Printing Press)

SALDRU (Southern African Labour and Development Research unit (1993) South Africa's Rich and Poor: Project for Statistics on Living Standards and Development (Cape Town, University of Cape Town)

Schrire, R. (ed.) (1978) South Africa: Public Policy Perspectives (Cape Town, The Rustica Press)

Scheider, B. (1991) Politics Within the State: Elite Bureaucrats and Industrial Policy in Authoritarian Brazil (Pittsburgh, University of Pittsburgh Press)

Sechaba (1990) The ANC/COSATU Economic Conference (London, Sechaba Publications)

Seekings, J. and Nattrass, N. (2002) 'Class and Distribution in post-Apartheid South Africa', in *Transformation* 50, pp. 1-30

Seidman, G.W. (1994) Manufacturing Militance: Workers' Movements in Brazil and South Africa, 1970 – 1988 (Berkeley and Los Angeles, University of California Press)

Selden, R.T. (1975) "Capitalism and Freedom' Problems and Prospects. Proceedings of a Conference in Honour of Milton Friedman (Virginia, University Press of Virginia)

Shomsul, A.B. (1977) 'The Economic Dimension of Malay Nationalism' The Developing Economies, xxxv, 3, pp. 240-61

Symour, S.M. (1970) Bantu Law in South Africa (Johannesburg, Juta and Co. Limited)

SACP (South African Communist Party) (1981) The South African Communist Party Speak – Documents from the History of the South African Communist Party, 1915 – 1980 (London, Inkululeko Press)

SACP (South African Communist Party) (1997) Central Committee Report (Johannesburg, SACP)

SACP (South African Communist Party) (1999) Discussion Document. Document Prepared for a policy conference held in Johannesburg, 31 August 1999

South African Foundation (1996) *Growth for All: An Economic Strategy for South Africa* (Johannesburg, SAF Publication)

SAIRR (South African Institute of Race Relations) (1994) Race Relations Survey – 1994/94 (Johannesburg, SAIRR)

SAIRR (South African Institute of Race Relations) (1995) Race Relations Survey – 1994/5 (Johannesburg, SAIRR)

Slovo, J. (1990) 'Has Socialism Failed?' *South African Labour Bulletin* 14 (6)

Slovo, J. (1992) 'Negotiations: What Room for Compromise?' *African Communist,* 3rd Quarter (Johannesburg, SACP)

Sikkink, K. (1991) Ideas and Institutions: Developmentalism in Brazil and Argentina (Ithaca, Cornell University Press)

SARB (South African Reserve Bank) (1996) 'Quarterly Economic Review', in *Quarterly Bulletin,* December 1996 (Pretoria, SARB)

SARB (South African Reserve Bank) (2001) *Quarterly Bulletin*, December (Pretoria, SARB)

Stadler, A. (1987) *The Political Economy of Modern South Africa* (Cape Town, Creda Press)

Stalin, J. V. (1976) *Problems of Leninism* (Peking, Foreign Languages Press, Peking)

Stalling, B. (ed.) (1995) Global Change, Regional Response: The New International Context of Development (Cambridge, Cambridge University Press)

Stewart, P. (1997) 'The RDP: 1994 – 1996', in Liebenberg, S. and Stewart, P. (eds.) *Participatory Development Management and the RDP* (Johannesburg, Juta)

Strange, S. (1996) The Retreat of the State – The Diffusion of Power in the World Economy (Cambridge, Cambridge University Press)

Streak, J. (1997) 'The Counter – Counter Revolution in Development Theory on the role of the State in Development: Inferences for South Africa' *Development Southern Africa*, (Johannesburg, Development Southern Africa)

Streak, J. and Dinkilman, T. (2000) 'Critical Perspectives on Southern Africa', *Transformation* 41, 2000

Stutz, M.N. (1974) *The Nationalists in Opposition*, 1934 – 1948 (Pretoria, Human and Rousseau Publishers)

Suckling, J. and White, L. (eds.) (1988) After Apartheid: Political Renewal of the South African Economy (London, James Curry)

Sunday Times 09 April 1995

Sunday Times 04 September 1996

Sunday Times 14 October 2002

Sunday Times 17 November 2002

Swanson, M. (1977) 'The Sanitation Syndrome: Bubonic Plague and the Urban Native Policy in the Cape Colony, 1900', *Journal of African History*, Vol 18, pp.387 – 410

Tan, G. (1995) *The Newly Industrialising Countries of East Asia*, Second Edition (Times Academic Press)

Terreblanche, S. J. (1976) Policy Objectives and Priorities in the South African economy', in Truu, M. (ed.) *Public Policy and the South African Economy* (Oxford, oxford University Press)

Terreblanche, S. and Nattrass, N. (1990) 'A Periodization of the South African Political Economy' , in Nattrass, N. and Erdington, E. (eds.) *The Political Economy of South Africa* (Cape Town, Oxford University Press)

Terreblanche, S. (2002) A History of Inequality in South Africa: 1652 – 2002 (Pietermaritzburg, University of Natal)

The Economist 17   February 2001

The Star 25   September 1993

Thomson, L.M. (1960) *The Unification of South Africa*, 1902 – 1910 (London, Oxford University Press)

Thompson, L. and Prior, A. (1982) *South African Politics* (London, Yale University Press)

Thomas, D. and Martin, G.W. (1992) 'South Africa's Economic Trajectory: South African Crisis or World Economic Crisis?', in Viera, S., Martin, G.W. and Wallerstein I. (eds.) (New Jersey World Press)

TIPS (Trade and Industrialisation Policy Strategies) (2002) *Tips Annual Report 2002*

TIPS (Trade and Industrial Policy Strategies) (2010) Inequalities in emerging economies: What role for labour market and social policies? (OECD Workshop, Paris)

Tsie, B. (1996) 'States and Markets in the Southern Development Community (SADCC): Beyond the Neo-Liberal Paradigm', *Journal of Southern African Studies*, Vol. 22 (1), pp. 75 – 90

Todes, A. and Watson, V. (1984) 'State policy: Restructuring Local Government in South Africa, 1948 – 1984', in Hal, M. (ed.) *Africa Seminar Collected Papers*, Vol. 4 (University of Cape Town)

Tokman, V. E. and O'Donnel, G. (eds.) (1998) *Poverty and Inequality in Latin America*, (Indiana, The University of Notre Dame Press)

Tooze, R. (1993) 'Conceptualising the Global Economy', in McGrew, A. and Lewis, P. *et al, Global Politics: Globalisation and the Nation State*, (Polity Press)

Turok, B. (1999) *Beyond the Miracle – Development and Economy in South Africa,* (Cape Town, University of the Western Cape)

Turok, B. (2014) With My Head Above the Parapet: An Insider account of the ANC in Power (Jacana Media, Johannesburg)

UNDP (1992) Human Development Report 1992 (New York, Oxford University Press)

UNDP (1997) Human Development Report 1997 (New York, Oxford University Press)

UNCTAD (1991) United Nations Conference on Trade and Development – *State of the World Population* (New York, United Nations Fund for Population Activities)

UNECA (2015) United Nations Economic Commission for Africa – High-Level Panel on Illicit Financial Flows Report

UG (Union of South Africa) (1945) 'Report of the Investigation into Manufacturing Industries in the Union of South Africa', Board of Trade and Industries, RP282/1945

UG (Union of South Africa) (1958) 'Commission of Inquiry into the Protection of Industry' (Viljoen Commission) UG No. 36/1958, Office of the Prime Minister: Economic Development Programme (EDP) (Government Printers, Pretoria)

UG (Union of South Africa) (1958) 'An Abstraction of Agricultural Statistics of the Department of Agriculture', Table 51 (Government Printers, Pretoria)

UG (Union of South Africa) (1960) Report of the Department of Bantu Administration and Development for 1958 -9, (Government Printers, Pretoria)

Uys, S. (1988) 'The Afrikaner Establishment', in Johnson, S. (ed.) *South Africa: No Turning Back* (Macmillan, London)

Van der berg, S. and Bhorat, A. (1999) The Present as a Legacy of the Past: The Labour Market, Inequality and Poverty in South Africa, University of Cape Town (Development Research Unit)

Van Holdt, K. (1991) 'Towards Transforming South Africa's manufacturing Industry: A 'Reconstruction Accord between the Unions and the ANC?' *South African Labour Bulletin*, Vol. 15, No. 6 March

Van der Horst, S. T. (1971) *Native Labour in South Africa* (Frank Cass & Co. ltd, London)

Van Wyk, G. C. (1994) 'Money and the Restructuring of the South African State' (PhD Thesis, Warwick University)

Vartiainen, J. (1999) 'The Economics of Successful State Intervention in Industrial Transformation', in Woo-Cumings, M. (ed.) *The Developmental State* (Cornell University Press, Ithaca)

Voice of Business (1994) Annual Report – 1994 – JACOB, Johannesburg

Wade, R. (1990) Governing the Market: Economic Theory and the Role of Government in Taiwan's Industrialisation (Princeton University Press, New Jersey)

Webster, A. and Adler, G. (1999) 'Towards a Class Compromise in South Africa's "Double Transition": Bargained Liberalisation and the Consolidation of Democracy', Politics and Society, Vol. 27, No. 3

Weekly Mail and Guardian 02 February 1996

Weekly Mail and Guardian 04 April 1996

Weekly Mail and Guardian 12 April (1996)

Weiss, L. and Hobson, J.M. (1995) *States and Economic Development* (Polity Press, Cambridge)

Weiss, L. (2000) 'Developmental State in Transition: Adapting, Dismantling, Innovation, Not 'Normalising', *The Pacific Review*, Vol. 13 (1)

White, G. (1984) 'Developmental States and Socialist Industrialisation in the Third World', in *Journal of Developmental Studies* 21 (1)

White, G. (1988) (ed.) *Developmental States in East Asia* (Institute of Developmental Studies, (Macmillan Press, London)

White, G., Howell, S. and Xiaoyuan, S. (1996) In Search of Civil Society, Market Reform and Social Change in Contemporary China (New York, Oxford University Press)

Williamson, J. (1990) 'What Washington Means by Policy Reform', in Williamson, J. (ed.) *Latin American Adjustment – How Much has changed?* (Institute for International Economics, Washington DC)

Winsome. J. L. (1987) The World Bank and Structural Transformation in Developing Countries: the case of Zaire (Lynne Renner Publishers, Colorado, USA)

Wolpe, H. (1972) 'Capitalism and Cheap Labour Power in South Africa: From Segregation to Apartheid', *Economy and Society*, Vol. No. 3 (Nov)

Wolpe, H. (1995) 'The Uneven Transition from Apartheid in South Africa', *Transformation*, 27: 88 – 101

World Bank (1993) *The East Asian Miracle: Economic Growth and Public Policy* (Washington, World Bank Policy Research Department)

World Bank (1994) World Development Report, (New York: Oxford University Press)

World Bank (1995) 'A Successful Approach to Participation: The World Bank's Relationship with South Africa', *HCO Working Papers*, No. 57, July 1995, Washington

World Bank (1996) ' Technical Assistance', Lessons and Practices', (www.worldbank.org/oeddclib.nsf/812f64a83d93ba)

World Bank (1997) World Bank Report, New York (Oxford University Press)

World Trade Organisation (1995) *Trends and Statistics* – International Trade (Publications Services, WTO, Geneva)

Wong, Gangwu (1997) *China and World Since 1949,* (London, The Macmillan Press)

Woo, Jung-en (1991) Race to the Swift: State and Finance in Korean Industrialisation, (Columbia University Press, New York)

Woo-Cumings, M. (ed.) (1999) *The Developmental State* (Ithaca, Cornell University Press)

Yudelman, D. (1983) *The Emergence of Modern South Africa: State, Capita and the Incorporation of Organised Labour in the South African Gold Fields, 1902 – 1939* (Greenwood Press, London)

Yudelman, D. (1987) 'State and Capital in Contemporary South Africa', in Butler, J., Elphick, R. and Welsh, D. (eds.) *Democratic Liberalisation in South Africa: Its History and Prospects* (David Philip Publishers, Cape Town)

Interviews

Philip Dexter: (ANC/SACP/COSATU leader) – 21 August 2002

Princeton Lyman: (US Ambassador to SA in 1992 –1995) – January 2003

Jonathan Grossman:(UCT Senior Lecturer, Sociologist and Activist)13 June 2001

Andre' Fourie: (CEO – National Business Initiative) – 12 September 2002

Tebogo Phadu: (ANC RDP Office) – 22 August 2002

Patrick Bond: (Wits University Academic and social activist) 30 October 2002

Ed Hall (Corporate Affairs Director, Unilever South Africa) 13 June 2001

Ben Fine (SOAS Economist and member of MERG) 16 December 2002

John Sender: (SOAS Economist and member of MERG) – 16 December 2002

Lutz Franz: (Communications Manager, Shell Southern Africa) June 2001

Micheal Samson: (Senior Economic Advisor, Economic Research Institute, Cape Town)

Lord Renwick: (British Ambassador to South Africa, 1987 – 1991) 07 April 2003

Baroness Linda Chalker: (British Overseas Development Secretary and Minister for Africa between – 1986 – 1997) 21 January 2003

Index

V

W